PICKING UP THE PIECES
FROM PORTUGAL
TO PALESTINE

Quaker Refugee Relief in World War II

A MEMOIR

Howard Wriggins

University Press of America,® Inc.
Lanham · Boulder · New York · Toronto · Oxford

Copyright © 2004 by
University Press of America,® Inc.
4501 Forbes Boulevard
Suite 200
Lanham, Maryland 20706
UPA Acquisitions Department (301) 459-3366

PO Box 317
Oxford
OX2 9RU, UK

Library of Congress Control Number: 2004102471
ISBN 0-7618-2797-8 (paperback : alk. ppr.)

To Sally:

Partner in all things, source of
unending inspiration and support.

To Peter Davis
fellow worker in the
global field
with my thanks

Howard
Jul 04

TABLE OF CONTENTS

Part I
PORTUGAL, 1942-1943
Refugee Casework and Migration

Part II
ALGERIA AND EGYPT, 1943-1944
Refugees and Internees

Part III
ITALY, 1944-1945
Stateless Refugee Services and Rebuilding Abruzzi Villages

Part IV
FRANCE, 1945-1946
Spanish and Stateless Refugees and Normandy Reconstruction

Part V
GENEVA AND GAZA, 1948-1949
Palestine Refugees

LIST OF FIGURES

PHOTOGRAPHS

MAPS

FOREWORD

The United States came of age as the world's preeminent power during World War II. Millions of mostly male Americans enlisted or were drafted into the military services. Millions more, many of them women, worked in the defense industries, producing the weapons of war. Thousands became involved in humanitarian programs helping people all over the world who were suffering from the war, including refugees from the war zones and from persecution. Among the humanitarian aid workers were some Americans who, for religious or other reasons, were excused from military service as Conscientious Objectors. One of these was Howard Wriggins, the author of this book.

The number of people who suffered from the war and from persecution by the Nazi, Soviet and Japanese regimes is incalculable. The work of those who tried to relieve the suffering was extraordinarily arduous, performed under quasi-war conditions. All supplies, from food and medicines to transport and shelter, were scarce. The work was round-the-clock and overlaid with the horror stories of the sufferers. It was also dangerous.

Howard Wriggins worked for the American Friends Service Committee (AFSC), a Quaker organization, from 1942 to 1948 (with a short break after the war to pursue graduate studies), in Portugal, Algeria, Egypt, Italy and France, and in Palestine after the first Israeli-Palestinian war. His description of the nature of the work, of his courageous colleagues in his and other humanitarian organizations, of the hardships they endured, of the mammoth task they confronted in trying to help tens of thousands of people lacking basic human needs--all of this and more make this book a compelling story.

Wriggins at one point, in a sort of "by the way" comment, mentions that after the war AFSC was a co-winner, with its British counterpart, of the Nobel Peace Prize for their many years of Quaker international relief and the spirit with which it was given.

In my own Foreign Service career (1949-78), I was seldom involved in the kind of humanitarian crisis that Wriggins describes. I do remember one incident, however, in 1954 in the small university town of Tuebingen in southern Germany, where I was running the American cultural and information center. Former president Herbert Hoover visited and gave an address at the university. Adults and children lined the streets and waved German and American flags as his car came into town, all in recognition of his role in providing humanitarian assistance to needy Germans after both world wars. Hoover was thus more honored in the country of our defeated enemy than in his own country, a testament to the gratitude of people who had been helped by organizations such as AFSC.

Howard Wriggins went on to a distinguished career in the academic world and in government. After receiving his Ph.D. from Yale in International Politics, he served for ten years in Washington. He supervised the foreign affairs division of the Legislative Reference Service in the Library of Congress, was a member of the State Department's Policy Planning Council and a senior member of the National Security Council staff. He later was granted leave from Columbia University to serve as US Ambassador to Sri Lanka, and retired as Bryce Professor Emeritus of the history of International Relations.

He was one of many Americans who emerged from the experience of the war with a strong desire to help make the world a better place--more peaceful and more democratic. His is a generation which, imbued with idealism, came face to face, first with the Nazi regime and then with Stalinism, and went into teaching and government in order to pursue their ideals. He tells in his book of his personal struggle in justifying to himself his Conscientious Objector position while so many men of his generation were fighting the war. What he saw close at hand persuaded him that there are times when force may be necessary, though it should never be taken up lightly. Moreover, if force is used the victors have a responsibility to help set things right again. His story confirms that there are courageous ways, other than fighting, in which to achieve great humane ends.

This book illuminates the huge task confronting governmental and non-governmental organizations, now and for the foreseeable future, of assisting the constant and often overwhelming flow of refugees in every continent of the world. The experience of organizations like AFSC in the 1940s is relevant to today's refugee crises and to the policies of nations like ours that are so often the country-of-choice for refugees. The United States' refusal, in World War II, to admit more than a trickle of Jewish and other refugees trying to escape the Nazi death camps, is shocking. That record should be on our consciences today, and the achievements of the AFSC and other humanitarian organizations should help guide our policies toward refugee populations into the future.

Theodore L. Eliot, Jr.
Foreign Service Retired,
US Ambassador to Afghanistan
Dean Emeritus, the Fletcher School of Law and Diplomacy,
Tufts University

PREFACE

This is a wartime memoir with a difference. It tells the story of how I, a young idealistic Quaker, was changed by my encounter with the harsh realities of Europe during World War II. Thanks to my volunteer service with the American Friends Service Committee, the relief arm of the Religious Society of Friends, I was brought face to face with the results of Nazi cruelty. As I listened to "my" refugees' tales of woe and as I gained a clearer view of what Europe would be like if the Nazi leaders reshaped it to suit their perverse ambitions, I was no longer able to hold to the Conscientious Objector position I had grown up with.

Three other themes drive this memoir:

- how the American Friends Service Committee (AFSC) set about assisting refugees and other victims of the period in each of the places where I served;
- how the historical and political background in each affected how we could help the refugees and civilian victims of war;
- how the AFSC and United Nations brought emergency assistance to Palestinians who fled their homes during and after the first Arab-Israeli war and crowded into the Gaza strip and neighboring Arab states.

It is a tale of Quakers picking up the pieces and helping refugees during and after World War II. It is the story of how people coped or could not--the fear of the hunted refugee repeatedly peering out the window during an interview fearful police were on his trail; the bitterness of refugee parents having to choose whether or not to send their children to safety in the United States; the experience of Quaker workers watching helplessly as their refugee workers and clients were deported from the south of France.

Chance played a major part in my story, as it did for so many of us at that time. When most American men of my age were mobilized and did the fighting, I was permitted to alleviate some of the pain inflicted by government intent or by the side-effects of war. I am profoundly grateful for the opportunity offered me, six months before the attack on Pearl Harbor, to enlist in the Quaker overseas relief service. In the end, the four years stretched to six.

In the spring of 1942, I began working in Portugal. I went to North Africa briefly at the end of 1943 and then on to Egypt. Italy was next--I moved north behind the advancing Allied armies. After Italy, I worked a year and a half in France. With a year of graduate studies at Yale in between, I volunteered again in 1948 when the Secretary General of the United.Nations asked the AFSC to take responsibility for emergency assistance to Palestinian refugees in Gaza after the first Arab-Israeli war.

Everywhere I went, I batted out long letters to my family, reporting on the surrounding misery and human resilience, trying to make sense of the pain and destruction. Luckily, my mother, the family squirrel, captured most of them, on flimsy onion skin and the eye-straining V-mail. In my letters, I discover a world where, in the midst of war, there is an idealism hard to find in today's market-driven world.

It will quickly be obvious that this is a memoir based on my own experience; it is not a complete record of the American Friends Service Committee's activities during and after World War II in Europe or the Middle East. I have, however, tried to capture for the reader much of the substance of the Quakers' activities on behalf of refugees and civilian victims of war in Europe from 1942 to 1946 and later in Gaza. Alas, fifty years later there has been no resolution of the Palestinians' plight. Millions of refugees elsewhere remain homeless, part of the world's unfinished agenda.

For those old enough to have experienced the forties and fifties with the Second World War and Korea, years before the Vietnam trauma, this memoir will recall a period of anguish and brutality, but of idealism and hope as well. For those who grew up during the 1960s, it will show a war very different from the one we fought in Vietnam. For those many, young and old, who are now engaged in non-governmental organizations providing relief throughout the world, this account can provide insights that may be useful for their work.

Howard Wriggins
Hanover, New Hampshire
September 2003

ACKNOWLEDGEMENTS

Unknowingly, my mother began by collecting my letters. Years later David Hapgood shoved me off the bank when I hesitated. Charlotte Brooks, Tom Bodine, Eunice Clark and Mary Elmendorf started the recall. They reviewed the chapters on France, as did Hugh Jenkins and Micheline Lyons. Robert Paxton of Columbia University gave indispensable advice. Bill Fraser, an indispensable colleague in Paris, later shared his understanding of the anguish among French Friends during and right after the Occupation.

Without Ellen E.M. Roberts of Where Books Begin this memoir would never have been completed. She encouraged me from the start. By her lively spark, ready wit and sharp editorial eye, she helped give it shape as did Vanessa Constantine. Jenny Cuasapaz patiently oversaw the finishing touches. Corinne Johnson went far beyond the call of friendship in her experienced editorial review. Betsy Alexander's skillful and sensitive hand helped me ready the final text.

Stephen G. Cary, Gilbert White, Andy and Bob Burgess, Marjory Walker, Avery Post, Gordon Browne, Peter Bien and Ann Adams read and commented on the entire manuscript. Jay Hurewitz, as always, reminded me of the importance of what had gone before. Comfort and Channing Richardson, Joan and Alan Horton, Don Peretz, Dick Nolte and Lee Dinsmore commented on the Gaza section. Ken and Louise Kimberland reviewed the Algiers chapter. Michael Barrat Brown provided useful background on the Egyptian chapter. Micheline Salmon Sriber shared hours of recollections of Secours Quaker. Alice Resch Synestvedt of Copenhagen, who helped spirit Jewish children to safety in Switzerland, generously shared her own internment camp photographs and comment. The family of David Hartley was kind enough to share a tape of his reminiscences and provided a vintage photograph for inclusion in this book.

Jack Sutters and Joan Lowe at the AFSC archives in Philadelphia gave me a desk and useful files. Jack Sutters' remarkable memory continued to surprise; Joan Lowe's diligence turned up numerous gems. Suzanne Levi at Kendal, Elizabeth Potts Brown at Haverford College Library, Shelley Helfand at the Joint Distribution Committee's New York Archive , Mary Ann Leonard and Leslie Swift at the Holocaust Museum in Washington were each helpful in their own special ways. My debts to the Baker Library at Dartmouth are many, particularly to Mimi Curphey and John Cocklin who responded ingeniously to my more obscure questions.

This essay cannot do full justice to the contributions made by so many others--those who worked for the American AFSC, the British FRS, French Friends in Secours Quaker and the FAU in Egypt; the volunteers in Gaza and the many dedicated local people working for us in all these efforts. Willis Weatherford and John Elmendorf AFSC Commissioners for Europe visited Paris occasionally. Among those volunteers in the French Program not mentioned in the text include M.C. and Libby Morris; Nancy Fraser and David Jenkins in Paris; David Cadbury and Molly McCrae in Marseille; Allen Haigh in Montauban; Hilda Davis, Mary Garrett and Charles Thum in Perpignan; Cliff and Stan Cain, Becky Taylor, Joe Howell and Burns Chalmers in Normandy; and indispensable in London Fred Tritton, Margaret Backhouse and Lettice Jowitt. Apologies to these and others not mentioned in the text, without whom these Quaker services would not have been possible.

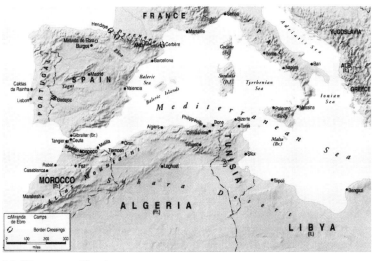

Mediterranean Coast

Six months before Pearl Harbor, I enlisted in the Quaker overseas relief effort by joining the American Friends Service Committee. Their work in World War II earned the Committee a Nobel Prize in 1947. My four year commitment to that effort stretched to six as I worked from Lisbon, at the Western end of the Mediterranean to Gaza, at the eastern end.

PART I PORTUGAL 1942-1943
Refugee Casework and Migration

The American Friends Service Committee, like every human enterprise, sometimes disappoints, but I honor it still for being out in the world year after year, grubbing around amid the ugly realities of violence and hatred, seeking to feed the hungry, reconcile the estranged, and restore faith in the despairing.

Stephen G. Cary, *The Intrepid Quaker* (forthcoming)

CHAPTER ONE
PREPARATION

In 1940, hanging over all of us in my age group was the looming shadow of war in Europe. Commencement time at Dartmouth College in June coincided with newspaper reports of the collapse of France and the hair's-breadth escape from Dunkirk of what remained of the British army. Because I had spent my junior year at the *Ecole libre des sciences politiques* (popularly known as the *Sciences Po*) in Paris, these dire developments were more than a distant drama; they were threats to the land and lives of people I knew and cared about deeply. A number of my fellow Dartmouth students volunteered to serve with the British armies or the Royal Air Force (RAF), and went off right after graduation. I too wanted to help, but in some other way.

My opportunity came in April 1941, when I was taking a graduate year in International Relations at the University of Chicago. A letter from Elmore Jackson of the American Friends Service Committee (from now on AFSC) invited me to join a group training for overseas relief and reconstruction. The training would start in September at Pendle Hill, a Quaker retreat and study center outside Philadelphia. We would have to commit ourselves in advance to four years of overseas service, as volunteers on a maintenance basis, and be ready to serve anywhere we might be needed.

Jackson's invitation came as a surprise; but it came at an important moment. I have never been certain how it originated. Did it go back to the summer of 1940, when I met Elmore Jackson at Penn Craft in a summer volunteer work camp? Penn Craft was an experimental "subsistence homestead" community run by the Quakers in western Pennsylvania. Working as stonemason assistants, we were building low-cost housing, rather like Habitat for Humanity today. Elmore and I had a long talk then about overseas relief and reconstruction. However the invitation had originated, after consulting my parents I accepted with gratitude.

I was 23, a member of Germantown Friends Meeting in Philadelphia, having attended Germantown Friends School for all 13 years of my early schooling. Although my mother was Episcopalian and my father Congregationalist I had found the Quaker environment inspiring. It was a quiet, comfortable community, with gentle people helpful to each other. I was impressed by the warmth of Quaker family life and the Quaker concern for the unhappy state of the world. These Quakers profoundly influenced me.

From about age 16 I had regularly attended their Sunday Meetings for Worship. "Unprogrammed," free of paid ministers and the ceremonial that go with worship in many churches, the gathered congregation meets in silence.[1] Those attending may rise "when the Spirit moves" them, as the Quakers say, and share their thoughts. Messages by members of the Meeting are usually devout. They stress the power of love. Quakers believe people should seek the overarching common threads that bind us together, all equal in God's sight regardless of race, creed or color. As a teenager, I was impressed by how much those women and men were at home with the hopeful New Testament; the stormy Old Testament was rarely referred to. While some might give sentimental messages, others, more serious, stressed the importance of following founder George Fox's admonition to find "that of God in every man" and to live in such a way as to "do away with the occasion for war." A number of these Germantown Quakers knew the art of combining wit and uplift. Many commended the simple, modest life. All held that it was greed, vaulting ambition, fear and a readiness to hate that led to conflict.

After Sunday Meeting, a study group for adults and teenagers drew speakers who talked about the inequities in our society at the time, the plight of the unemployed coal miners in western Pennsylvania, the despair of Depression-driven farmers. Others underlined the virtues of nonviolent approaches to social and political conflict. Frequently, they stressed the importance of a life of service in education or health. They described Quaker activities in the coal mining communities, in the big city slums and on the small farms that were not surviving the Depression.

The Quaker tradition of refusing to bear arms went along with helping civilian victims of war. In 1870, during the Franco-Prussian war, British Quakers had been active in France. During World War I, they had promptly organized a Friends Ambulance Committee that served in France. A War Victim's Relief Committee helped the many refugees driven from their homes in Belgium and France during the early years of the war. When America entered that war, at first only members of three Peace Churches—the Quakers, Mennonites and Church of the Brethren—had been exempted from bearing arms and were assigned to the medical corps or other "non-combatant service." The American Friends Service Committee was founded in 1917 by Rufus Jones and others so that conscientious objectors could provide alternative humanitarian and relief service to civilians overseas. Later, members of other churches who could demonstrate their religious scruples against bearing arms could also be assigned to "non-combatant service" or were allowed to join the AFSC units abroad.[2]

In our study groups in Germantown, former AFSC workers told how some 100 Conscientious Objectors underwent strenuous training before heading for France to erect temporary housing or work with British Friends in civilian hospitals in bombed-out France. We learned how the AFSC had been asked to organize the extensive child feeding *Quakerspeisung* in Germany and Austria after the war. There was also a small team offering medical help in the Russian civil war's typhus epidemic, and in Serbia rebuilding destroyed houses.

A long tradition lay behind the Quakers' stand against all war. Since the late seventeenth century, the Religious Society of Friends had been unequivocally opposed to war, believing it contrary to what Jesus would have us do. In 1804, London Yearly Meeting reaffirmed what had already been well-established by George Fox, the movement's founder.

> We feel bound explicitly to avow our continued unshaken
> persuasion that all war is utterly incompatible with the
> plain precepts of our Divine Lord and Lawgiver...and that
> no plea of necessity or of policy, however urgent or
> peculiar, can avail to release either individuals or nations
> from the paramount allegiance which they owe unto Him.[3]

The Society of Friends has always enjoined its members not to
bear arms or have anything to do with preparations for war. However,
the Quaker emphasis on the primacy of the individual's conscience
required an individual to decide his or her own path. At the same time,
anyone who took the C.O. position was also admonished to seek an
alternative form of constructive service—as Rufus Jones put it, a
service of love in wartime. In view of the Quakers' prominence in good
works and public advocacy, it always surprised me that the Society of
Friends that loomed so large in my Philadelphia has fewer than 100,000
registered members in the United States and fewer than 20,000 in Great
Britain, though there are many Friends of Friends who attend their
Meetings for Worship but never join.

In addition to Quaker influences, I had studied enough
diplomatic history at Dartmouth and in Paris to see the folly of many
international struggles, which seemed to go on and on forever. One
ambitious ruler after another sought predominance, at great cost to his
and his opponent's people. Barely twenty years had passed, but already
World War I's terrible slaughter and the Versailles settlement were
being roundly criticized. Even Sidney Fay's detailed study, *The Origins
of the World War*, could not quite explain the start of World War
I.[4]Rather than the ambiguities of history-in-the-making, I found
comfort in the certainties of clear-cut rejection of "the way of
violence," so often arbitrary, ill-directed, and destructive. An important
book for me at the time was Richard Gregg's *The Power of Non-
Violence*.[5] He argued the possibility and utility, as well as the virtue, of
nonviolent struggle against oppression and war. He drew examples
from Gandhi's resistance to racial and imperial oppression and other
historical nonviolent actions that then seemed persuasive.

The Selective Service legislation that Congress passed in 1940
provided for those with conscientious objection if their seriousness
could be confirmed by their local draft boards. Soon, Civilian Public
Service camps, rather like the Civilian Conservation Corps camps of
the Depression era, were organized by the Peace Churches to provide
alternative service for those of draft age. Despite my personal
identification with France, which was then facing the German armies in
what the French called "une drôle de guerre," or phony war, I asked for

C.O. status. In filling out the daunting Form 47 I argued the importance of holding up the ideal of an alternative way, that of nonviolence.

> For me, if one believes in the spirit of Christianity as seen in the light of the spirit of the Bible and as best exemplified by the life of Jesus Christ, one cannot conscientiously participate in war. The two are incompatible. One believes in love as a vital, ongoing force, or one repudiates it. In the latter case, one can accept war; in the former it does not seem possible to do so.

As George Fox, the principal inspiration for the Quaker movement, put it, "there is that of God in every man." I continued, "Since there is this essential characteristic of likeness common to all people, . . .it is wrong for me to deliberately kill my fellow man." I took Fox's famous precept as seriously as I knew how.

While totally consistent with my Quaker involvement, taking the C.O. position had not been without stress. I was standing out against mainstream choices, in effect setting my own judgement against most of my contemporaries and national leaders I respected. Despite those influences, I had chosen the C.O. position. Moreover, I was in one sense turning my back on my friends in France, who were hard-pressed by the war. But for me, arguments about either/or choices and on ideal principles seemed persuasive. For many others, seeking C.O. status was far harder. Family, friends and their community might disapprove. Many could expect to be socially ostracized or face extended prison terms. They generally lacked the channels for useful service that I could hope for. Their draft boards could be severe in blocking their choice. For me, six years with the AFSC were filled with such ambiguities and paradoxes that I now look back on my simple thinking in 1940 with some wonder.

Soon I was recognized by my draft board as a conscientious objector and given a IV-E (or C.O.) classification. Because I was underweight, I was classified for "limited service." During the spring of 1941 I was notified that I would be subject to call to a Civilian Public Service camp when my number came up in the lottery.

As I finished the spring term at Chicago I wondered where AFSC's training would lead. I recall my rather exaggerated notions of the hardships I saw for myself as a relief worker for the AFSC because I had known that the people in Germantown Meeting who had worked in Russia during the typhus epidemic had served in truly awful working conditions. It never occurred to me that the following May I would find myself walking down the gangplank at Pan American's Art Deco marine terminal in New York at 1:00 a.m., about to step aboard a luxurious PanAm Clipper flying boat bound for Lisbon. Nor did I foresee that work with the AFSC would lead me into so many varied and challenging experiences.

In September 1941, four months before the Japanese attack on Pearl Harbor, I became part of the AFSC training program for overseas relief and reconstruction. In mid-October, in light of this preparation and at the request of the Service Committee, I was reclassified by my Draft Board as II-A, "work of national importance," a classification I retained throughout the war. That they had asked me early and I had volunteered promptly made it possible for me to serve in this way.

FOUR MONTHS TRAINING AT PENDLE HILL

When our four-month study program at Pendle Hill began in September 1941, we were seven, called the "guinea pigs," because we were an experimental group. Fellow students included Spencer Cox, who subsequently drove supply trucks and ambulances in China and later headed the American Civil Liberties Union in Philadelphia; Tom Bodine from Germantown; and Marydel and Walter Balderston, who went on to help humanize the program for interned Japanese-Americans during the war. We lived collectively, each helping in the kitchen, maintaining the study center, or doing chores. We studied Quaker history, including the complicated interweaving of different trends in the Quaker movement and the origins and evolution of the Quaker "peace testimony," or religious pacifist principles.

We also explored the principles and practice of Quaker relief service during and after World War I. One story that remained in my mind suggested the Quakers' scrupulous concern for meeting human obligations. At the end of World War I, Bulgarian prisoners of war had been assigned to help Quakers rebuild destroyed homes in Serbia. These Friends were forbidden by the military officials to pay the POWs anything beyond bare maintenance. Based on careful records, and long after the program was finished, an AFSC worker tracked down each Bulgarian helper and paid for the time he had worked for the AFSC.

Among our preparations was the study of whichever language we would need—German for me—though our language training was rather informal. Rudimentary German would be indispensable for connecting with those refugees who did not know English or French. We visited the Service Committee's headquarters at 20 South 12th Street in Philadelphia and early met Clarence Pickett, Executive Secretary of the Service Committee. A warm, encouraging presence to us all, he was clearly the dynamo at the center of the staff. Although he was in his sixties, he had a youthful spring in his step, a fine combination of shrewdness in assessing who might help the Committee's enterprises and a fundamental optimism about the people he met. Based in Philadelphia, he could commute to Washington or New York with equal facility. I later learned he had a wide network of friends and admirers among religious leaders across sectarian differences and across the country. He was also remarkably at home in Washington, a close friend of Eleanor Roosevelt and many New Deal officials, from the Farm Security Administration to the TVA.[6]

We heard reports from the field in France and Portugal and from the Anglo-American Friends Ambulance Unit then forming to bring medical skills and medicines to the hard pressed people of China. We came to appreciate the careful discussions that preceded AFSC policy decisions. No votes were taken in these meetings, but the Clerk, after listening to all views, would present, in a beautifully crafted minute, an inclusive sense of the meeting which gave generally clear policy advice. If there was no consensus, the issue was put over till the next meeting. While all felt free to speak, it was clear that some voices carried more weight than others.

I will never forget the shock and deep gloom that settled on our Sunday afternoon tea at the home of the headmaster of Westtown School on December 7, 1941. A classical music concert was interrupted by the announcement of the Japanese attack on Pearl Harbor. After a stunned silence, the headmaster quietly called on us to remain calm. He warned us to avoid chauvinist excitement and urged us to find our own ways of being helpful in the next unpredictable time.

The president went before Congress the next day to ask for a declaration of war. It was impossible to imagine what lay ahead; hardships, personal losses and destruction were bound to follow. For those of us already enlisted for the long term with AFSC, this event only intensified our impatience to get to work.

FOUR MONTHS' APPRENTICESHIP AT THE AFSC OFFICE, PHILADELPHIA

In January 1942, our four-month training program at an end, I was assigned to the Refugee Division AFSC headquarters in Philadelphia. James Vail, one of the country's leading specialists in silicates, formerly vice-president of the Philadelphia Quartz Co., was secretary of the Foreign Service Section. I came to appreciate his deep concern for what we were doing, his encouraging management style and the breadth of his interests, from crystallography to Scriptures. The committee expected me to join the refugee and child feeding programs in France in three or four months.

Marnie Schauffler, my immediate boss, was an energetic source of cheer and human concern. Bursting with enthusiasm, she had a warm smile, her brown eyes projecting both encouragement and an impatient urging to get on with the next task. Outraged by our government's refusal to grant visas to those being driven out of Germany, Austria and Poland, she applied ingenuity and charm in her efforts to assist them. She was a great guide to Washington and New York, understanding that the more of the senior people in the relief committees in Washington and New York I knew, the more useful I might be in Europe.

The AFSC was a sprawling organization, tucked away in dozens of offices crammed into a kind of warren surrounding the Friends Meeting at 20 South 12th Street. A Peace Education section worked on campuses, organizing public speaking occasions and publishing brochures aimed at keeping us out of the war. Once the United States was in the war, they stressed the humanitarian needs of the civilian populations in the war zones. Another section dealt with work camps and social issues. They had been concerned with assistance to communities poverty-stricken from the Depression. With the war, a number of the staff turned their hand to help in organizing the Civilian Public Service camps for C.O.s. By now the Foreign Service Section had the largest budget, supporting relief programs in France, collaborating with the British Friends in China, backing refugee assistance programs in Portugal and Central America and refugee reception centers in the United States.

Marnie Schauffler reminded me that the AFSC had worked with refugees in the early 1930s, responding to the rising tide of refugees fleeing Nazi persecution and terror. Jews now declared stateless, individuals Hitler claimed were Jews but who considered themselves not Jews, politically active opposition elements (often Socialists or Christian Socialists), intellectuals, artists, and musicians, all needed help. The AFSC had established offices in Berlin, Vienna, Paris and Rome that were kept operating as long as possible to help threatened individuals and families to emigrate. By the spring of 1942, however, our outposts were limited to southern France, Portugal and Geneva.[7]

Marnie Schauffler, head of AFSC's refugee division and my mentor in the winter of 1941-42, joined Secours Quaker in France in 1945.

The Spanish Civil War, beginning in 1936, had also awakened Quaker concern. British and American Friends developed child feeding programs in areas controlled by both the Republican government and General Franco. As Franco's troops advanced in 1938/39, some 300,000 Spaniards fled into southern France. The Quaker child feeding operations crossed the Pyrenees with them. The French, still suffering from the economic Depression and highly suspicious of the "communists" among the refugees, set up rough and ready refugee camps. The Quakers provided food supplements, medicines and documentary assistance to refugees in a number of these camps.

By 1941-42, however, the main effort of the staff in the Refugee Section of AFSC focused on attempting to obtain visas for people in Portugal or North Africa who had fled Nazi persecution. American immigration regulations required that all visa applicants had to have an American with considerable wealth or a recognized organization willing to sign an affidavit guaranteeing that the immigrant would not become a public charge. The individual consulate officer had considerable discretion in deciding whether the individual's papers provided the government with adequate guarantees. This was a laborious and discouraging process, both arbitrary and costly. In view of what was happening in Europe at the time, the United States presented to us a virtually closed door.

AFSC, along with numerous Jewish organizations, the Unitarian Service Committee and Catholic Relief, tried to persuade administration and elected representatives to ease their strict constraints. But we ran into the stone wall of anti-Semitism, fear of fifth column penetration by the Germans concealed among the refugees, and Depression-induced fear of future job competition. The Federal Government had also organized the President's War Relief Control Board to ensure that the charitable organizations were in fact doing what they promised and were not covers for some other purpose. In the meantime, persecution intensified and more and more Jews sought to flee.

The charitable non-governmental organization (NGO) scene in those days was far simpler than it is today. Nevertheless, most east European states by now were under Nazi control, and their people organized large fund-raisers in New York, Washington and Chicago. Church groups were organized by denominations. By all odds, the most energetic were the Jewish organizations, whose appeals were understandably among the most desperate. For many years, the United Jewish Appeal had been raising funds for the kibbutzim and other Jewish programs in Palestine as well as for the support and rescue operations of the American Jewish Joint Distribution Committee's (JDC). Marnie and I also checked in with the Mennonite Central Committee, Church of the Brethern and Unitarian Service Committee.

My short-term job was to visit U.S. government agencies that could, if they only would, simplify the affidavit process. I was also supposed to learn the who's who of agencies like the JDC, the International Rescue Committee (IRC), the Hebrew Immigrant Aid Society (HIAS) and other organizations dedicated to relief. The JDC was occasionally able to arrange special ships for refugee movements, or reserve blocks of tickets. For this reason, in addition to the huge burden they carried, they were important to the smaller agencies like AFSC in cases in which we had been able to obtain papers for someone we needed to get out in a hurry.

Ray Wilson, Executive Secretary of the Friends Committee on National Legislation, was the large, affable and skillful Quaker-on-the-Hill. He contacted congressmen and senators on peace issues, the arms budget, legislation affecting C.O.s, and farm issues. Later, when the war started for Americans in December 1941, he vigorously protested the internment of nearly 100,000 Americans of Japanese descent living mainly in California and elsewhere on the West Coast who were herded into internment camps in the mountain states. The Friends, incidentally, were one of the few groups who openly challenged the government's Resettlement Program at the time and quickly set up services for those in the internment camps. Tom Bodine, one of my fellow guinea pigs, later spent several years helping to arrange college placements for young internees, and the two Balderstons worked in the San Fransisco AFSC office on the internees' problems.

FLIGHT TO LISBON

All of this was behind me on May 29, 1942, as I walked down the gangplank onto the Pan American Clipper flying boat. It is hard for us now to think back to the excitement of the PanAm Clippers. Bill Masland, one of PanAm's pioneer pilots, had been ahead of me at Germantown Friends. To be following in his footsteps was special. Only four years after the first scheduled transatlantic mail flight, here I was flying across the Atlantic on a humanitarian mission to Lisbon.

The flying boat finally took off after the third try—each of the previous nights the departure had been canceled at about 4:30 a.m. for reasons never explained. Security was such a concern that whether things happened or didn't happen no one ever expected that ordinary people deserved an explanation.

The some thirty passengers were of course very mixed. One of them, a friend of Marnie's, was going to Monrovia, Liberia, as the new Consul General. Fishman's Lake in Liberia became an important transit stop for planes crossing from Brazil to Africa and then on to Cairo and India. Aboard was someone from the Unitarian Service Committee bound for Lisbon and beyond. In those days, no one talked about themselves or where they were going or what they were up to. We fastened our seat belts and with a great roar of the four motors we rushed along the surface of Flushing Bay and finally were airborne. For the most part, everyone settled into their books.

The flight was incredibly comfortable. There was room to stretch out, since the seats turned into berths of a sort. Tables folded out from the wall to receive tablecloths before the food arrived. Stewards in short white jackets served meals and arranged the bunks. As our plane headed for the British island Bermuda, I could not help thinking of my good fortune to be engaged in AFSC's humanitarian enterprise. In Bermuda, all the mail was unloaded for censoring, and our passports and our identities were checked.

From Bermuda we flew overnight to the Azores, landing at Horta. The landing and take off in Bermuda had been smooth, in a protected bay, but we landed in the Azores into a choppy sea, and taking off was not so easy. Twenty-eight hours after leaving New York, at about dusk we flew up the Tagus River and circled low over the lovely city of Lisbon, scattered across rolling hills, before landing.

The map contains the following labels:

Atlantic Ocean

Bay of Biscay

FRANCE

Bordeaux
Oviedo
Cordillera Cantabrica
Bilbao
Pamplona
Toulouse
Narbonne
Pyrenees
Perpignan
Vigo
Burgos
Ebro
Zaragoza
Andorra
Porto
Valladolid
Duero
Barcelona
Coimbra
Sierra De Guadarrama
Caldas da Rainha
Sierra De Gredos
Madrid
Tagus
Toledo
Baleric Sea
PORTUGAL
Lisbon
Setubal
SPAIN
Guadiana
Valencia
Baleric Islands
Sierra Morena
Cordoba
Guadalquivir
Cartegena
Mediterranean Sea
Sevilla
Malaga
Algiers
Cadiz
Gibraltar (Br.)
Strait of Gibraltar
Tangier
Ceuta
ALGERIA (Fr.)
Oran
SPANISH MOROCCO
Melilla
Azores
Atlantic Ocean (Port.)
Horta
MOROCCO (Fr.)

Gurs Camps
0 50 100 150
miles

0 50 100 150
miles

Cartography by © Philip Schwartzberg, Meridian Mapping, Minneapolis

Spain and Portugal

The Lisbon office of the AFSC had opened in 1941 to assist the refugees who had escaped across the Spanish frontier hoping for a boat out of Europe. "The individual human being ceased to exist," Erich Remarque noted. "Only one thing counted, a valid passport."

The coast of Portugal had become the last hope of the fugitive... If one could not reach it, you were lost, condemned to bleed away in a jungle of consulates, police stations and government offices, where visas were refused and residence permits unobtainable. A jungle of internment camps, bureaucratic red tape and ...a withering indifference.

Eric Remarque, *The Night in Lisbon*, 1964

CHAPTER TWO
LISBON: REFUGEE ASSISTANCE

ARRIVAL AND FIRST IMPRESSIONS

We were cleared quickly through Portuguese customs. When I pushed the bell at the AFSC's heavy door a shriveled concierge cautiously cracked the door and peeked out. By dint of sign language, showing her my black AFSC passport and speaking the names of people in the office, I was able to persuade the suspicious lady that I was indeed legitimate. Reluctantly, she let me into the AFSC office and I put down my light-weight luggage—a twenty pound cardboard suitcase and a parcel of magazines. Eventually Phil Conard, the head of the Lisbon office, and Russell Richie, whom I was to replace, came in, astonished at my arrival, of which they had had no advance word. They were delighted to hear all the messages I had for them and particularly pleased to have magazines from home as they had had none since

January. Magazines were too heavy for the limited weight allowance on the Clippers, but a package I carried by hand was all right.

The office, which had obviously been a residential apartment, was spacious though austere. Phil had an office with two desks; Russ had a smaller office with a single desk. We had one room, which I guess had been the dining room, for conferences and meetings, which doubled as a kind of sitting room and where there were magazines and books. A radio could get the BBC. Dorothy Thumwood, our remarkable secretary, had an office she shared with an assistant typist. And our Portuguese errand boy who carried letters to the post office, the cable office, etc., had a corner in the hall. Phil had a bedroom, I had a smaller bedroom, and we had a spare bedroom for visitors. There was a cold water shower flowing into a large brass tub that had to be bailed out into the toilet.

Later that first evening as I took a brief walk with Russ Richie, I was struck that Lisbon was all light. I knew that Paris, London, Berlin, Oslo and all the cities in the fighting or occupied countries were blacked out. But in Lisbon, being in neutral Portugal, street lights, restaurants with sidewalk cafés, all were bright.

The Avenida da Liberdade, marking Portugal's liberation from Spain in 1640, was then a small-scale grand boulevard. It was lined on each side with swanky shops and restaurants, with café tables on the sidewalks. It led down to the Rossio, and then down to the Praça do Commércio and the Tagus River. This central artery was surrounded by hills, some marked by large government buildings and one by a former royal palace. The remains of a large Moorish castle dominated the highest hill. Other hills were covered by minute, piled-up houses. Up the slopes along steep lanes and alleys were houses with tile roofs built after the disastrous earthquake in 1755. Trams wound their way on a maze of tracks through the narrow streets, the conductor's bell clanging as he tried to get donkey carts, horse-drawn wagons and the few cars out of the way so he could pass. A cable car/funicular moved slowly up and down a steep hill between our hillside office and the Tivoli Hotel down on the Avenida da Liberdada, where we had lunch and dinner.

LISBON PROGRAM AND IMMEDIATE TASKS

By the time I arrived, our office had several related tasks. First was to receive any and all refuges who knocked on the Quaker door. We would welcome them, listen to their stories, often long, tragic and for me, fresh from the United States, unbelievable. All had been forced to flee, often with nothing but the clothes on their backs. They had lost their homes, their livelihood. Members of their family had been arrested and taken away. Their lifetime savings had been confiscated. Intense anti-Semitism, bureaucratic perversity and what in the United States later became known as Catch-22 entrapped them. We did our modest best to ease their plight. We also regularly visited refugees sent by the police to live in an isolated summer resort or even less fortunate, men jailed in abysmal conditions in an ancient prison. A different duty involved receiving supplies—food, medicines or used clothing—sent from the United States or purchased in Portugal and shipping them on to the AFSC offices in southern France.

Phil Conard, head of our office, was a vigorous man in his early 70s who had twice come out of early retirement. He was of medium height, with graying hair, a carefully clipped mustache and a smile in his eyes and on his face that I learned to attribute to his strong religious faith.[1] His years as a representative of the Protestant YMCA in Catholic Brazil and Uruguay had honed his diplomatic skills, which included a fund of amusing observations about *la comédie humaine*. Understandably, he had close relations with the Mexican ambassador, who was well able to help Spanish refugees who might be politically at risk in either Portugal or Spain.

We first had to decide whether an individual refugee should be supported by the Joint Distribution Committee (JDC), or the Unitarian Service Committee, or the Hebrew International Aid Society (HICEM/HIAS), or Catholic Relief Services. Those of French nationality who wanted to join General Charles de Gaulle's Free French movement would go see a M. Grolier at the Free French office. The Unitarian Service Committee specialized in those who were at some risk because of their past political activities at home. Others became our responsibility—those made stateless by the Nazis because of Jewish ancestry though they did not consider themselves Jews (according to the distressing vocabulary of the times, they were dubbed non-Aryan Christians); partners of mixed marriages of Jews with non-Jews; fallen Catholics, German, French or other Protestants and a wide variety of others of many nationalities and conditions. The AFSC helped a variety of forlorn individuals stuck in one way or another.

My immediate job was to learn all I could about the refugee service program so that I could relieve Russell Richie of his duties in Portugal. Russ was an affable, outgoing, energetic man who clearly enjoyed life. A man about town, he was at ease with everyone—refugees, Portuguese officials, waiters at the Tivoli hotel, secretaries from the British Embassy and American officials.

Most important, he introduced me to the refugees who came into the office during the two weeks we were together; he also took me to Caxias, a fortress where refugees who had entered Portugal illegally were held in large cages. Before his departure for France, Russ took me to Caldas da Rainha (Baths of the Queen) where over a weekend we interviewed at length some thirty families the AFSC was trying to help. Not all of them were on our relief rolls, since some were being cared for by another agency, but for some historical reason we were the primary committee to help with their immigration to anywhere we could find. Russ then left for Marseille, where the AFSC had moved its headquarters after the Germans had occupied Paris in June 1940. He would work either there or with the three other offices in Toulouse, Montauban or Perpignan.

The Lisbon office of the AFSC had been opened in the spring of 1941, somewhat after the peak of the refugee flow into Portugal, when perhaps 200,000 people had arrived after the shattering Nazi German victory over the French armies in June 1940. Every available boat in Portugal had been filled, taking people away to the United States, Great Britain, or Latin America. Some even held visas for Thailand. A number of Americans were finally coming home; others were fortunate citizens of European countries who carried full documents. But most were stateless. If they couldn't find individuals, a committee or a government to sponsor them, they had to remain in Portugal.

Many arrived at our door without proper papers. They managed to come via France at great physical risk, avoiding the French frontier guards and crossing Spain illegally. They feared being picked up by the Portuguese police and put into their awful jails. The deepest fear of stateless Germans and Austrians, and the French who had left France without permission, was of being turned over to the Spanish police who were thought to be working so closely with the Gestapo that refugees might be passed back to the Nazi police. It was not unusual for a refugee, while talking to me, to stare out the window the whole time, just to be sure the police had not been on his or her trail.

In *The Night in Lisbon*, Erich Remarque captured the situation well:

> The coast of Portugal had become the last hope of the fugitive. . . . If one could not reach it, you were lost, condemned to bleed away in a jungle of consulates, police stations, and government offices, where visas were refused and work and residence permits unobtainable, a jungle of internment camps, bureaucratic red tape, loneliness, homesickness, a withering universal indifference. As usual in times of war, fear and affliction, the individual human

being ceased to exist; only one thing counted, a valid passport.[2]

Every refugee knew AFSC funds were limited, of course. And everyone who managed to get to the office without being arrested felt compelled to show his or her need to be the greatest and most urgent. We knew that there were others about to arrive; it was not easy to be always as open and Quakerly as we would have liked. On the other hand, a sympathetic ear was a boon for so many who had been hunted by Nazi, French or Spanish police as they had crossed frontiers illegally, at night, in forests where the bark of a dog could mean being tracked down.

More dramatic—and distressing—were the men who had been picked up by the police before reaching us. They were taken to the infamous military fortress Caxias, just out of town by the river Tagus, and put into cages originally designed for 10, which might now hold up to 30 men each. These men were of all nationalities; their clothes were often mere rags. They had no privacy, even when going to the stinking toilet in the corner. They had come to Portugal without documents—no passport, no birth certificate, no identification at all. The unlucky ones were not able to speak Portuguese, French, Spanish, Polish or English, the languages of the relief agencies. The lucky ones were able to speak one of these, and the more variety the better. For French speakers, the favored strategy was to try to pass themselves off as Québecois, as a way of getting to Canada or into the Canadian services.

Philip Conard was the head of the AFSC's delegation to Portugal from 1941 to 1945.

On my monthly visits to Caxias I could at least help them get in touch with their consul, if there was one in Lisbon. But most were out of favor with their native countries; otherwise they would have been in their armies. Lacking a place for private talk in this infamous jail, I had no way to get facts that might aid their release.

However, I was able to bring to these wretched refugees with little hope of freedom supplies like underwear, t-shirts, note pads, envelopes and pencils, and some candy bars. Whenever I was discouraged by the tide of human misery and evidence of official disdain, and it was time for my prison visits, I always emerged from the fetid atmosphere so glad to be able to breathe the outside air, see the sky and walk freely. I would then chide myself for having been so self-regarding as to allow the luxury of discouragement.

CALDAS DA RAINHA—ASSIGNED RESIDENCE

Caldas da Rainha was a summer resort, a watering place which had been requisitioned by the government. It now housed refugees waiting for transit to their final destinations. The houses were typical of modest Mediterranean resorts of that period. They were small, without insulation, with one stove for cooking, perhaps one wood/coal stove for a bit of warmth on a cold morning. The refugees were permitted to live in any unoccupied house they could find, but had to report to the Portuguese police in Caldas each day. If they needed to go to Lisbon to visit a consulate or a doctor, they had to obtain a police permit for the day and report back on their return that evening.

My responsibility on visits to Caldas da Rainha was to talk to all the refugees on our list. I would hear how things were going, discuss how their visas were progressing, and assess what money they would need for the next month. On my first visit I needed to reassure them that, while I was not Russ Richie, I nevertheless would continue his work. I listened to hear enough of their individual stories to know who had been in which concentration camp, whether they had escaped or been released, who in their families had been lost or taken away by the authorities, whether they had come into Portugal legally or illegally. For each, the past was the most significant part of the self, since the present was a hiatus, and the future a total unknown.

On these trips I felt drained by making decisions about next steps for each of some thirty families in deep trouble. On his visit to Caldas, Russ had stayed with a White Russian family, and I followed the same practice. They understood my need for rest after an intensive day of sharing many distressing experiences.

One of the hardest tasks, I found, was deciding just how much money each individual or family needed. Eric Johnson, a close Quaker friend from school, was temporarily in Lisbon en route to the AFSC program in Morocco. He was an athletic man of medium height, with thick dark hair, a firm chin and quick movements. Horn-rimmed glasses made him appear somewhat owlish, but thanks to his warmth and openness he could make a quick connection with anyone. He traveled with me once to Caldas. In a letter home he wrote that since these refugees had been through terrible experiences, understandably they painted as black a picture of their plight as possible. Their aim was to win the sympathy of young Howard Wriggins (aged 23) from America. The hard fact, Eric reported, was that some of the interviews took on the aspect of a contest as each head of family sought to gain as much as possible. As an AFSC worker, I could stray only so far from our normal allowance scale.

Even so, one reason for going to Caldas was to help the refugees cope with the awful burden of bureaucratic indifference. If they had a passport of the right color, there was no need to worry; or, if not the right color, then the stamps within the passport could make the difference between prison and freedom, between being stuck in Caldas or free to move whenever there was shipping space. This chaotic world was one of great arbitrariness and total unpredictability. I could never see any rhyme or reason why some people managed all right and others ran into nothing but trouble. As the AFSC saw it, my task was to keep alive a sense of common humanity and belief in the possibility of mutual trust.

At the time, I may have exaggerated the power I had. The allowance I gave them would carry them until my next visit. I wasn't always certain the requests I heard were valid. This was especially true of medical necessities, which were often ambiguous. The most common treatment for nearly everything—back pains, irregular bowels, ear aches—was "injections." Some of them I suspected were more for providing psychic comfort to the patients or a small fee to willing doctors. But if the attention brought some respite to our charges, I concluded that Philadelphia's donors would not object.

Figuring out the appropriate level of money help was one problem. Equally challenging was strict honesty over migration possibilities. Having seen the resistance in Washington to refugee immigration, I was doubtful that many on the overloaded quota lists were likely to make it before the end of the war. Even though just enough refugees received visas to the United States or other places so that the outside world was not totally shut down for innocent civilian migrants, honestly keeping up their morale was difficult.

Helping them was also limited by communications. To those of us now used to e-mail everywhere, overnight mail and parcels at home, and nearly instantaneous voice link anywhere in the world, our difficulties fifty years ago are hard to imagine. Mail might be held up for weeks by US or British censors in Bermuda. Transatlantic telephoning for civilians was almost impossible; one might wait for a week to get a connection. When a call came through, it could well be fuzzy; furthermore, the other person might not be there. To send a telegram required getting a typed message to the post office down on the Avenida da Liberdade. Imagine the delays in getting immigration papers passed back and forth under such circumstances.

As I wrote in December 1942:

> The world is at war and I am comforting refugees, holding out hopes which, when I hold them out, I myself am almost convinced cannot be fulfilled. And the next time I see this person I may have to slap down one hope and substitute another to give them enough strength to go on. And it all must be done so gently, since they are near the edge already, and a shock would be the last shove over the lip. Some do go off the handle in my office. Although I can stand it reasonably calmly when a woman cries in her troubles, when a man breaks down I am badly stirred, I must admit. They come to me for money. . . . The evidence for making a decision on how much a person needs is very slight . . . hunch, guesswork, some objective evidence which may be put on for the trip to my office, nothing you can be sure of. But a decision must be made and on the spot. At the end of a day of interviewing I quietly prayed to myself that I had done the best I could.

ADVOCATES TOWARD TWO GOVERNMENTS

As I tried to figure out our role, I realized that we and the other relief organizations were the refugees' advocates before two very different governments. The first was Portugal—after all the authorities were permitting refugees to stay, however restrictively, in Assigned Residence. However, we were the ones who had to speak up for them and assure the government they would not become a public charge. The harder nut to crack was the ultimate end of their troubles: a visa to enter the United States or anywhere else. And that requires a few words about American immigration policy at the time.

(A) Portugal under Salazar:

Our activities depended on maintaining good working relations with the Portuguese government. Portugal was then under the repressive grip of Dr. António d'Oliveira Salazar.[3] He had been placed in power by the army in 1926, after a period of protracted political disorders. His government served the interests mainly of the landed, the army and a small capitalist elite. A devout conservative Catholic inspired by the papal encyclicals of Leo XIII, this former professor of political economy established the "Estado Novo," a corporatist state like Mussolini's Italy. All economic activity was grouped under large "corporations" that theoretically combined labor, capital and consumer interests. In reality, however, only a small elite of conservative families prospered.

Salazar saw virtue in moving as slowly as possible into the modern world. Just how slowly was dramatized for us one Sunday morning. Eric Johnson and I were returning from Caldas to Lisbon via a picturesque Portuguese town, Obidos. We were up early, walking on the Moorish ramparts. To our astonishment, from the walls we watched a medieval pageant. The village was on its way to the nearby market town, the week's production going to market. Peasant donkey carts carrying pigs, chickens and ducks; wheels of cheese; donkeys with bulging bags of hay were slowly moving forward. Long-skirted women leading children by the hand, men wearing knitted tasseled green and orange caps, some with substantial pipes, leading cows or tethered goats, or an occasional horse. Some old men and women rode in carts, but otherwise everyone else slowly walked. Priests with their low-slung black platter hats, nuns in their strict and voluminous habits—they were there, too. Geoffrey Chaucer himself might have been in the company. It was a dramatic eyeful, confirming Salazar's hope for Portugal: as little social and economic change in the countryside as possible.

Under Salazar, the place for women was in the home; trade union activity was forbidden; literacy was the lowest in Europe. Like the neighboring fascist regime in Spain, Salazar's gave highest priority to public order, permitting as little overt opposition and public contention as possible. Those of us who had been aware of Nazi rampages and pogroms in Germany and Austria, or French labor disorders or extreme rightist parades in the 1930s, could not quite believe the public quiet on the surface of Salazar's Portugal. He himself was reclusive and shy of public appearances.

In the summer of 1940, the Portuguese had been swamped with thousands of people who had fled before the advancing German armies. Most central Europeans and many others who had earlier managed to escape to France fled south. They desperately wanted to get to Portugal, the sole remaining escape hatch as Hitler's armies appeared unstoppable. In that year, some estimates suggest 10,000 Jews entered Portugal. The Portuguese consul in Bordeaux, a humane man, issued thousands of visas. According to the story we heard, he mobilized his whole family to rapidly stamp the necessary papers so these harassed people could leave France ahead of the German armies and cross Spain into Portugal.[4]

Even though Portugal was neutral during the war and since the fourteenth century had been an ally of Great Britain, it was still subject to a strict naval blockade as Britain sought to limit the flow of goods to German-occupied Europe. As a result, Portugal's resources were stretched thin; there was little to spare for these unexpected foreigners. Moreover, overly generous help to refugees fleeing Nazi Germany, the Portuguese argued, could be seen as unneutral and might invite German retaliation. Their policy was to maintain obvious pressure on the refugees so they would keep moving on and out of Portugal. The police had wide popular support for their restraints on refugee activities.

Portugal was clearly a police state, and remained so long after the end of World War II. Informers were thought to be everywhere—at railroad stations, post offices, and in stores. Telephones were assumed to be bugged, travelers without proper identity cards could be arrested at train stations, on trains or buses, and summarily jailed. There were rumors of jail waiting for anyone acting against the regime. We knew from direct observation that the jails were medieval affairs.

To be sent to the fortress of Caxias might mean at least six months if one could not show clear identity papers or that one had external sponsors such as a consulate or foreign relief committee. Spaniards in these Portuguese jails were particularly vulnerable, as the regime feared "political infection" from former Spanish republican sympathizers. Although censorship was strict and the government prohibited open political debate, unlike in Franco's Spain, there were few reported cases of political liquidations.

Antonio Tabucchi's novel, *Pereira Declares*, clearly evokes what life was like in the late 1930s for a modest journalist who was constantly being badgered by his boss to be more responsive to the Salazar government's sensitivities.[5] The drama of that story revolves around the growing sense of futility of a minor journalist who accidentally meets a young Portuguese dissident, whose cousin comes from Spain to recruit for the International Brigade. In the end the police catch up with this young man, beating him so badly he dies. In a final spurt of courage, the journalist writes a detailed account of the police brutality, something everyone knows about but never dares mention. He arranges to have it published on the first page of the newspaper, his literary commentary, for which he has full responsibility. With a false passport he was able to get from the hoard collected by the dissident, he flees on a boat leaving immediately for Argentina. The book, published in 1992, touched a live chord in Europe and, according to the blurb on the jacket, has been translated into at least fifteen languages.

Like everyone else, we too felt that we were being watched; continuing our work depended on being very careful. Most of our day-to-day dealings were with the Foreign Department of the PVDE (Vigilance and State Defense Police), whose primary responsibility was said to be to root out any activities that might threaten the regime. They reportedly enforced the censorship, policed the work force, and vetted people for jobs. Compared to the Nazi police they were discreet, but their reputation was intimidating all the same. It was to officers in the PVDE we had to go to obtain the release of someone from the military prison, to get permission for refugees to come to Lisbon for medical treatment or to see a consulate about their visas. Often it was a routine matter, requiring only a simple letter identifying the person in question. Sometimes, however, it would require a visit to the PVDE headquarters. The officers who received me were all polite and adequately well spoken in either English or French. Their boots were always high gloss and their uniforms very well pressed.

(B) United States Immigration Policy

The American officials presented a quite different problem.[6] They were all very civil; they found us useful on occasion. Some of the younger ones were personally friendly enough, but they had strict orders limiting their flexibility on immigration questions.

Since the 1920s, American immigration had been organized around annual country quotas, designed to favor immigrants from northern Europe. With the Depression, there were strong labor lobbies, nativist groups and anti-Semitism as well as the Treasury and Labor Departments opposed even to using these quota numbers to the full. Anti-Semitism in the Congress and the population was considered so strong that even spokesmen for Jewish organizations were reluctant to push for the full use of existing quota numbers for fear that any raising of the issue of immigration would lead to Congress canceling existing legislation, however limiting. A number of efforts in Congress to grant special entry permits for 20,000 refugee children from Germany following the *Kristalnacht* pogrom were effectively blocked. Tragically, these awful events in Germany coincided in the 1930s with the economic collapse of the Depression. The slow-down in economic recovery in this country only strengthened the anti-immigration lobbies.

In addition, there were administrative decisions within the Visa Division of the U.S. State Department that imposed time-consuming and often onerous conditions before a visa could be issued. As I have mentioned, a prospective immigrant would have to have an affidavit from a relative or a reasonably prosperous American, either offering a job or assuring the visa issuing officer that the candidate would not become a public charge. It was often up to the consul who issued the visa to assess whether a proposed affidavit was sufficient. Moreover, quota numbers required before an authorized visa could be issued were trickled out very slowly. On this point, we tended to blame the officials in the Visa Division whom the AFSC had to deal with.

Later on I learned that the responsibility lay with someone higher up, Assistant Secretary Breckenridge Long, then head of the Office of Refugee Affairs. He seems to have been determined to allow in as few refugees as possible. Breckenridge Long periodically changed the procedures, adding new complications. As Long reported to his colleagues in the summer of 1940:

> We can delay and effectively stop for a temporary period of indefinite length the number of immigrants into the United States. We could do this by simply advising our consulates to put every obstacle in the way, and to require additional evidence and to resort to various administrative devices which would postpone and postpone and postpone the granting of the visas.[7]

Eveline B., a German, was a good example of Breckenridge Long's success. She reached Portugal from Italy before I arrived in May 1942. She came our way because of a painful case of nephritis. She was a tired, thin woman, part Jewish, who walked with a cane. She received from us a supplement to help cover treatments. She had originally fled from Germany to friends in Italy when Italy seemed a safer place. When she heard that her United States visa had been authorized, she came by train to Lisbon expecting to pick it up at the U.S. Consulate. Unfortunately, because travel was uncertain and getting transit visas took time, she could not arrive until only two days before her boat was to leave Lisbon. Since it seemed to the shipping company that she was not likely to arrive on time, they sold her reservation to someone in Casablanca who was equally desperate to leave an area under Vichy French control. The boat left Casablanca en route to

Lisbon the day before Eveline arrived in Lisbon, so she was out of luck. This was in April 1941. While she was waiting for another space, the U.S. visa regulations were changed. When she went to the consulate, she was asked whether she had relatives in occupied countries. As she later told the story, "my hair stood up on its ends and I felt cold chills run down my spine because I had to admit that I still had relatives in Vienna." By July 1943 she was still waiting for her visa. One of Marnie Scauffler's aides reported that during the year from December 1942 to December 1943 only 7,000 refugees entered the United States, and FBI clearance could take up to four months.

Following Pearl Harbor and the United States' direct involvement in the war, there was much talk of how the Nazis had weakened their neighbors by advance infiltration of spies and Fifth Column agents. The rounding up of Americans of Japanese descent and putting them in internment camps in the mountain states reflects some of the same anxieties. About the time I came to Lisbon, security anxieties had become so urgent to the authorities that any cable about an individual would not be delivered unless it contained the person's full name and address.

Similar fears were expressed directly when I paid a courtesy call on George Kennan, who was U.S. Minister in Lisbon at the time. He was civil but severe, with an impressive forehead and a very well starched shirt. Compared to my disheveled visitors, he was immaculate. Toward the end of a thoroughly correct conversation, he leaned forward, looked at me intently and said, to my surprise: "Of course you realize, Mr. Wriggins, that the activities of your committee and the others are tearing a hole in the security of the United States." He went on: "You have no way of really knowing about the identity of the people you are helping. You have their stories but you have no way of confirming their veracity." My answer was "Sir, if you sat listening to their stories the way I have, and saw the fear and anxiety in their eyes, I think you would be able to make some distinctions."[8]

About this time, as further evidence of Washington's anxieties, we were told by Philadelphia that we had to include the birth date of the person referred to, as well as his or her full name and address, or the telegram would not be delivered.

INDIVIDUAL ACCOUNTS

Some of the stories I heard in my office were unforgettable. Heinz W. was Austrian, a young man of about 25. He told me his story while hiding behind the curtain at my little office's second story window. He was a spare, tense young man, his hair neatly combed, his clothes obviously the worse for wear. Every few moments he glanced at the street below to see whether the police were waiting to arrest him.

> My father, who was half-Jewish, was arrested in our apartment in Vienna by the Nazi police and taken away. Luckily, I was not at home at the time. A neighbor, knowing where I was working, came running. She told me not to return or I too would be arrested. I didn't know what to do. I decided it was better to disappear, and managed to cross the frontier into Hungary, where I had a cousin in Budapest. I never knew quite how it happened, but the Jewish community there was able to buy or somehow obtain a Danube steamer and a large number of us were able to escape down the Danube. It was so crowded that if all of us had been on deck at once, the boat would have overturned; so we were divided into three groups, only one group allowed on deck at any one time. It was indescribably crowded; food and water were scarce. But somehow we managed to get down the Danube and to Burgas on the Black Sea. We stopped at Istanbul for supplies and extra fuel, through the Sea of Marmora and then sailed into the Aegean, bound for Palestine. Unhappily, a storm came up, with strong winds and huge waves. The boat was not built for the Aegean. Rather than see us all drown, the captain ran aground safely on the Island of Rhodes. Under pressure from the Germans, the Italian authorities put most of us Jews in an internment camp in Italy. Luckily, the Italian camps were not strictly run, so I was able to escape. I managed to cross into France and then Spain. Last week I crossed the Pyrenees near Badajoz at night and luckily have not yet been arrested here in Portugal. Can you help me?

All the while he was telling me, his eyes kept returning to the pavement below. He was obviously hungry, scared, too, but a bit proud of the ingenuity and luck that had brought him through so much. We helped him get squared away with the Portuguese police. The JDC helped him with support. I saw him whenever I went to Caldas, and we often had coffee together. He tried to be up-beat. He was thankful to have arrived safely in Portugal, but was impatient to be off.

When he finally reached America several years later I heard through the Service Committee that he tried to get into touch with me. In 1968, when I was at Columbia, he joined me for lunch at the Faculty House. He had a wife and two children and a small house on Long

Island, and was selling advertising space for *Playbill*, New York City's theater program.

A former Hungarian citizen, Lazlo M. had had to flee Hungary with his wife because, when he was a university student, he had become known as an opponent of the regime. In France, where he had originally felt safe, he had renounced his Hungarian citizenship and sought to connect up with the British office that was welcoming additional volunteers. But with the collapse of France the operation was stopped, and he was now stateless. The rush from Paris, "l'exode," had been so hectic that he and his wife had become separated and had lost touch with each other. He was now in Lisbon, with their baby, hoping still to go to Britain. I later learned that he and the baby were able to get to Britain, where he was absorbed into the British forces as an interpreter. I never knew what happened to his wife.

Jacob P. had been a lawyer in Germany. He and his wife had been stuck in Lisbon for several years. He was a short man, heavy set, who walked stiffly with a cane. When he crossed his legs he used his right hand to help. He wore thick glasses in black frames. His forehead was deeply furrowed by a permanent frown. They had just received word that his parents had recently been "sent off to Poland." They had sought help in tracing their parents from the Polish Red Cross. However, the PRC could not help locate individuals, so he had come to the AFSC. With my encouragement he tried to tell me what it had been like to be deprived of his German citizenship and to suddenly lose his respected position in Munich. Like other Jewish lawyers, he was forbidden to enter the courts; doctor friends were prohibited from practicing, professors no longer could teach; nurses and social workers lost their jobs. He and his wife had to wear a Star of David arm band. Their children could no longer go to the public schools. They were forbidden to go to their old shops or public parks. They watched Jewish shops broken into, everything stolen and then the shops burned. A synagogue they attended had been torched. Most hospitals no longer would treat them. Then some of their friends were arrested for trumped up charges; sometimes they were warned to leave Germany right away, sometimes they were beaten. "Anxiety hung about us all." Sometimes friends disappeared, sent to concentration camps and required to do work quite beyond their strength. They were supposed to deposit all their money in registered accounts. Banker friends regretfully told them they were no longer allowed to protect their savings, so their life savings were expropriated. His parents refused to leave Germany and they did not want to leave their parents alone at such increasingly terrible times, so they stayed on. When their apartment was requisitioned they had to contract into a miserable, crowded slum two room apartment. After Jacob was arrested, beaten and then released on condition he promptly emigrate, they finally decided to leave. That was not easy; it took all their remaining money. They fled to France, passed through several of the camps and ended up in Portugal with no money and no visas. He had friends in Argentina who, he said, were working on visas. So Phil Conard helped him draft a cable to them in Spanish.

This account and that of many others who came to our office vividly brought home to me what was really happening in Occupied Europe. At first it was incredible that in the twentieth century such things could be happening; but there could be no doubt any longer. The miserable people I worked with were really the lucky ones.

People were stuck in Portugal because the regulations were now so complicated they often could not be properly matched. Each piece of paper depended upon others. Even before the Nazi occupation of southern France, the most exasperating was the exit visa required to leave France. You couldn't get that unless you had a clearly valid transit visa for Spain. However, that wouldn't be given until you had a valid transit visa for Portugal. But that required a confirmed space on a ship. And for that you had to have a visa to somewhere. Not infrequently, by the time one had obtained all the necessary authorizations, the transit visa for Portugal had expired, so the transit visa for Spain would not be recognized at the Spanish border, nor would the exit visa be granted for leaving France. And so one would have to begin all over again.

One high-strung young woman told of a nightmare that recurred frequently. It seemed as if she was lost in a jungle of consulates, all of them having closed doors that could only be opened by insistent knocking, to be greeted by a sleepy porter whose only message was "No visas today."

Franz Kafka was a favorite literary reference for these educated refugees. *The Castle* beautifully described their situation. In Kafka's world, authority was pervasive but unreachable, the bureaucratic world arbitrary and baffling. "The Castle moves slowly and the worst of it is that one never knows what the slowness means. . .

One can never find out what is happening, or only a long time afterwards." They saw many examples of "ludicrous bungling which may decide the life of a human being." [9] Indeed, in my more imaginative moments I saw us as intermediaries between the refugees and The Castle. We knew more about the workings of the American Castle than they did. While we knew the details of penetrating the ramparts, there seemed no way we could persuade the authorities inside the ramparts to grant prompt entry to our refugees.

The uncertainty that also beset us came home to me one day when Phil and I were at dockside, happily seeing off a number of our charges. We realized that a young couple who had been in separate jails for some months as illegal arrivals in Portugal and who were supposed to leave on this boat were nowhere to be seen. We had worked hard to help them complete their papers, confirm their reservations and arrange with the police their timely transfer to dockside. Finally, Phil scribbled a note and handed it to a relief worker about to go on board. He disappeared up the gangplank. After fifteen minutes we had the thumbs up sign. We learned later that the couple were being held in the ship's brig until the ship sailed. No one in the police dared take the responsibility to set them free even to leave the country.

Fortunately the JDC (or "the Joint") had its European headquarters in Lisbon. A most remarkable man, Dr. Joseph Schwartz, was chairman of the European Executive Council of the American Jewish Joint Distribution Committee (JDC) and headed the office. Quiet and thoughtful, he was originally trained as a rabbi at Yeshiva University and had a Yale PhD in Semitic Studies. He was tall, with a mane of black hair, a large mouth and prominent nose. He had a deeply sad face. I thought at the time he bore the marks of the awful events he was doing his best to ameliorate. The burdens of his generation's diaspora lay upon his shoulders. At the time, in 1942, I did not comprehend the true horror of what we now understand as the Holocaust. He was an important source of encouragement to me when Phil Conard went home on leave. He had deep circles under his eyes. Because of all he did for the hunted stateless Jewish refugees, I suspected he rarely slept. Never for a moment could he really rest, knowing that a particular effort of his might save a trainload of people. Yet, when he greeted an old friend or was impressed by a good piece of work by a member of his staff he had a broad, winning smile. Joe Schwartz's organization more than any other was critical for the survival and movement out of harm's way of thousands if not millions of threatened Jews. Until the occupation of all of France, he traveled there frequently and to Switzerland. On occasion, he included me in evenings at his flat after he had returned from a trip. It was then that he told us of what he had seen—the visits to the deplorable French internment camps of Gurs or Le Vernet, for example.

Occasionally he managed a diversion from these awful events; he and several of his colleagues, including some from the HICEM/HIAS, would turn to card games or swap stories. They were great on Jewish jokes, telling stories on themselves, which they were free to do but no goy ought to try. Herb Katski, one of his aides, and I became friends; we sometimes met for lunch and cheered each other up when we were discouraged.

Another source of support was our office secretary and manager, Dorothy Thumwood.[10] Luckily for us, the short, blue-eyed, tireless Dorothy was a source of guidance in the intricacies of doing business in Portugal. From the first, when she was hired by Marnie Schauffler in 1941, she was one of the anchors of the AFSC enterprise. She carefully guided us fumbling Americans, helping us deal with the petty officials whose sympathy and support we needed to enlist. She was totally reliable and took pride in working for the Quakers. She was somewhat motherly, yet liked to be squired around in that male chauvinist society.

Dr. Joseph Schwartz was head of the JDC in Europe. The burden of his generation's Diaspora lay on his shoulders.

DIPLOMATIC CIVILIAN EXCHANGE

Occasionally some unexpected but urgent need cropped up requiring the fullest attention of all of us. The American consulate asked us, the JDC, HIAS, and the Unitarian Service Committee (USC) to rally around. Based in Boston, the USC, with the help of the International Rescue Committee, looked out for those refugees who had obvious anti-Fascist political credentials. There has long been an interstate tradition that when a war begins, as time and logistics permit, officials and ordinary civilians of enemy nationality are returned to their home country by means of a diplomatic exchange arranged through the International Red Cross. Reciprocity works normally to make likely a humane exchange. In July 1942, the International Committee of the Red Cross (ICRC) had arranged an exchange of American and German civilians to take place in Lisbon, using the Swedish vessel *Drottningholm*. Germans who had been residing in the United States were exchanged for Americans who had been living or working in Germany, Italy, Scandinavia and Spain. At the request of the consulate, "welfare organizations," as we were known by the consulate, arranged to feed them on their arrival by train and help steer them to a temporary consulate set up in the station to process their papers. Dorothy called on one of the hotel caterers to provide simple but solid sandwiches and refreshments. The JDC and HICEM, with a much larger staff, handled the logistics of hotel assignments, baggage handling and buses to take them to their hotels and *pensions*.

The first train was from Italy. The most colorful group were priests, all in black, with black rimmed spectacles and black pancake hats. They were run a close second by a number of well-dressed women with elegant poodles, in from the Italian Riviera. Both the women and the dogs looked singularly well fed; but everyone else looked quite hungry, as if they had been on short rations for quite a time.

In a twinkling all the sandwiches were gone, though we were expecting other trains shortly. We counted noses, checked on the original number of sandwiches. How could they all have been eaten so quickly? A large black bag fell open and five sandwiches went bouncing along the station floor. Once we assured all the passengers that they would be fed at their hotels and *pensions*, more sandwiches miraculously reappeared. Most people laughed, some a bit sheepishly. But under the circumstances, we should not have been surprised.

The next group of trains steamed in from Norway and Scandinavia. These Americans looked far less harassed; they were obviously not as hungry as the group from Italy. Other Americans came from Germany. They seemed to have been reasonably well cared for, too. But I was distracted by an unexpected sight: the escort for the German group did not at all fit the stereotype of the spick-and-span German official in polished boots. To this day I have not forgotten the slight little man with wire-rimmed glasses who seemed nervously in charge of the documents for this group. His trousers had suffered a big tear in the seat.

For those of us who remember the movie *Casablanca*, refugees there wanted above all to get to Lisbon. Like the celluloid Casablanca, those of us in Lisbon thought of the city as a "seething cauldron of espionage and counterespionage," as the U.S. Minister George Kennan put it.[11] It was hard to see anyone of foreign nationality and not to wonder what he or she was *really* doing. The British were very much in evidence, with a good deal of talk about the Anglo-Portuguese treaty as one of the longest running treaties still in force. No doubt the British had the place well under surveillance. One jolly looking Englishman invariably sat at the bar of the Tivoli Hotel, where he could see who came in and who came out, having his coffee after lunch. But he also seemed to be there when we came in for our lunch, too. He always smiled at us as Phil and I came in. I sat down beside him more than once if Phil was not with me, to have my coffee, too. But we never got beyond "I'm in the import-export business." Lisbon gossip often turned to the preemptive race between the Allies and Berlin to corner the Portuguese wolfram (tungsten) output, as neutral Portugal sought to keep both protagonists reasonably happy while letting them compete over the price.

Once in a while, an avuncular former British Foreign Office retiree, a friend of Dorothy's, would give me a call, inquiring about my impression of a hyper-active German refugee lady who periodically came in to share with us a letter from a friend of hers in Theresinstadt. Somehow she had permission to live in Lisbon, not at Caldas da Rainha, and that must have raised questions about how she had managed to circulate so freely. At that time, most people who knew about it thought Theresinstadt was some sort of a German-organized Jewish community, and that those who were being "deported" would be eventually sent to labor camps in Poland or to work in German war industries. The woman had good reason to be worried.

Sometimes the elderly diplomat would inquire about other refugees. He was properly apologetic when he did so. And since every time I was able to reassure him, I felt he was doing this simply to be able to report to the office at home that he had inquired of some other source than the internal intelligence he normally received.

There were numerous Germans in Lisbon, too. Sometimes we would run into them on the crowded sidewalks. At first, my Quaker instincts whispered that they were people just like us, and I ought at least to make eye contact to confirm that fact. But their faces remained obviously blank, as if I didn't exist. After hearing many of the first hand accounts of what the "stateless" had had to bear at the hands of the officials of the Hitler government, I lost interest in such gestures. There were restaurants and entertainment places that catered to their tastes. Sometimes, of an evening, one could hear through the window their chorus singing "Lili Marlene" or the "Horst Wessel".

CHAPTER THREE
SERVICING QUAKER
ACTIVITIES
IN FRANCE AND SPAIN

In Lisbon, in addition to helping the refugees who were unable to flee farther, we supported the Quaker civilian relief programs in France for Spanish refugees and victims of Hitler's policies. The AFSC had begun in France in 1938-1939 at the end of the Spanish Civil War, when some 300,000 Spanish refugees had fled to safety in southern France. In a desperate effort to gather in and provide for these hard-pressed people, the French government had established a number of austere refugee camps scattered in the south. As the Spanish refugees had fled to France, the Quaker relief staff had flowed to France with them.[1]

Less than two years after this influx from Spain, in June 1940 the government of France was overwhelmed in a mere six weeks by the German Blitzkreig. The defeat was stunning. The French army disintegrated and nearly two million French soldiers became prisoners of war. The French state, that great creation of Richelieu, Colbert and Napoleon, was shattered. The remains of the French government, under Premier Paul Reynaud, fled south, first to Bordeaux and then to Vichy, a spa famous for its health-giving waters. They improvised a government as best they could, set up in many requisitioned hotels. Marshal Philippe Pétain, the hero of Verdun, became Head of State. The Armistice had already been signed that gave Nazi Germany nearly complete powers over all aspects of French life. France was divided in two by a strictly enforced Line of Demarcation. The Occupied Zone included Paris, all of the northern and central regions and the western Atlantic coast. Unoccupied France, the area under the Vichy administration, included the southern and southwestern regions.

Despite the fall of the national French government, local bureaucratic structures of *Préfets* and *Sous-Préfets* came back to life remarkably quickly. An extensive policing system and special militias were rapidly assembled to follow orders from the Pétain government in Vichy, more responsive to the presumed than the real wishes of the German occupation forces at that time. Refugees and foreign Jews who had earlier found asylum in France were rounded up and put in internment camps by those French police and militiamen. Even Jews of French nationality were subject to arrest. [2]

After the defeat, the AFSC had access only to the southern zone, where our four branch offices (known as *délégations*) at Marseille, Toulouse, Montauban and Perpignan continued their efforts. The challenges they had been facing were now many times multiplied when a huge influx of some six million Dutch, Belgian and French citizens had fled south before the advancing German armies! Along with them came thousands of refugees of other national origins, many of them now stateless, who earlier had sought safety in France from Nazi authorities.

With the new influx and the draconian Vichy policies, many foreign Jews who managed to reach the south were arrested and sent to these internment camps. Rivesaltes, Gurs, Récébédou, Les Milles and Le Vernet were among the camps we knew about. Arthur Koestler's moving *Scum of the Earth* memorably evokes his incarceration in Le Vernet. It was hastily enlarged to hold the rapidly expanded *indésirables*. Its accommodations were awful; sanitation was nearly nonexistent. The inmates had to dispose of the daily accumulated excrement into a local river. [3] Real people who never knew of the book confirmed Koestler's reporting. Having listened to numerous accounts of life in the camps, sometimes I had nightmares, like a number of "my" refugees. I dreamed I was trapped in Le Vernet, wasting away for lack of food and the forced labor the camp guards demanded.

As harassed people came through our office, we heard more about the internment camps in France. Numerous refugees had had a brief taste of camp life before they were able to get papers to leave France. Les Milles, we learned, had been set up in an abandoned brickyard. It now contained mainly Jewish exiles from Germany and Austria; a number of the people we knew had passed through it. We heard that food was short; the principal meal was soup and that but a watery liquid. Brick dust was everywhere—in the air, in the water, in what little food they were given; the thin straw they slept on was permeated by it.

Held in an extermination camp, along with the 70,000 other, mostly foreign, Jews, this woman was most likely deported.

According to one visitor, prisoners were ordered to pile the bricks in an orderly way in one part of the brickyard. When that was done, they were ordered to pile them in the other side of the camp. We heard of Rivesaltes, a desolate camp near Perpignan, where the famous tramontane blew what seemed like a thousand days of the year. It was particularly hard on the children, whose lungs suffered from the constant wind, particularly in winter, and the lack of sufficient food.

Gurs, one of the numerous camps where the Vichy government interned "undesirables," foreigners and Jews including those of French nationality.

Refugees who came through our office in Lisbon confirmed that each month in the autumn the rations became smaller and more difficult to obtain. As local diets worsened, the four offices had opened modest supplementary feeding programs for undernourished French children. At one time in the early 1940s, some 80,000 were receiving supplements of milk and a fortified biscuit. A number of "children's colonies" had been established by charitable groups and individuals to care for hundreds of orphans or refugee children whose parents were interned or lost in the chaos. The "colonies," too, were regular recipients of AFSC supplies. "Surplus" dried milk could still be purchased in the U.S. But after the 1940 armistice with Germany, the British blockade prevented all shipments directly to France. If we obtained the proper documents from the British, order by order, it was still possible to ship to us in Portugal and for us to forward from there to our delegations in France. From time to time, some food supplies could be purchased on the market in Lisbon—sardines, tinned tuna, nuts and dried fruits. These had to be under strict controls, and shipped only by specific permission for each shipment, authorized by both the Portuguese and the British. Understandably, the Portuguese were bent on preventing foreigners from buying up precious food stocks or running up prices that would trigger a widespread galloping inflation.

The bulk shipments we managed to send were mainly for the refugees interned in the camps and for school feeding programs organized by our four *délégations.*

Used clothing came from the large AFSC clothing workshops in Philadelphia, Boston or Chicago that collected tons of clothing every year. If their stocks were temporarily low but shipping space was offered, other collaborating NGOs rallied around. Quite often addresses on the shipments would not be as exact as was ideal; or the people in Portugal could not read the address correctly. We would have to locate the very warehouse where the goods were lying idle and make sure they were forwarded as promptly as possible. We tried to expedite whatever was addressed to us for forwarding to Marseille or one of the other offices.

The following account from Marnie, written in April 1942, dramatizes the unpredictability and emergency character of shipping space:

> You would have been greatly interested in the furor of excitement of the departure from here of twenty tons of clothing for the internment camps, consigned to you . . . As we have written you we have been holding the Navicerts for some time awaiting shipping space in one of the Portuguese boats. We were warned that all that could be offered was a last minute vacancy, which finally occurred. At seven o'clock one evening, we were advised that we could have space for twenty tons if they were on board (in New York) by 3 o'clock the next afternoon. Only about six tons were already in New York, several more were in Philadelphia and a number of tons at the Mennonite Service Committee in Akron, Pennsylvania. Lillian [Traugott] by the feat of performing a miracle, secured trucks and the whole clothing warehouse turned out to select and load the bales by flashlight. The shipment from Philadelphia left about midnight and goodness knows what time the Akron load was sent. But it was all loaded and everyone has had a warm feeling of satisfaction ever since. We wish we could offer to you the same helpful crew in arranging the next lap of the journey.

It took us a long time to track down this particular shipment since, in their haste, the labeling had not been clear. When we finally read this letter, we better understood their difficulties.

We could also send food parcels from Lisbon to individuals in France through a Portuguese shipper. While it was hard for us to imagine just how important these periodic food parcels had become, we did have a list of people who needed them. They often wrote back expressing their gratitude. We also sent them to members of the AFSC staff working in the French program. A letter from Gilbert White working with the office in Marseille reminded us how necessary these packages were for the morale and effectiveness of the Marseille staff. Two and a half years later, when I arrived in Paris and tried to live off the Secours Quaker canteen, I realized how quickly one's mood and energy level were affected by insufficient food.

Before I left home I had heard from Mme. Thierry, the short, dynamic, talkative French woman in whose apartment I had lived as a student in Paris. With the collapse of France, she and her daughter had been able to go south and were living in Haute Garonne. They were not suffering in 1942 as much as the severely deprived city people. But the sardines, nuts and dried fruit I was able to send them personally were very much appreciated. In some small measure, I was able to repay a part of my debt to them.

ONE BIG MISTAKE

There is one big mistake I made that cost the Service Committee some $60,000, big bucks in those days. It concerned claims arising from an undeliverable shipment that had spoiled while waiting for the necessary Navicert permissions. In July 1942, Thorkild H., a pleasant, well-spoken Norwegian working part time with the Marseille delegation of Secours Quaker, came to Lisbon to sort out this longstanding affair. A substantial shipment of sardines, chocolate and breakfast food had been purchased sometime early in 1941 by Wilhelm Holst, Marseille office's purchasing agent, from A.P. Delmas, AFSC's normal Portuguese supplier. The French Secours National was also involved. This was the large French governmental organization that covered the administrative costs of many welfare agencies operating in France, and was AFSC's sponsor vis à vis the French Government. Naturally enough, the Secours National office in Lisbon also purchased supplies for its own operations and for other hard-pressed welfare agencies in France. The Norwegian, who apparently knew well all the staff in Marseille, explained that both AFSC and Secours National were working together to get the money back from M. Delmas, who had really been responsible for the loss.

In this case, unlike all the other shipments that Delmas had sent to Marseille, the fish had gone bad before he had been able to get the necessary Navicerts from the British. I was invited as an observer to an all-day meeting between the visiting Norwegian, a French representative of Secours National and M. Delmas. There were long complex arguments as to the original quality of the fish, which should not have gone bad, and as to why the Navicerts had not been obtained, and so forth. Delmas seemed clearly to blame.

In the end, a secretary who had been standing by produced a *procès verbal*, drafted I think by Thorkild H. He assured me that it had been only a record of the conversation, so that each party had a record of what had been discussed. As one present, wouldn't I please sign? Like the naive beginner that I then was, I put my signature on what I had just read, which seemed to me a fair account of the discussion. While it blamed Delmas for not getting the proper inspections and Navicert clearances on time, it confirmed that the shipment had been on behalf of AFSC. This turned out to be a "contingent liability" of AFSC that was only settled in Lisbon in August 1945!

I learned a lesson, but the AFSC paid the bill.[4]

DEPORTATIONS FROM FRANCE

In June and July 1942, reports filtered through of awful things happening in France. Suddenly the French authorities, first in Occupied France and by September in the southern part under Vichy rule, were issuing orders to their Prefects to arrest large numbers of foreign Jews and deport them to "destination unknown" in the East. The numbers were staggering at the time—20,000 to 30,000 from the Occupied Zone and 10,000 from "Unoccupied France."

The camps, such as Les Milles near Marseille, Le Vernet near Toulouse and Rivesaltes near Perpignan, were scenes of heartbreaking separations as French police vans were backed up to the camp entrances and men, women and children forcibly loaded and sent off. In some cases, parents had the choice of taking their children with them to an unknown future or leaving them behind in the hopes that friends and neighbors would care for them and raise them. We assumed at the time that these unfortunates were to be sent to work in military industries far into Poland and further east. However, it was hard for us to imagine how many of these uprooted people—especially the old and decrepit— could be useful in war industries.

We heard rumors of extermination camps. In 1942 we simply could not believe that, in the midst of a desperate war, the Nazis would waste their energies—and scarce railroad cars—on non-military objectives. We were also well aware that the British during World War I had used exaggerated stories of German brutality toward the Belgians to help justify the slaughter in the trenches. Could these be similar exaggerations? But the deportations, we knew, were real enough.

Russ Richie, my predecessor in Lisbon, wrote in his diary for Sunday, September 6, 1942:

> Last Wednesday morning saw the worst departure yet... children down to 2 yrs, families separated... some broad exceptions made, some sent on the train with the promise that they'd be got off in the morning. The visit of the Intendent de police, dePorgic and his chef de cabinet, Auseneau, topped it off. They took the list of exceptions drawn the night before and called them from the crowd at 7:30 in the cold morning —and sent them on the train—not dressed, no food, no baggage.

As Gilbert White wrote to us in Lisbon:

> While safe themselves, [the AFSC staff] have felt the heavy responsibility of those who by a few words or a little extra care, can perhaps, save the future of others. So rushed and casual have been some of the deportations that a single word of intervention has sometimes been sufficient to save a man from going.

At least for the moment. Many families preferred to leave children behind in France rather than take them to share their uncertain fate. Agencies that ran children's colonies, the Quakers among them, were besieged by parents seeking a safe haven for their children.

Naturally, these barbaric deportations intensified the discouragement if not despair of the refugee community in Caldas da Rainha. Individuals we knew who had hoped soon to see friends or relatives they had left behind in France, now feared the worst. In France large numbers of possible candidates for deportation went into hiding. At this time, the French authorities stopped issuing any exit visas, while the numbers who tried to escape from France sharply increased. They ran great risks to cross the Pyrenees at night, using inconspicuous but perilous trails and by-ways to avoid the more obvious border posts. By January 1943, Phil Conard's reports suggested that some 12,000 refugees had found their way to Barcelona, perhaps one fourth of them Jews. Since most had no Spanish papers and often had come without identification at all, they were quickly put in jail or into internment camps. Even those with valid visas for the United States or beyond got caught in the system and were unable to get to the consulates.

We guessed that the horror of the German and French arrests and deportations from France must have finally provoked the American government to release 1,000 quota numbers to the United States

Committee for European Children (USCOM). We learned that some thirty highly dedicated, active and competent women involved in children's agencies left New York in late October by the Portuguese boat *Nyassa* for Lisbon, to serve as escorts for these children.[5] They expected to escort the French children from the Spanish-Portuguese frontier to the U.S. and help settle them temporarily into American families to sit out the war.

Somewhat earlier there had been talk of my being transferred to the Marseille office, as a number of new delegates were arriving from the States and one of them could replace me in Lisbon. At the time I was delighted at the idea. But after consultation with Marseille, it became clear it would be more useful all around if I were to remain in Lisbon to help with the USCOM children. Had I gone to France then, just before the November 1942 Allied landings, my further utility for the AFSC would have been short-lived as I would have been interned in Germany with the others.

CHAPTER FOUR
ALLIED LANDINGS
AND LISBON LIFE

THE LANDINGS IN NORTH AFRICA AFFECT OUR ACTIVITIES

On November 8, 1942, we heard on the radio that combined Anglo-American units were landing on the beaches of Morocco and Algeria. It took several days before all French contingents stopped resisting. The very first news produced obvious though properly restrained excitement in neutral Lisbon.

The Allied presence in North Africa brought a marked change in the public mood. The palpable fear of a Nazi march through Spain into Portugal lifted; new hope infused frightened officials and the public in Lisbon. As a Portuguese friend put it, "Until then, we had always feared a German thrust through Spain to the Atlantic coast. These landings brought us hope that the Nazis were stoppable. Germany no longer seemed invincible."

Prudent neutrals, who understandably had held their fingers up to the shifting winds, now felt emboldened to be more helpful. People who hitherto had walked by on the street without seeing us now greeted us with smiles. Police authorities who had been strictly "correct" now shortened the time we might be kept waiting before an interview. Refugees who had been close to deep depression now were less despairing

The immediate effects on our activities were less salutary. Very soon after the Allied landings, German troops flooded the rest of France and Italy seized a portion of the maritime Alps. The 1,000 exit visas obtained for the child refugees by the JDC, AFSC, and the other relief agencies suddenly were in doubt. I later learned that, before and right after the Allied landings in North Africa, Roderick Davidson, an AFSC colleague, with a French doctor and a social worker, had criss-crossed "unoccupied" France, visiting camps, children's colonies and orphanages.[1] They interviewed frantic parents and their anxious children, taking on the heavy responsibility of choosing the 1,000 children from among several thousand candidates, to be sent to safety through Lisbon. He reported in his unpublished memoir that

> some of the children had come across Europe on foot,
> or almost so, from Poland and some without adults.
> Some had suitcases of stone hard stale bread; they
> saved it when hungry and kept it when being fed
> regularly as a psychological security measure.

For at least six weeks these three colleagues prepared their lists, gathered what paper work they could, and hoped the American consulate would be able to issue the necessary visa papers promptly and to arrange the exit visas with French authorities. It became harder and harder to communicate with Marseille. One message that did come through asked me to warn Philadelphia that "if the arrival of the children in the United States is accompanied by demonstrations unfriendly to any power, it will prevent future emigration, including the second half of the project." As it turned out, the intensified German presence in the south and Premier Laval's opposition precluded any chance of regularized exit from France for the refugee children.

We now heard numerous stories of additional children, some with families, others without, being rounded up and deported to Germany. Some hid in the woods to escape deportation. Hundreds were crossing into Spain each night. Many others tried to escape to Algeria or Morocco by whatever means they could.

AFSC IN FRANCE BECOMES SECOURS QUAKER

The AFSC staff in Marseille had anticipated for some time the Nazi occupation of all of France in 1942. With French colleagues they established Secours Quakers on paper, with all official approvals. Should the Americans have to depart, all funds and materiel were to be transferred to this new organization. All hoped that programs would continue so long as supplies could be had. The transfer duly took place in December 1942 in Gaillac, a town in the interior zone. German patrols were expected to be less frequent there than along the coast, where Allied landings could be expected. Shortly the American staff was instructed by the Germans to go to Lourdes, where Americans were being gathered. They were interned in Baden Baden for a year and a half before they were exchanged through Lisbon.[2]

For those of us in Lisbon, this newest threat to refugees in southern France heightened our sense of purpose. As shortages intensified, it was all the more important to forward supplies on to France or Spain promptly. As refugees still managed to get to Portugal despite frontier guards, it became even more vital to maintain friendly working relations with Portuguese authorities, to spare these new arrivals time in prison. Now each day seemed to count even more.

THE USCOM ESCORTS IN LISBON

By the time the USCOM women arrived in Lisbon, the Germans had already occupied all of France and the women's mission became very uncertain. There was nothing for them to do, and it could be weeks before we would know when or whether they could help with the children's transport.

Keeping committed and energetic women occupied during an enforced and unwanted stay was not easy. They were all professionals with considerable responsibilities at home. For these women all of whom were concerned with refugees and children's rescue, the war sharpened their sense of purpose. This was no time for a holiday in beautiful Portugal, but that's what was in the cards for them. Dorothy arranged tours to historic sites, some trips to the beach, some evening parties, too. More than once I heard one say to another, "Mental hygiene, Ruth, mental hygiene," or "Go take a nice hot bath, Mary", or "let's go for a brisk walk; that will help."

Whenever I recall the "USCOM ladies," as we dubbed them, I am reminded of one Saturday before the Sunday weekly PanAm Clipper departure with our mail. One of the USCOM team, a soft-spoken, gray-haired woman, came in late in the afternoon and asked rather diffidently if she could talk with me. I was in the office late that day, with a long evening ahead of me, catching up on some letters to Philadelphia on behalf of individual refugees. I looked at my desk, piled high, and with a rather helpless gesture said, "I'm beset by the mail deadline; I'm sorry I can't talk this afternoon. But I will be here tomorrow from nine in the morning. We could talk at length then." She quietly said, "Thank you; perhaps we can talk then." She did not turn up the next day. Late the following afternoon her shoes were found, next to each other on a cliff where the sea came quietly in at high tide. So far as I know, her body was never found. I felt dreadful. Phil Conard tried to cheer me up with the thought that if she was that deeply distressed, one conversation was not likely to have made the difference. But for a long time, I have wondered.

In Caldas da Rainha, some parents had long been ready to send their children to safety, even if they themselves could not go. They believed that any chance to get a member of the next generation into the United States was worth taking even at the cost of splitting the family for now. The refusal of the French government to allow the selected children to leave France gave these parents in Caldas de Rainha just such a chance. But with that chance came a terrible choice. If they grasped this opportunity for their children perhaps the parents would never see them again. Much would depend upon many unknowns. How long would be war go on? Would the United States open its doors again after the war? Would their children become too attached to their foster parents? As we talked in Caldas, worried parents tried to decide. I could only listen, asking an occasional counter question or voicing a possible alternative answer. After hearing her husband voice these awful questions as he sought a reasoned answer, one anguished woman burst out "We have already lost so much! Must we now give up even our children?"

The USCOM escorts now were indispensable. They took medical histories, talked at length with the parents about the best kind of placement and with the child to learn what kind of person that child was. I handled the documentation. None of the parents or children could go from Caldas to the Consulate in Lisbon without permission obtained from the police by Dr. Baruel, head of the Lisbon Jewish community. The strict Orthodox Jews could not travel on the Sabbath, a further complication. After a medical exam by the USCOM doctor acting for the Consulate, two stenographers filled out the necessary immigration forms. I retrieved the photostats and originals from the photo shop and returned them to the Consul, the kindly but scrupulous Mr. Miller. With the Unitarian Service Committee, the JDC, HICEM/HIAS, AFSC and the Consulate staff all working together, some of the children got through these formalities in five hours, which seemed miraculous compared to what most people experienced.

The AFSC office in Spain located a number of children whose parents were prepared to send them to Lisbon and on to the States. I have been in correspondence with one of them, long since married and living in England, who was four when she was sent with her half-sister:

> When my mother crossed from Vichy France into Spain in the autumn of 1942, we were put in prison with the possibility of being returned to France. The Friends approached my mother about the possibility of our being sent to the U.S.A. But the Americans were only giving visas to children, so she did not want us to go without her. At the time, Spain was expected to fall and they were able to trace my father, who had crossed into Spain and from there to Portugal where he was able to join the Polish Free Forces taken to England. It was he who gave permission for my half-sister and I to go to the USA. Of course Spain did not fall, and my mother never forgave him.[3]

In the end, the USCOM escorts cared for some 300 European children on their way to the States. Most had been selected from among refugees blocked in Casablanca and Spain. They and twenty-two from Caldas finally sailed on the *Serpa Pinta*. We all breathed a sigh of thanksgiving for the new opportunities opened up for those children, and for relief that the USCOM ladies finally had a task worthy of their talents and energy.

About this time we had fresh evidence that Portuguese officials were now more helpful to people who fled from France. A Frenchman whose name I do not remember found his way to our office and told the following extraordinary (but believable) story.

> It's a long story of how I was able to travel by freight train and on foot, crossing the frontiers at night, from southern France and across Spain. I entered Portugal late last week. Outside Lisbon someone was kind enough to let me clean up in his barn. This morning I came by bus into the main square of Lisbon. I got off the bus and tried inconspicuously to mingle in the crowds. But no luck. A policeman came up to me, and politely but firmly held me by the arm. He had

little English and French flags on his uniform lapels. He first tried English, then French, which he spoke wretchedly, but I could understand him. He looked me straight in the eye, "Are you here legally?" I thought for a minute, should I tell him the truth right off, or try some kind of a story? Sooner or later, my story would be found out, so I decided to tell him straight. "No", I said, "I have come from France; I could not even try for papers. Could you please tell me how to get to the French consulate?" He replied: "But the French consulate will not help you. Since the German occupation they have already changed everybody and if you couldn't get papers to leave France, they will send you back. You'd better go to the Quakers; they're more likely to help you." He knew your address without even looking it up and he then showed me how to get to your office.

I was surprised -- and pleased -- that we had such a reputation among the police. We gave him directions to the office of M. Grolier, de Gaulle's Free French representative.

THE BLOCKADE TIGHTENED

Bureaucratic controls on food shipments to France now became more complex. We had had to obtain a NAVICERT from the British authorities for shipments of supplies coming to us by sea. Now that all of France was occupied this became increasingly difficult, since the British (and U.S.) were all the more determined to stop the flow of supplies to German-occupied areas. I had to negotiate with a Monsieur T, the Lisbon representative of the Secours National, the French welfare organization that provided Secours Quaker with part of its child feeding ration.

He reported that Secours National was willing to receive goods from us for delivery to Secours Quaker in France. However, we first had to obtain the necessary LANDCERT from the British. The Ministry of Economic Warfare insisted upon this document before goods could move from Lisbon to France through Spain. We persuaded the International Red Cross to take responsibility for these shipments. In that way, we calculated, the British would have less reason to say no to our shipment. In the end, the British agreed and the International Red Cross moved our goods, delivering them to the French Secours National. Finally, they turned the goods over to the Secours Quaker for distribution to schoolchildren. By such laborious and round-about means we kept up a flow of limited resources to these child feeding and internment camp programs despite wartime restrictions.

SUPPORT FOR REFUGEE ACTIVITIES IN SPAIN

Phil Conard had special links to the Spanish-speaking community so we knew that conditions in camp Miranda de Ebro, near Bilbao in Spain, were very bad. Some 3,500 illegal entrants were crowded into a camp originally built for 700. Food was scarce, the sanitation abysmal, health conditions really awful. A number of refugees with authority to leave France with visas for Latin America had had to enter Spain illegally, since their visas to, say, Argentina would have expired before the Spanish and Portuguese transit visas would be granted. Those were the types of snarls we came to call Catch-22.

Once in a camp, the internees found it nearly impossible to communicate with the authorities, let alone get out to visit the consulates in question. The largely illiterate guards, fearful for their own futures, did not dare take any chances; only rarely would they let individuals out to visit their consulates. Yet most consulates would not grant visas without interviewing the candidates, and few had the spare personnel or the desire to visit the camps.

We were therefore relieved when David Blickenstaff and his wife, Janine, came through Lisbon in February 1943, assigned to establish refugee services in Madrid. A short man with carefully combed hair and dark brown eyes that seemed to have a special energy, he was experienced in the ways of the Iberian peninsula. David was a member of the Church of the Brethren and had worked in the Brethren aid program during the Spanish Civil War.[4] He first set up shop in their Madrid hotel room. Later the American Ambassador Carlton Hayes, the historian, offered him office space in the Embassy, where he acted on behalf of the JDC and the Unitarians as well as for the AFSC.

Many of David's needs for supplementary food supplies and clothing could not be met in Spain. Before we could ship anything to him we had to get permission from the Portuguese. Similarly, special permission was required even to forward from our office imported goods addressed to David Blickenstaff in Madrid. Anyone he was able to release from a Spanish camp or jail needed to be met by one of us at the Lisbon train station. They had to be accompanied to find food and lodging where they could wait for the next boat that, by some chance, might have a space.

David reported an amusing though rather desperate game that some undocumented inmates in Miranda de Ebro were trying. Sometimes the Polish Government in Exile in London would be unusually ingenious and a supply of food or clothing would suddenly appear at the camp, addressed to the Poles. Opportunities to leave via Gibraltar might be worked out by one or another London group. Or later, an authorization for x number of Czechs to leave via Gibraltar might come from Madrid. Or the Yugoslavs might receive a shipment of winter clothes in December. The number of stateless claiming any one single nationality would suddenly swell, depending upon where opportunity seemed to lie. But claiming Canadian citizenship seemed to be a favorite for French speakers in Spain who were not yet ready to go with de Gaulle.

About this time, we discovered what had happened to five tons of clothing shipped from Philadelphia. It had been sitting in a Lisbon warehouse down by the river, no one having advised us that it had arrived some months before. How we discovered it I do not recall and the record does not show. We wanted to forward it right away to David Blickenstaff for distribution in Miranda de Ebro, but the documentation did not tell us whether it was men's clothing, women's clothing or mixed. Imagine the frustration of the camp authorities or the welfare agencies if they had struggled with the customs authorities to have the goods released to them, only to find it was all women's clothing! I don't know what happened to that particular shipment, but we did get some men's clothing to David for distribution in Miranda.

Some time later, we learned that David had been able to spring 300 "stateless" men from that camp, by arguing that since stateless men were without nationality they were not likely to be subject to military mobilization if they were released. That persuaded the Spaniards that these men would not be likely to help the Allies. They were then established in the same kind of Résidence Forcé as our refugees in Caldas, and the JDC was able to cover most of the costs. In Spain, Caldas de Malavela was set up for women and children, while the husbands and fathers were sent to camps like Miranda. Lisbon would be the principal route for any who obtained documentation for Mexico or Latin America; Gibraltar was one exit men of military age could use to avoid Spanish prohibitions against allowing military men to leave.

With the German Occupation of southern France, the Vichy government had been overwhelmed. There could no longer be any pretense that the French Legation in Lisbon still represented a sovereign government.

LIFE IN LISBON

I could never quite shake the sense of the arbitrariness of this world. So many of my refugee friends had lost so much—family members, home, position, life work. So many family members were no longer in touch, perhaps in prison, deported or killed. So much in Europe had made it a hellish place. There was no apparent reason why I should be free and holding the power to give or withhold what others needed, and they should be penniless, facing a future of great uncertainty. I held a passport of a recognized nation. Because of depraved decisions made in their home country, these people were now stateless, unable to return home or to look ahead. Sometimes I would imagine the wasted years of waiting. Surrounded by so much tragedy and signs of human cruelty, it seemed essential to seek sources of refreshment.

Lisbon itself was full of opportunities for recreation. Dorothy knew all the jewel-like beaches within easy distance of Lisbon, and from April to October the water was wonderful. Now all the nearby beaches are built up with high rise hotels, but at that time they were untouched except by fishermen. So a Saturday or Sunday expedition, with one of Dorothy's picnic hampers, enabled a total change of mood. Once I knew where the beaches were, I did not need her guidance. Swimming, of course, was the best kind of exercise to help one forget the troubles we knew.

I came to know a young American, Bob Kemler, who was working in the Foreign Economic Administration, paralleling the British Ministry of Economic Warfare. By a tacit convention, we never talked about his work, though I had no such inhibitions about mine. He was living in a very fine pension, where the food was delicious and the company agreeable. In a nearby pension lived Joan Crossland-Taylor, about the same age, a handsome, energetic British Catholic woman, a secretary in the British Embassy. She enjoyed walking with a long loping stride like mine. I liked being with her and from her point of view, this puritanical Quaker was "safe" as a temporary wartime friend. We liked to stroll along the waterfront, munching sardines roasted on tiny charcoal fires on the quayside. Occasionally we went swimming on a Saturday when things were quiet.

Sometimes Phil would propose taking the air at the end of a hard day or on a Sunday afternoon, and we would go for a vigorous walk around the city. On the eastern side of Lisbon there is a largish hill with a park on the top. We sometimes walked up there to see the city laid out below us, with the ships moving up and down the river. In the evening Lisbon was particularly attractive, a sparkling city lit up like so few in Europe, most ships with their lights on.

Busy rivers are almost always a feast for the eye, and during the day the Tagus was dotted with ferries crisscrossing back and forth. Lateen rigged freight boats slowly moved upstream while those coming down moved more smartly. In the European spring showers were frequent but hardly heavy. The summer in Lisbon could be very hot, but there were often compensating breezes in from the Atlantic. I recall with pleasure the light in Lisbon, brilliant at noon but ever-changing as the day wore on. Toward late afternoon, the multi-colored houses changed their tints, the ochre-orange roof tiles taking on a deeper tone.

We would sometimes choose out-of-the-way side streets, many down by the docks smelling of fish, echoing to the calls of women announcing their fish, fruits or even light weight kitchen utensils in baskets balanced on their heads. In the spring, I recall, flowers were hanging everywhere, on little baskets outside windows, and, even in wartime, lightening the scene on the major Avenidas. Many houses were enlivened with ceramic tiles embedded in the walls, a reminder of 400 years of Moorish presence. There were tiled roofs everywhere. Without a camera, I imagined the compositions I might have made out of lights and shadows.

THE C.O. QUESTION

During my time in Lisbon, I became aware of nagging doubts about my C.O. position. Was I really a "pacifist" when I saw what a disaster it would be for all the people I was helping, even for the Portuguese, if the Nazis should come to control Portugal? Even worse would be a Nazi victory. Richard Gregg's proposals seemed far less persuasive in a world threatened by panzer divisions and the Gestapo.

In Lisbon we had a more than ringside seat to the war. The comforting hand of disbelief that had so often served me in Germantown, or even Chicago, was gradually pushed aside by stories of horrors brought to me daily by our refugee victims. The relieved response of the Portuguese, to say nothing of the relief of the refugees following the Allied landings in North Africa, showed me that they foresaw a very different world whether the Allies won and the Nazis were defeated, or vice versa. At a transatlantic distance it had been possible to think that it would make little difference whether one imperialist or another won in the end, by stressing all the evils of British and French colonialism, for instance, or discounting what the Nazis were really doing. But in Lisbon, I could not discount any longer.

I had studied enough European diplomatic history to know that the contests between great states seemed to go on and on, no matter who had won a particular war. First it was Francis I, then Charles the V, then Louis XIV, then Napoleon, then the British and French overseas. Portugal itself was full of evidence of the evanescence of imperial power. All this had confirmed for me the virtue of keeping out of such historic contests. This knowledge had helped to reinforce my pacifism. But as seen from near at hand in Lisbon, I could no longer dismiss this particular struggle as historically insignificant or morally inconsequential.

In Lisbon I read in The Times Literary Supplement a number of articles by E. H. Carr on the "Conditions of Peace." He held the only chair in International Relations in Great Britain, at the University of Aberystwyth in Wales. In the Spring of 1940 he had lectured at Dartmouth, so I was alert to his name.[5] He was then warning the British (and the Americans) that economic or military power in international affairs mattered greatly. After World War I, he argued, statesmen had spent all their time drawing frontiers, rather than considering how these small states could possibly survive situated where they were between two large, often contending states.

As important, the statesmen at Paris in 1918-19 had refused to think about how the German people were to be allowed their legitimate place in post-World War I Europe. Hitler, Carr seemed to argue, was more a result of these statesmen's folly than any other cause. You can imagine how controversial his views were in 1941-42. I saw how the presence of Allied forces across the Straits in North Africa made a real difference to the way the Portuguese looked at their world. I still remember seeing every day the changed way the Portuguese dealt with us after the landings in North Africa. This suggested that there was something important to what Carr was arguing about the role of power in international affairs—not what I understood as a Quakerly line of thought.

Thus, there were moments when doubts assailed me about my pacifism; but at this time, these were not deeply disturbing. There was so much to be done that could be helpful to other people; so many times when we could soften the inhumanity of bureaucratic systems. The well-recognized, distinctive Quaker role permitted us to assert the legitimacy of humane values when so many others were preoccupied with the power struggle. We had unusual opportunities. We were fortunate to be part of this affirmation, in itself a justification for our presence and our work.

CHAPTER FIVE
REFUGEE RESPONSES
TO ADVERSITY

Before laying down the work in Lisbon in the late summer of 1943, as I prepared for my next assignment in Algiers, I drew a few generalizations from my year and a half effort to enter into refugees' experience. To be sure, one of our goals had been precisely not to do that. We sought to see each as an individual deserving our full attention. And I vividly recall how differently individuals faced their particular challenges. Nevertheless, some points did strike me.[1]

While the refugees who got as far as Lisbon were spared the fears of deportation, each faced his own special kind of psychic hell. They knew that they were physically safe, particularly following the Allied landings in North Africa. But if their own escape had in any way put others at risk, they could not help feeling a special form of guilt. Even if, so far as they knew, they had come without adding to others' risks, they often felt guilty anyway. Simply to be alive while the future of loved ones left behind was so uncertain preyed upon their minds.

We were not aware of the Holocaust at this early date. In 1996, I reminisced in New York with Herb Katski, one of the JDC representatives in Portugal at the time. We agreed that in 1942 and early 1943 we had not known what was in store for Jews in Germany and Poland. It came as a relief to the two of us to recall that we both had been ignorant of this. We both had feared we had dismissed in disbelief what should then have been obvious to us both.

For most of the refugees, all that they had carefully accumulated (in the matter of things, but also in the matter of place, position and reputation) had been taken from them. They had to start over again. Moreover, while they were in Lisbon they lived in a hiatus, rather like a patient with an unknown disease who waits anxiously for an unknowable diagnosis.

Perhaps the greatest source of strength for them, apart from whatever religious belief they might still hold, was all of those around them shared the same uncertain life. For all, their fate depended upon documents, pieces of paper with the proper information, the proper stamps, the necessary signatures. At the same time, however, since visas and shipping space were scarce, they were bound to be mutually competitive.

For many there seemed to be nothing to do but sit at cafés. They would stretch a cup of coffee for hours, particularly in winter. They stayed as long as possible in the café's warmth, and waited — and talked. They were deeply vulnerable to rumor, the "refugee telegraph," as we called it. There was talk of no more boats; of special ships chartered by the Committees; of quite specific quota numbers, especially for such as they. After the Allied landings, there were rumors that the war would soon be over. Most of these rumors, like dreams, proved chimerical.

It was also difficult for the refugees to decide whether to be active or just be patient. They must have been constantly wondering: what should I be doing to help me out of here? Most had got as far as Lisbon by great and ingenious effort. They had friends who had pulled strings. They may have had just plain luck, *fortuna* as Machiavelli had called it, or used bribery at the right moment. I imagined the refugee musing: "To whom can I write in America or Argentina? Stamps are expensive. My address book has been lost. How can I pick up the tenuous threads that may be there? If only I could be clear on what I ought to do. Perhaps it is already hopeless." It was my job to moderate despair—perhaps after all there was something I, and they, could do.

These conditions exaggerated a person's character. Most of us most of the time can live within a broad spectrum of ups and downs. But when hard pressed by uncertainty, by fears of an unknowable future, by short rations over many months, by sheer loneliness, our inherent characteristics become more marked. Some people became more aggressive, egotistical, ready to sacrifice anyone for their own advantage, for food, for some link to authority. Others, on the surface not very different, became more saint-like, sharing what little they had, helping others in unexpected and inconspicuous ways. At Caldas, there were those who could think of no one but themselves. There were also some who were actively concerned about others, really aiming to help them while seeking nothing in return.

Some allowed themselves to rot, intellectually or physically. Others made the most of their enforced leisure. I recall an older man, a German professor of philology, who somehow continued to work on a major manuscript from notes he had managed to bring with him across Europe. A Hungarian, a non-Jew probably having fled Budapest for political reasons, took regular violin lessons from Maestro Jacobsohn, the Berlin Philharmonic's first violinist, who had had fled because he was a Jew. During the year and a half I was in Lisbon, the Hungarian became a really good violinist. I spent one long weekend in Caldas, when, after my interviews were over, Jacobsohn took me in hand for an afternoon to see if I could make something of my childhood efforts on this demanding, marvelous instrument. Occasionally, I was able to draw some sweet sounds from one of his violins, but I was not persuaded the fiddle was for me.

I had grown up believing that strict loyalty to one's wife or husband was one of the highest values. But I saw that men or women who were perforce separated from their spouses seemed to survive with greater vigor and better health when they found temporary partners for mutual comfort and reassurance. My sample was small; I didn't know the circumstances of their married life or separation; nor do I know the longer-run results. But the solitaires, men and women, did less well. To face their many difficulties alone for many was overwhelming.

Women who knew how to knit were much in demand as winter came on. Those with money ordered knitted vests, sweaters or caps. AFSC organized a volunteer knitting project for those in the Miranda de Ebro camp in Spain. I thought the knitters were the lucky ones; they were always needed. Many others had no such contributions to make. But a letter from Ross McClelland, the Quaker representative in Geneva stressed their resilience. Referring to the humiliated and the demoralized refugees he recalled those

who for so long had been unfortunate outcasts, so flagrantly
denied the most elemental claims of human
dignity...gradually sink into despair...[How]almost magical
is the effect on their personalities of relief from the constant
material anxiety... if they can at least count on some regular
assistance from someone like the Quakers.

NEW ASSIGNMENT: NORTH AFRICA

In mid-summer 1943 the AFSC decided that, when Phil
Conard returned to Lisbon from the States and a quick visit to Spain
and a new delegate arrived in Lisbon to help him, I should transfer to
North Africa to join Ken Kimberland, David Hartley and Eric Johnson.
Leslie Heath, our principal delegate there, was preparing to go home
after an intense year initiating the program. Ken, taking his place, was
moving the main office to Algiers, where the U.S. Office of Foreign
Relief and Rehabilitation Operations (OFRRO) had its headquarters.

To say good-bye to Phil Conard was not easy. He had been a
wonderfully understanding, gentle boss. He had also had the courage to
recommend to Philadelphia that the operation would be safe in my
hands while he was in the States. I had over four months running the
show; and on his return he expressed his satisfaction. It had been a
wonderful apprenticeship.

PART II   ALGERIA AND EGYPT
Refugees and Internees 1943-1944

Iberian Peninsula and North Africa

Spanish Civil War veterans, victims of Vichy's policy towards the undesirables, Libyan civilians, and refugees from Greece and Yugoslavia were among my charges in North Africa. Working with the Friends Ambulance Unit in Egypt, I had a heady taste of what international cooperation can accomplish.

Living conditions (in the camps) were dramatic...persecutions, illness, short rations, racism, xenophobia...The bulk of the internees are without clothing, without money and without means of improving their own conditions.
André Kaspi, *La mission de Jean Monet à Alger mars,* October 1943

CHAPTER SIX
SPANISH REFUGEES, VICHY INTERNEES AND LIBYANS

TRANSFER TO ALGIERS

In August 1943, with Anglo-American troops now in North Africa, a regular courier air service had been set up. I climbed aboard my first DC-3 flight stopping at Gibraltar and then landing in Fez. At the Fez airport I got one of the shocks of my life. From the quiet Lisbon backwater I was pitched into the middle of the Allied military machine, surrounded by jeeps, personnel carriers, trucks and planes. I was taken on a bumpy jeep ride into town, down a curving drive lined with stately palms, to the Palais Jamaï, a grand hotel in the Saracenic style.

After an unremarkable dinner of army food with some Arab flourishes, I was urged to visit the Great Market of Fez. I walked a short distance toward town, turned left through an imposing gate and was suddenly back in the fifteenth century, in my first Arab *souq.* Everywhere I looked were sellers and shoppers, donkeys loaded with sacks of grain or fuzzy Kabilye rugs, shrouded women. Branching lanes were bordered by tiny stalls, a *patron* sitting cross-legged near the front. Customers were drinking a colored drink from a glass or sipping coffee from a tiny cup. Tinny speakers blared out Arab music. I saw leather wallets, wool rugs and leather hassocks of the type that had been hawked around the cafés of Paris when I was a student there. However, I was not there to shop or gawk, and soon found my way back to the hotel.

The next day I jeeped back to the airport with travel orders for the short hop to Algiers. This time my DC-3 had bucket seats, very uncomfortable but convenient, as they could be folded up to transform the plane into a cargo carrier.

The AFSC flat in Algiers was an airy fourth floor apartment with tile floors that proved to be cool in summer, but a cold wake-up when winter came.

THE HUMAN PROBLEMS

Leslie Heath arrived in Morocco in July 1942, four months before the landings, to head the three-man Quaker team. He was a large balding man, warm-hearted and friendly with a way of settling his considerable bulk on his heels as he launched into his stories. At that time there were about six million Muslims in Algeria, 850,000 Christians (mainly French settlers known as *colons),* and some 140,000 Jews. Apart from a very small elite, most of the Muslims lived in poverty. It was clear that the AFSC could do nothing significant for that large group. After a quick survey, Leslie concluded that the most urgent need the AFSC could tackle was that of the 6,000 men in deplorable internment camps.

The most immediate need was for clothing. Three years into the war there was none available in North Africa, but clothing was something the AFSC could contribute, from its centers in Philadelphia, Boston and Chicago. After consulting with the International Red Cross representative and making careful approaches to selected camp commanders, Leslie and his crew began their quiet work.

Most internees were Spaniards who had fled to Algiers in 1938-1939 as the Spanish Republicans were defeated. French officials and businessmen in the *Maghreb* (Morocco, Algeria and Tunisia) were deeply suspicious of these presumed communists. As a result, many were still in the camps. Those who managed to get out did not have proper work permits. There were already thousands of poor Arabs and even Europeans out of work in depressed Algeria and, although free, the Spaniards were living a hand to mouth existence.

Other internees, of many nationalities, designated by the Vichy government as *indésirables,* had originally fled to France to escape arrest by Nazi or other police. They risked crossing to North Africa on the collapse of France in 1940. Others had been arrested by the Vichy regime and shipped to North Africa for internment. Perhaps three quarters of these were stateless Jews.

Leslie Heath, Ken Kimberland and David Hartley evolved a three-point program. They provided used clothing from Quaker stocks for the worst-off internees. With the help of French social workers, they identified destitute families of internees and provided small cash supplements or emergency food. They assisted disabled veterans among Spanish refugees who were not in camps. On occasion they were also able to act as intermediaries between the internees and the authorities.

THE ALLIED LANDINGS

The Allied landings proved crucial for the internees and for the scope of the Quaker programs. In November 1942 some 110,000 American and British troops with all their equipment landed on the beaches of Morocco and Algeria. Eight hundred ships had sailed in convoys directly from the United States or Great Britain. It is not surprising that this successful landing had greatly cheered the refugees in Lisbon and in North Africa, as people now saw that the Nazi machine might be stoppable.[1] These effects also influenced my views on conscientious objection.

From Portugal the landings had seemed to go very smoothly. In fact, however, they had been highly complicated and could easily have ended in disaster. Most unexpected of all, Admiral Jean François Darlan, President Pétain's heir apparent and Minister of the Marine, happened to be in Algiers at the time of the landings! He had flown from Vichy to see his son who had been stricken by polio. The key French officers who had been secretly enlisted to call for an immediate ceasefire once the landings began were outranked by Admiral Darlan. It took three days before he would call for an overall ceasefire.

Robert Murphy, the principal American representative in Algiers, commented on both the difficulties and yet the importance of relations between the allies and the French.

> It was not always easy for Americans to work with disparate [French] personalities, whose volatile temperaments were enhanced by their feelings of defeat, humiliation, pride and exile, but we could have done nothing without their generous assistance.[2]

Understandably, many Frenchmen resented the unheralded invasion of the Anglo-Saxon troops. Algeria had been treated as an integral part of France since 1840. The American and British forces saw the landings as "liberation." But for the French they were a blatant invasion of France itself. Almost as offensive, these intruders soon acted as if they owned the place. In addition, though I did not know it then, the French authorities were all too aware of nationalist stirrings among the Arab population. Appeals for constitutional changes had been vigorously opposed in Paris and by French settlers. No doubt Algerian nationalist leaders drew confidence from the collapse of France and the growing influence of America and Britain, co-authors of the Atlantic Charter that supported the hopes of colonial peoples.

Perhaps even more consequential to the French view of the Allies was the British naval attack, after the armistice in 1940, on the French fleet at Mers· el Kebir. Churchill had wanted to insure that France's sophisticated navy would not be added to the German capability to harass the hard-pressed Royal Navy in the Mediterranean.

It need not have surprised us that French officials were not immediately responsive to the Allies on such matters as dealing with the men in the internment camps. To reduce the chances of military resistance to the landings, the Allies had assured key French officials that the Allied forces were coming only for military action against the Nazis with no intention to intrude on the internal affairs of Morocco or Algeria. On news of the landings, most of the men in the internment camps expected to be released within a few days, but local officials made no move to free them. Because of the promises of non-interference in domestic affairs, Washington could not press very hard.

That the internment camps were not immediately opened provoked a public uproar in Britain and the United States. Within two weeks, President Roosevelt "requested" that all those imprisoned for opposition to Nazi policies should be freed. However, Vichy officials were not ready to release these *indésirables* to further complicate French rule.

A few of the internment camps were not far from some of the GIs' transit camps or supply depots. Following the landings, a considerable number of the inmates managed to escape and were hired by the armies as unskilled labor. Without work permits, they were routinely rearrested by the Algerian police. The AFSC encouraged hiring officers to give work contracts to each new employee, so the police would be less ready to rearrest them. But this was clearly a stopgap measure.

To examine the troublesome jurisdictional and police

questions, General Eisenhower established a Joint Commission for Prisoners and Refugees, co-chaired by senior British, American and French officials. Eric Johnson, who had come down from Lisbon in March 1943, became the commission's acting secretary. His report on visits to the camps and interviews with officials, police and refugees provided the International Commission a detailed view of the situation, and the police were given more consistent and humane instructions.

By March 1943 more than half the internees had been released and the more notorious camps closed. The able-bodied found work with the British and American forces, which usually included mess privileges and access to work clothes, shoes and overcoats. French authorities periodically asked AFSC how far Allied authorities should privilege the displaced persons when there were so many French nationals and Muslim Algerians also needing assistance. Alas, we never found an answer to this conundrum.

When the American Office of Foreign Relief and Rehabilitation Operations (OFRRO) came in some months after the landings, they found that the small AFSC team already knew a good deal about conditions in the camps and the French officials dealing with them. Fred Hoehler, the first head of OFRRO, was a humane and bureaucratically flexible man. In effect, he appointed the AFSC team as his Office of Refugee Affairs. The new relationship gave the AFSC a recognized status and immediate access to army messes and to reliable vehicles and it quickly brought the new arrivals up to speed on the needs of the stateless and other internees.

By the time I arrived in August 1943, Leslie Heath had left and Ken Kimberland was head of the AFSC mission. Nearly six feet tall, slight of build, with sparse sandy hair and gray eyes, he was energetic and well-organized, a no-nonsense man with a quick step who got things done. Trained as an economist, he had considerable banking experience. He was very persuasive. Several times I watched him quietly continue a conversation that had begun with an early "no" until, in the end, the official would say the desired "yes." He knew how to find the right buttons to induce the system to work for our purposes. His example was useful to me when later I worked with the Intergovernmental Committee on Refugees in Italy and much later in the State Department.

The Spanish internees had their own special difficulties. By 1942 they had been in the camps there for over five years. Distrusted as communists and without work permits, they were leading a precarious existence. David Hartley oversaw a number of mutual aid societies organized for them. Shorter than Ken, he had light brown hair and hazel eyes, a high broad forehead and a warm smile. Dave was a reflective man;he moved more slowly than Ken, as if considering each step. In my impatience I sometimes thought him unduly phlegmatic for urgent times, while he thought I was unduly wound up. When we got to know each other better in Italy, I found him to be imaginative and quietly effective.

My colleague David Hartley oversaw mutual aid societies for Spanish veterans who, distrusted as communists and without work permits, were leading a precarious existence.

With him I visited a number of *amicales* or resident centers for wounded Spanish veterans who eked out a living making high-quality woven *espadrilles* (sandals) that fetched a premium price in the local markets. Though seriously maimed, each was wonderfully adroit, compensating for whatever limb was missing. One man with only one good leg and a makeshift peg moved amazingly quickly from his work bench to the pile of raffia in the corner when he needed more materials. Another with only one good arm sewed the edging by holding the nearly completed *espadrilles* with his feet. Veterans of the famous International Brigade, who fought with the Republican forces against Franco's Fascist regime, continued to send modest help to these beleaguered comrades. AFSC found some sewing machines so they could work more rapidly and provided clothing for the coming winter. AFSC clothing also went to Spanish refugees in Morocco and to a number of children's colonies outside Oran and Algiers.

For these two groups the former camp internees of many nationalities and the remnants of the Spanish exodus outside the camps – the AFSC presence in Morocco and then Algeria was able, by moving in Allied and French governmental circles, to remind the otherwise preoccupied authorities of human needs it had been easy for them to ignore.

A third group of refugees, who came to take a lot of my time, were so-called Libyans, whose French grandparents had migrated to Libya before World War I. They had retained their French citizenship for two and sometimes even three generations. When Italy entered the war in June 1940, Mussolini expelled from Libya, an Italian colony, the thousands there who held French citizenship. Moreover, as the war in the desert between the British (based in Egypt) and the Italians and Germans (then based in Libya) swept back and forth in great lunges of advance and retreat, many civilians fled to seek safety in Tunisia and Algeria. The result was that large numbers of civilians from Libya were in these countries, perhaps a third or more of them Jews.

British authorities took over responsibility for Libya as the Germans and Italians retreated. They had promised that these civilians could return home as soon as the Allies won in North Africa. The French government was anxious to have them gone as soon as possible. Large numbers of Algerian Arabs were also very poor and might hope to do better elsewhere than in Algeria. Understandably, however, the British were reluctant to have just anyone return to Libya. Why anyone who had not lived in Libya would want to live thereafter it had been devastated by that very mobile war, I could not imagine.

There were no good records of who these Libyan refugees were, where they had lived before, or where they might want to go. I explained to the new head of OFRRO the paucity of information that was preventing the Libyan refugees from going home promptly. He proposed I survey the displaced Libyan communities in Algeria and Tunisia to gather the necessary data.

OUR WORKING ENVIRONMENT
The working situation in North Africa was very different from that in Lisbon. There I had had direct access to Portuguese and American authorities, and a modest but workable budget. As already noted, Leslie Heath and his small AFSC staff became, in effect, OFRRO's Office of Refugee Affairs quite promptly after the Allied

landings. However, now OFRRO personnel began to arrive in considerable numbers, the director changed and a government bureaucracy began to emerge. Instead of our group functioning with nearly full autonomy, we found ourselves gradually being drawn ever closer into OFRRO. Written communications between our staff in Casablanca and in Algiers were supposed to go through government channels. Thanks to Ken's years with Chase Bank, he accepted these bureaucratic niceties with equanimity. I admired Ken's way of making the most of the added resources and organizational clout this arrangement gave to our activities, but I did not like what seemed like the bureaucratization growing up around us.

SEARCHING FOR LIBYANS

The "Libyans" faced special problems. Once we decided I was to find out more about them, the head of OFRRO made sure I checked with British authorities, who were delighted. It was easy within the American community to forget about the British role; they were far fewer in number and their equipment was largely American. On the other hand, the British and American headquarters staffs were often combined. Indeed, one of the gratifying things about this period was the intimate and cooperative relationship between the Americans and the British. My next work in Cairo would only confirm this.

For the survey of Libyan refugees in Algeria, a captain in the Air Force ground crew was assigned as driver with a command car, a glorified jeep with a folding canvas top that was a great help against the North African sun. We had good times together, much talk and relaxation as we pushed right along from town to town. For the first few days of the journey Jim Falk, visiting for the JDC, came along as a liaison to Jewish communities where we would visit. While I talked to French officials—*préfets, sous-préfets*, local police or military officers —and heads of the Libyan community, Jim paid especial attention to the Jewish refugees who were among them.

Following the collapse of France, the situation of 140,000 North African Jews sharply deteriorated. They had been considered French citizens since 1870. But by September 1940, only three months after the armistice with Germany, the Pétain government had withdrawn French citizenship from them. Now stateless, they were susceptible to being arrested and sent to labor camps. Anti-Semitism in North Africa was strong among French settlers, who, in addition, distrusted the Jews as potential political anti-French allies of the far more numerous local Arabs. Jewish professional and economic activities were more and more circumscribed. The JDC had been able to help community organizations, but anxiety among individuals was palpable.[3]

Most of the community appeared to be of modest means— small shopkeepers and the like—though some were schoolteachers and I met a medical doctor or two. A number made clear that their ancestors had been part of the Sephardic exodus from Spain in the fifteenth century. Having lost their French citizenship and being without work for many months, they were having a hard time, and they were careful in what they told me.

When I explained our mission concerning the Libyans to the officials, as likely as not, they would respond politely with a shrug of the shoulders:

> Of course, Monsieur, I will see that you meet the persons who can help you interview *"les pauvres Libonais."* You are quite right, these unfortunates from Libya have had a very difficult time. *Hélas,* others, too, face severe shortages. Indeed, dear Sir, I hope you realize that throughout Algeria there are far more citizens of France who are virtual refugees, who are no better off than these. They came to escape "les événements" in France. Their resources, too, have been exhausted, and the hospitality of their family and friends has worn thin. But what can one do?

We would then be shown to the official concerned with refugees and to the local social worker who knew how to find them and put them at ease. We would gather details of their present circumstances. Where did they want to return to? Where specifically had they lived before? Were there people still there who might help the British find their addresses, in case they would want to get confirmation? How had they earned their living? In the course of visiting about fifteen towns we were able to document the condition of some 200 "Libyan" families of French nationality.

On the second half of the trip further east, we interviewed considerably more. When they heard an American was to visit, some families had all their goods and chattels packed. It took more than a few minutes to explain that we were information gatherers and not in command of a convoy of trucks just over the horizon organized for their benefit. They were pretty miserable and wanted to go home as soon as possible, believing they could make do better there than in Algiers. I was sure they had no idea of how devastated their homes had become as the armies lunged back and forth across Libya.

One morning, quite unexpectedly, we happened upon a set of

Roman ruins. Timgad was a North African outpost founded at the time
of Trajan, about 100 CE. It was well preserved due to a volcanic
eruption that had covered the whole site with a deep layer of volcanic
dust. The street plan showed clearly. Some columns had been placed
upright again, a triumphal arch stood at the entrance. Walls of buildings
showed the differing quarters, with a sharp contrast between the villas
of the well-off and the tiny cubicles of the poor. This area, ancient
Mauritania, had been one of Rome's breadbaskets. We could see the
chariot and cart tracks worn into the stone paving; they evoked the
galloping horses drawing their light chariots through the gates and
lumbering cart horses dragging wheat down to the Mediterranean shore
for shipment to Rome.

Alas, time pressed, and we hurried on. But that surprise
spectacle has stayed with me. It was one more reminder of how great
imperial structures wane or even disappear, suddenly collapsing as
elaborate or delicate systems are disrupted, and are never reestablished.

Late one hot afternoon we were driving hard along the
northern edge of the Sahara, heading toward Laghouat. We were
thirsty; the road seemed to go on and on; the oasis we sought never
came. As we climbed slight rises in the road that wound in great curves
among the low lying dunes, we always hoped we would reach it. Then,
without warning, we came upon a steep declivity, perhaps 100 feet
below the surface of the plain, and saw a jewel of an oasis, with small,
watered emerald green fields of rice, and dozens of stately date palms.
The road dropped down to the oasis; we already felt better.

We found a teashop, with welcoming shade under a grape
arbor. To run water over our faces and wrists was delicious. We avoided
the ice offered, but the cool bottles of *limonade* taken from a
dilapidated kerosene refrigerator, overly sweet though they were,
quickly restored our humor. After a rest, we pressed on to the much
bigger town that lay a good long drive away, nearer the main lines of
travel, where we would first pay our respects to the local Commissaire
de Police.

In the end, we provided a detailed report to the British and to
Washington of where several thousand Libyan refugee families were
living, where they were from, and where they hoped to go in Libya.
OFRRO then reminded and encouraged French officials to accelerate
the refugees' return, when bureaucratic sloth might otherwise have
postponed and postponed the extra trouble such a move would require.[4]

MEMBER OF OUR STAFF REARRESTED

On my return to Algiers I learned that Gerard Schmidt, a

young German Christian and a former POW on our staff, had disappeared. He had been released from one of the camps, on our responsibility, to work for maintenance. He did yeoman service delivering supplies and handling office chores. Ken Kimberland immediately suspected he had been rearrested and checked with a number of the police and security authorities. No one he contacted would acknowledge such an arrest. Ken dropped everything else and went from one prison to another, speaking directly to the commandant or to his deputy. Finally, he found our man. Because Gerard did not yet have an official work permit and was still without a proper passport, the local police considered him an *indésirable*. They had locked him up in a cell by himself, with a tiny window high in the wall. He received only watery soup for food. A stinking toilet stood in the corner, and there was no way for him to keep himself clean. He had not been allowed to phone or send a letter to us.

Had Ken not taken the trouble to pursue it personally, Gerard might not have been released for months. That evening Gerard told me, "I was really discouraged. I imagined how long I might be left here, perhaps for years. You have no idea of my relief when I heard Mr. Kimberland's voice outside the door." So long as Gerard remained in Algeria, he could not rest entirely easy.

A PERSONAL TURNING POINT

My intimate work in Portugal with victims of Nazi persecution compelled me to face the harsh reality of Nazi brutality toward all Jews and anyone who opposed their brutality.[5] I came to believe that the forces then seeking to dominate Europe and gaining ground before the American intervention, would bring abomination to all of the continent. No longer was I the detached neutral I had thought myself to be. I gradually became persuaded that the outcome of this war would make a huge difference to the future of Europe and the United States.

Moreover, I could not help recalling how relieved the Portuguese neutrals were at the Allied landings in North Africa. The German threat no longer loomed so darkly. They dared to be more hopeful. In Algeria, I could see that the mere presence of Allied forces encouraged constructive steps. It bolstered the courage of those French officials who opposed Vichy's discriminatory policies. Although Gerard Schmidt had recently been rearrested, stateless and other *indésirables* were gradually being released and the worst internment camps closed. However much religious principles might decry the notion that military force could make a positive difference, I saw it happening before my eyes. My commitment to nonviolence had become conditional.

Non-violence might well have a place within the British and American world Quakers had known historically, and in domestic protests against an unresponsive government. A non-violent world was a great ideal. But I had seen or heard enough about the ruthlessness of the Nazi regime to persuade me that no amount of non-violent protest, however lovingly carried out, could have dissuaded it from its destructive course. Nor did I have faith in a God that knew what was happening and could comfort those who had suffered the most. The world I had seen was too arbitrary and harsh for such a benign belief. I regretfully concluded that there was that of the Devil in man as well as that of God. To love that of God in every man, as George Fox put it, was more than I was capable of. The demand was just too much. As a result of such thoughts I judged that I was no longer a religious conscientious objector to war.

Accordingly, in November 1943, after much heart-searching, I wrote to James Vail, head of AFSC's Foreign Service Section, that if I had to register again with Selective Service, I would no longer be justified in seeking C.O. status. I still thought the unusual opportunities for humanitarian service provided by the Service Committee in this unhappy world were of the kind the world badly needed then and for the long run. As I put it in a never-ending non-sentence, I stressed:

> the importance of encouraging a sustained belief in the possibility of integrity and disinterest on the part of others, the conviction that one can be concerned regardless of religious or political or national tags, that expressions of cooperation, sympathetic understanding and gentle friendliness are vital, necessary values, especially needed by the millions suffering as a result of the war and the political and other conditions that caused it.

Under the circumstances, I queried, did he think I should report to my draft board that I no longer could claim my former C.O. status?

At the time, to turn from the C.O. position so soon after taking it might indicate I lacked conviction. One part of me continued to argue that if I rejected the C.O. position I would be sliding into just going along with everyone else. In the end, the reality of the harsh violence of Europe proved to be more persuasive.

I acknowledged to myself that to continue in my present service rather than return home to enlist would be personally preferable. Perhaps I was finding AFSC more comfortable, a kind of rationalization for avoiding the least congenial and, more serious, the riskiest choice? There were twinges of guilt. If I were to continue with AFSC, I would have to justify my choice by strong performance toward

AFSC's goals. I hoped the humanitarian work I was engaged in could justify the course I chose. Much would depend on how James Vail responded to my letter. Later I found that Erich Remarque acknowledged that in wartimes men who were not in the fighting forces often felt guilty.

It was a big load off my mind to send the letter, for there was no one in responsibility within reach with whom I wanted to discuss this, though in Lisbon I had explored my changing position with Phil Conard, himself not a religious pacifist. I would not receive James Vail's reply until I was in Cairo, working with the British Friends Ambulance Unit.

THE BRITISH FRIENDS AMBULANCE UNIT (FAU)

In late November or early December, John Rose and Peter Gibson, leaders of the British Friends Ambulance Unit in Cairo, came to Algiers. They wanted to see how we were working within OFFRO. They expected that as the continent opened there might be opportunities in Italy and the Balkans for joint work, and they thought it would be useful for AFSC to be in touch with Michael Barratt Brown. He was the FAU member planning the cooperation of voluntary agencies (NGOs) with the British equivalent of OFRRO. The FAU visitors proposed a swap of personnel; an American should be seconded, as it was called, to the FAU unit in Cairo, and one of their number would join the AFSC unit in Algeria.

This was interesting to Ken and me, particularly because we thought that with closer links to the British headquarters in Cairo, AFSC might have larger opportunities in Italy and the Balkans. David Hartley was fully engaged in overseeing the *amicales* for the wounded Spanish veterans; Eric Johnson ran the Casablanca office, and Ken was in charge of the head office, handling AFSC clothing shipments and the distribution of special funds donated in Britain and the U.S. for Spanish veterans. I was the logical choice to go.

Cables were sent to Philadelphia proposing such a swap. We argued that American and British Friends had always worked closely together. We already had a joint Anglo-American effort in China; the French program had been an Anglo-American affair from the beginning. The AFSC came back with a positive response and in mid-December 1943, carrying out my new instructions to join the Friends Ambulance Unit in Egypt, I caught a plane to Cairo.

Cairo is the most densely populated large urban area in the world...The
pressure of people touches every aspect of life...it overwhelms public services.

Max Rodenbeck, *Cairo, The City Victorious* 1998

CHAPTER SEVEN
EGYPT: YUGOSLAV REFUGEES

THE FLIGHT TO CAIRO

The flight to Cairo stopped at Banghazi in Libya for several
hours. It was a sandy, unappetizing place, a run-down bit of the former
Italian empire. I hopped a jeep to the *souk el turk*, where some of the
Libyan refugees I had interviewed had their shops before they were
expelled. I was reassured to see trading was in full swing. I was glad to
send a report back to Algiers to reassure the British that sending the
refugees home would not necessarily add to public expense.   Flying
into Cairo was spectacular. After crossing miles of dun-colored sand, I
discerned a thin streak of brilliant emerald, winding far to the south. As
this bright ribbon approached the Mediterranean, the Nile Delta
broadened out into a great fan-shaped spread of green, pockmarked
with towns, and then huge Cairo, its large mosques accented by their
narrow minarets. Through the core of the city ran the brown Nile River.

Dumped from a British army bus into a central terminal, I found a dilapidated horse-drawn victoria to take me to the Bab el Louk railroad station. The station had been requisitioned by the British and part of it turned over to the Friends Ambulance Unit (FAU) for its offices and living quarters. I had never seen a city so crowded, so nearly overwhelmed with people. The sidewalks were solid people, the roads were choked with bicycles, donkey carts, dilapidated carriages and military vehicles. These last were always hurrying and honking — 4x4 trucks, many with canvas tops; jeeps, battered Land Rovers, officers, sedans. In addition were occasional military convoys, lines of trucks and tanks on long carriers.

When finally I got to Bab el Louk, I introduced myself and quickly received a warm welcome. I had become accustomed to the relaxed atmosphere of our fully civilian AFSC life. In contrast, the FAU establishment in Cairo seemed very well organized, even a bit military. Staff all wore British army battle dress uniforms, with army boots. There was a clear sense of who were the equivalent of officers and who the men. I was assigned a cot in a large room with six or eight others.

DEATH OF MY FATHER

Within two or three days of my arrival, I received a message from Ken Kimberland on the military line from Algiers, reporting that my father had finally died of emphysema, at age 62. He had never smoked, but was allergic to pollens and dust that in those days they could not counter. Each time he went to the hospital it seemed to get worse. I knew my mother would be both anguished and relieved and I was sorry to be so far away. It had taken some six days before I could send a message of my shared sense of loss.

In the spring of 1942, with some effort, my father had walked slowly from the car to train side to send me off for the Clipper flight to Lisbon. We both must have suspected that we would probably not see each other again. Now my suspicion had been realized. I was relieved for him, and for my mother, too, who had shared his awful periods. Our mutual reticence left me later wishing I had known him much better. My sadness was soon submerged, however, in intensely challenging tasks on this solo mission. The year and a half since our separation had been so full that it was some time before the reality of my father's death really hit me.

He was a gentle, kindly man. A graduate of Philadelphia's famous Central High School, he was well read in American and European history. According to the story in the family, he had wanted to go on to college and perhaps become a college teacher. But when his widowed, impoverished mother married the much older founder of B. F. Dewees, a carriage trade business in ribbons, gloves and notions, my father and his older brother Tom had to go into the family business. He knew in detail of the revolutionary war around Germantown and about the American Civil War. English history and the Italian Renaissance were also his hobbies and his chair at home was always surrounded by books. He was a pillar of the Germantown Boys Club, one of the first white institutions in Germantown to open its doors to the blacks who had flooded into Philadelphia in the 1920's and 1930's. I often thought he was not cut out to be a businessman, but he made a humane contribution to the store. Many of the staff were deeply fond of him. Thanks to the hard working "Tom and Charlie," B. F. Dewees became one of Philadelphia's leading women's specialty stores. I was proud that they had one of the first retirement plans for the sales "girls." My father quietly supported my interest in the Quakers.

IMPRESSIONS OF CAIRO

In the meantime, there was Cairo right outside the door with all its noise, its cries of human argument, and its gridlock. Overhead, kites circled lazily in the warm updrafts. Below, traffic was abominable. I discovered the standard practice when a military convoy came through: military police (MPs) blocked every crossroad well before the leading vehicles arrived, and held the cars stopped in the sweltering sun until the convoy had passed.

In one, possibly apocryphal incident a long, black, top-down car was stopped for a convoy. An agitated man in a well-pressed suit and a red *tarbush* got up from the back seat and demanded to be let through. "I am Nahas Pasha," says he, "the prime minister of Egypt. And I have to be at a cabinet meeting that began ten minutes ago." The huge American MP strolled slowly over to the agitated Egyptian official's car, put his foot on the running board and said, "Mister, you are not going to interrupt that convoy." "But I am the prime minister of Egypt, and I am chairing an important meeting." "Mister, that may be so. But to me, you are just another damn wog. You'll have to wait like everyone else." "Wog" was the derogatory term used by the British, roughly the equivalent of "nigger" in the old South. The Prime Minister had to wait.

The military presence was everywhere. Only ten months before, the decisive Battle of El Alamein, only 70 miles from Alexandria, had marked the high point of the German advance toward

Egypt. Cairo was headquarters for the British Middle East Command and Alexandria for the British Fleet, Mediterranean East.

The contrast between rich and poor in Cairo was palpable. On one hot afternoon walking back toward our railroad station, I saw a sky blue chauffered Cadillac convertible, with the top down, carrying a gorgeous woman who reminded me of the statuettes of Nefertiti in the Cairo museum. Her hair well groomed, she wore a huge necklace, as if going to a fashion show. What a contrast, what a provocative display! But the shocking thing to me was how quickly I came not to notice the dramatic inequalities, as if my sensibilities had become anesthetized.

I occasionally had to visit Shepherd's Hotel, that had become the symbol of the British occupation of Egypt. British officers, in their ample shorts, their socks, their officer's swagger sticks under their arms, their scotches in their hands, were standing, talking, greeting each other, telling stories. Right off the terrace, down on the street, shoeshine kids, beggars, pimps and touts sought the attention of anyone they could interest.

The hardest working people in the hotel were the telephonists, young women in a large but stuffy office, with banks of telephone switchboards with plug-in cables. They had to handle English, Arabic, French and Italian. Callers in the nearby phone booths, trying to reach a contact in a room upstairs or elsewhere in Cairo, competed with the endless stream of calls from outside. Many would end up tearing their hair, stamping their feet, even screaming, as they were unable to get through to their party.

As I think back, it is remarkable how little connection I had with Egyptian officials. Egypt had been a British protectorate since 1880. Nominally, since the Anglo-Egyptian treaty of 1936, Egypt was recognized by Britain as independent—except for four matters. These were defense, imperial communications (the Suez Canal and other facilities on the route to India), protection of foreign interests, and the non-Egyptian minorities. In practice, all important decisions were made by the British.

VOLUNTARY ORGANIZATIONS IN THE BRITISH TRADITION

In British parlance, "Voluntary Organizations" are roughly akin to our non-governmental organizations (NGOs). In Cairo the NGO scene was very different from the one I had known in Portugal and Algeria. In Lisbon we and the Unitarian Service Committee and Catholic Relief had dealt with refugees who were not the responsibility of the JDC or other Jewish organizations. In Algeria, AFSC was assisting Spanish civil war veterans and trying to help victims of Vichy's policy toward *les indésirables*. In and near Cairo, there were many more relief organizations and a wider variety of refugees.

The British Red Cross and Order of St. John Joint War Organization, Friends Ambulance Unit and Save the Children Fund were prominent, as well as the Australian Red Cross. The American Red Cross had a unique official standing in a military base area. Near East Relief was the major inter-denominational relief organization that had been active in the region since World War I. There were also war relief organizations for Greece and Yugoslav homelands, the YMCA, Mennonite Central Service Committee, and of course the Joint Distribution Committee.

All were officially connected to the British Government's Middle East Relief and Refugee Administration (MERRA), the rough equivalent to the American OFFRO in North Africa. MERRA was established first to coordinate assistance to 150,000 Polish refugees and demobilized soldiers, who had arrived via the Soviet Union and Iran many months after the 1939 collapse of Poland at the start of the war. Thousands of Greek refugees later fled across the Mediterranean as Greece fell to Italian and Nazi troops in the spring of 1941. MERRA helped the Voluntary Societies with residential, office and warehouse space, telephone lines and other logistics. The Cairo Council of Voluntary Societies coordinated the efforts of the many different organizations.

By 1945, the FAU had established a considerable presence in the Middle East. Mobile medical units served with the British Army in the Western Desert campaigns and a unit was attached to the Free French forces in Lebanon and North Africa. Some fifty FAU members were joined by sixty trained nurses, laboratory and mechanical technicians and drivers assisting in the Greek and Yugoslav refugee camps.

Michael Barratt Brown of the FAU was in a key position within the Council. A short, well-built man, he was a brilliant, witty analyst of social and economic class differences, a rapid thinker and a fluent talker. He was fun to work with, and he was a great help to me in Cairo. He was a useful link between most of the British and American NGOs and the British official community.[1] During this waiting period, it was his job to assist in planning for civilian reconstruction once the Continent became accessible, shaping regularized consultations between British officials and the NGOs.[2]

Meanwhile in Washington, Governor Herbert Lehman of New York had been appointed as the first Director of UNRRA (United

Nations Relief and Rehabilitation Administration). It was an exciting time, when statesmen could envisage a truly international organization especially created to meet the immediate postwar emergency needs of shattered countries and economies. How UNRRA decided to utilize the many eager NGOs would make a big difference to us all. Would its leaders understand the valuable role NGOs could play?[3]

AFSC had wanted me to observe and report to them on the Council's meetings, but to make no commitments on behalf of AFSC until we had further consultations. I saw my job as scouting for future overseas opportunities for the AFSC and conscientious objectors now assigned to Civilian Public Service camps at home. It seemed to me that Cairo could well be the base for entering the Balkans, since so many Greek and Yugoslav refugees were in this area. The British authorities already had ties to underground activities in Greece and Yugoslavia. After World War I Quakers worked in Serbia, so badly smashed during that conflict. In 1919 an AFSC team of fifteen men and women worked, with the help of Bulgarian POWs, to rebuild destroyed homes and establish an orphanage. With these traditions and the greater acceptance for NGOs in British areas, I urged AFSC to send out a senior commissioner for the Middle East to assess the possibilities for Civilian Public Service (CPS) men and to plan activities on the spot with other NGOs when the Continent should open up.

As I look back, I was the enthusiastic field man assuming there was a backlog of frustrated CPS people itching for service overseas. Unhappily, at the last minute a rider had been attached to the 1943 Defense Appropriation Bill explicitly forbidding able-bodied COs in CPS camps from serving outside the country. AFSC in Philadelphia was already stretched thin supporting all the activities then under way—including Lisbon, North Africa, overseeing famine relief in Bengal, and supporting the transport program in China. Nevertheless, I learned in late February that AFSC would send a commissioner to visit Cairo some time in the spring.

RECREATION

Life in Cairo was not all organizational talk and message shuffling. On Christmas day, 1943, Dennis Greenwood of the FAU and I climbed up the Great Pyramid of Cheops. We hopped a bus to Giza, and simply walked over to the enormous mound and started climbing. When we reached the marble facing three quarters of the way up we found hand and foot holds and were soon at the top. The day was wonderful—clear skies, not too hot. One could see far up the river to the south and out toward Alexandria to the north. What an incredible structure it was. There were no tourists crowding around; we were entirely alone.

On a Sunday afternoon, John Rose, the senior FAU leader, and I went for a leisurely stroll through the older part of Cairo. John was a shy older man and I enjoyed our quiet talks together. A well-established architect in one of Britain's Caribbean islands, he was sensitive to the architectural niceties in Cairo. Our objective was a series of Coptic Christian churches.

The Copts were converted to Christianity in the first or second centuries C.E. Their churches typically were entered by going down steps from the sidewalk, as street levels had risen over the centuries from accumulating debris. Only an occasional painting in the Byzantine tradition, a rare cross and the widely used form of the basilica gave an indication these were Christian churches. I was struck by the number of ostrich eggs that hung over the altars. Coptic women often wore traditional Egyptian dress, including ankle bracelets of heavy silver and a dark veil over the head, shoulders and face. Some of the men wore the red tasseled *tarbush*. The wood carving in many of the churches was exquisite. It was all very strange and, in a way, sad and lonely.

About this time, in the company of Philip Sanford (an Australian with substantial business experience in Argentina), I occasionally stole away from the regular FAU mess for a quiet dinner on our own. The masses of men in uniform, the swarms of military vehicles and the open misery of displaced persons on the streets and in the camps meant that the war was never out of our awareness. But one particular evening brought vividly home the cost to individuals of this terrible war. We got settled in a small French restaurant, and our eyes soon became used to the dim light. At the next table was a horrifying sight. He wore the uniform of a British Royal Air Force (RAF) officer. His face had been terribly burned and very poorly patched. One eye was completely closed. His left hand lying beside his plate was contorted into a kind of claw. He must have been shot down and pulled out of a burning plane. I had seen nothing like this before or since until I saw the movie based on Michael Ondaatje's novel *The English Patient*. Across from him sat a very brave young lady carrying on the conversation as if he were just another dinner companion.

Phil and I were reminded that while we might be engaged in planning future reconstruction work or were concerned about the needs of refugees, thousands in Allied forces had risked their lives to open the way for our humane activities.

GREEK REFUGEES NEAR GAZA

Sometime in early January, Michael Barrett Brown, two other FAU members and I visited Nuseirat refugee camp, just into Palestine south of Gaza across the Sinai desert, empty oil drums marking the edges of the tarred but narrow "road." Some 6,000 Greek refugees were housed there, having been rescued by British troops retreating from Greece in the face of German advances in 1941. It was a well-run camp, tents neatly lined, all their tent flaps rolled up to catch whatever small air was stirring. Just-washed clothes, some virtually rags, hung limply. There were many women and children and practically no men. Nearly all of them had been mobilized or were held by the Italians or Germans as prisoners of war.

We arrived during a distribution of second hand clothing. It was not easy to match the mixed up clothes to the individuals who needed them. My report to Philadelphia was filled with perfectionist advice to the clothing workroom about how to sort, label, and pack the different types and sizes. The recipients of that report must have shaken their heads. After all, "the field" was lucky to get any clothing at all as everyone faced a worldwide shortage that now is impossible to imagine.

MORE ON THE C.O. QUESTION

Just after Christmas, James Vail's reaction to my request for advice on the CO question finally caught up with me in Cairo. He began with condolences for the death of my father. He wrote that he could well understand how present events and my experiences in Portugal and Algeria could challenge my earlier convictions. He reminded me that some other Quakers were now serving in the medical corps or had joined the services. He was sure there would be future problems in our relationships with governments, and the chances of developing satisfactory working arrangements in the many fields of our interest would depend upon experienced personnel. In conclusion, he wrote:

> Unless you feel a strong concern to raise the issue [with your draft board], I am disposed to suggest you continue your present work, which you are doing progressively better and to the complete satisfaction of the Committee. Your experience can be of great value to the Committee. With the attitude of dedication to the task which you state I do not feel any change is indicated.

With that I was prepared to drop the subject and get on with tasks and life in Cairo. But deep down it was not as easy as that; I continued to feel torn between my earlier hopes for a non-violent world and my present view of the harsh, victimizing world I saw around me.

YUGOSLAV REFUGEES FROM ITALY TO EL SHATT CAMP IN EGYPT

Early in January, Michael Barratt Brown arranged a meeting for me with William Matthews, the head of MERRA. The three of us had a good exchange about the roles that NGOs like the Friends Ambulance Unit or AFSC might play in a MERRA setup. (Clearly, he had different views from those reflected by OFFRO on the virtue of NGOs retaining much of their autonomy while still working closely with governmental agencies.)

In January 1944, word came that some 2,000 Yugoslav refugees would soon need to be moved from Taranto, Italy to Egypt. These Titoist refugees had left their homes along the Dalmatian coast because fighting between the German army and local guerrillas had ruined the crops; there simply was no food. A Polish passenger ship, *The Batory,* was standing by to bring them to Egypt, where they could be housed and fed away from the battlefield in Italy. Matthews asked the FAU to send an escort party to accompany them from Taranto to the El Shatt camp at the southern end of the Suez Canal. The FAU asked me to head the escort party of four. We sailed in a small troop ship for Taranto in the middle of January. The first of the three days, the sea was rough, but the last two were fair and calm.

On board ship I read *Fontamara,* by Ignazio Silone, strongly recommended by Joe Schwartz in Lisbon. An Italian novel of life under Mussolini, it shows how fascism corrosively penetrated a peaceful Italian village until the whole population was at one another's throats.

By the time we arrived, the British army and Titoist partisans had the refugee movement well-organized. Two of the refugees spoke some English; a few spoke French or German and one of the FAU volunteers spoke fluent German. With that, my French and the two English speakers, we worked out a smooth loading of the ship and a very civilized transfer. The Titoist partisans had organized the people village by village, so they all moved with friends. Accommodations were troopship bunks, the food was generous and the four-day voyage to Port Saïd relatively smooth. On the boat, we worked out a careful registration. Each family was identified, children counted, their home village recorded; and each received a number to help identify their tent. We reflected afterwards that by acting as intermediaries between the military authorities and the refugee leaders, we made the journey easier for everyone.

At the El Shatt camp tents were already assigned to each family. Water connections were not too far from each tent and army food kitchens were within reach. But for the refugees, used as they were to the Dalmatian Coast, it must have been a harsh experience to find themselves in the desert. However, at least they knew they were physically safe and would have enough to eat.

This was not my first acquaintance with Yugoslavs. During the summer of 1939, after my study year in Paris, I bicycled down through the Balkans to meet my sister Edith so we could visit Istanbul and Greece together. On the way, in a Belgrade Youth Hostel a young Croat and I shared a meal, in the course of which he muttered darkly about those "uncouth, ruthless Serbs." Later, Ede and I visited the Dalmatian coast and we took a bus up to Setinja, then the capital of Montenegro. Sharing the rear of a bus as we swung left and then right up the switchback road that led from the sea to Montenegro, a young Serb and I got talking. In his turn, he muttered darkly about "those Croats. They think they're so superior. I'd like to kill every one I can get my hands on!" An English-speaking Yugoslav partisan, Durshan Curcia, became a spokesman at El Shatt camp. A young lawyer from Split, he was a tall, broad-shouldered man, with a bold mustache and earnest dark brown eyes. Over coffee, he eloquently argued that Tito and the *Partisanis* were going to put an end to those ethnic myths, as all the peoples of Yugoslavia from now on were going to work together. I had seen how well all the different peoples represented in this group were quietly organizing and smoothly working together. So perhaps Durshan Curcia would be proved right.

After depositing the displaced persons in El Shatt, Sanford and Michael and I reported personally to Matthews in Cairo. He was fascinated by our report. He was pleased it had gone so well, and quietly proud, as he had every right to be, of the humane and considerate way the British military had handled the whole affair.

I described to him my concern that in the long run the large number of young people would pose a challenge to the camp administrators. At home they would have had chores to perform for their families and opportunities for small-scale responsibilities. At El Shatt, under army organization, equivalent opportunities would not exist. A welfare office ought to be organized to promote schools, workshops, athletics and games. As we had found in North Africa, that office would need close liaison with military depots to obtain surplus materials. After a brief discussion, Matthews asked if the FAU might send someone down to the camps for a week to see what ought to be done.

WELFARE PROGRAM AT EL SHATT

John Rose asked me to undertake that task and Phil Sanford and I went down for about a week to prepare a report. It called for the camp administration to provide active support to Yugoslavs who wanted to organize elementary and secondary schools, sports clubs, woodworking shops, sewing circles. Army depots would be instructed to release "surplus" tools, sewing machines, and blackboards, and MERRA should allocate a modest budget line for small purchases.

On the strength of the report, Matthews asked me to go down on a four- to six-week assignment as director of the Welfare Activities Program, to help get it started. It may seem incongruous for an American Quaker to be dealing with the British army on behalf of Yugoslav refugees, but strange things were happening to everyone during this period. So I went down with his authorization in my hand, confirmed by instructions sent through channels.

The partisan network was already beginning to organize schools, but they needed official authority to scrounge from the military chairs or materials and carpentry tools to make chairs and blackboards. They also needed to apply for paper, pencils, and other supplies for education. Their schools were highly ideological and their organization authoritarian but their efforts to bury historical ethnic and religious differences were reassuring. The sports clubs came naturally, too. I spent a lot of time with British camp administrators and the leading Yugoslavs. We poked about in army supply depots and introduced key Yugoslavs to the officers in charge of the depots, authorizing them to go on their own to the officers in charge.

Life for the civilian staff at the camp was remarkably comfortable. Each of us had a separate tent, with space for a trunk or suitcase and a folding camp chair. The bed was a folding army cot; latrines and wash facilities were not far away. The most surprising wrinkle was the morning bed tea, brought silently by an Egyptian kitchen helper and left at the head of the bed. The British did manage to make the best of a hard assignment!

INVITATION FROM THE IGCR

At El Shatt I had a visit from Patrick Malin, then vice-chairman of the Intergovernmental Committee on Refugees (IGCR). He was a smiling, talkative Irishman, member of Swarthmore Friends Meeting, and had taught economics at Swarthmore College. I was very surprised to see him. As he explained, the IGCR had been established at the Evian Conference in France in 1938. Called jointly by the British and Americans, the conference was an indignant diplomatic response to the persecutions in Germany and Austria that generated the flood of Jewish refugees. Opposition to immigration into the UK and the USA at the time was so strong the IGCR never became more than a gesture of bi-national political concern. Looking back, it is shameful to note that between December 1942 and December 1943, when so many Polish and other Jews were being killed in the death camps, only 7,000 refugees entered the United States.

Now that the war was progressing, Pat Malin and his British boss, Sir Herbert Emerson, wanted to activate the moribund IGCR. The League of Nations' Nansen Office had provided support to stateless White Russian refugees after the Russian revolution. Emerson and Malin hoped the IGCR could play an analogous role after this war. They were hoping to open a number of offices in countries as they were liberated from Nazi control, the first to be in Naples. To start with, they would work with whatever experienced organization was available. Already, Sir Clifford Heathcote-Smith, then consul general in Alexandria and a seasoned British foreign service officer, had been named as the IGCR Resident Representative in Italy.

Malin said he had been in touch with AFSC Philadelphia. To my surprise, he then asked me if I would be willing to be the AFSC representative in Italy and at the same time to be Assistant Resident Representative of IGCR to help Sir Clifford Heathcote-Smith. This was an exciting proposition. While working in Lisbon, I had often wondered what would take the place of the League of Nations' Nansen Office. While in Algiers, I had puzzled over how the AFSC was to get a foot in the door in Italy. Here was an unsolicited opportunity to work toward that over a longer time instead of dealing only with the present extended emergency. It seemed like a great stroke of luck, but I could only express an interest since the decision belonged to AFSC in Philadelphia. As I thought about the job I had just begun at El Shatt, I believed that the enthusiasm and well-directed energy of the partisans would ensure that they would be able to make the most of the arrangements we had just begun, with or without me.

ONSET OF HEPATITIS

The very next day I began to have a marked fever. The nurse in charge took one look at me and sent me back to the FAU headquarters in Cairo, where I promptly went to bed. The next morning, I looked at myself in the mirror and saw the truth—my eyes were becoming a sickly yellow and I had contracted hepatitis. In short order I was driven to a civilian hospital in the Golf Club on the Gezira Island. The doctor reassured me: the malady was common in the region. The cure was simple—a fat free diet for at least a month and a slow regaining of strength for another month—two whole months out of action. While the first week was deeply depressing, as it often is with hepatitis, for the rest it proved to be an interlude for reading and taking stock while I slowly regained strength.

After the first week, FAU friends brought me many books and good company. Other visitors from the NGO community dropped by. Friends from Algeria sent good wishes. After a bit, I would deal with AFSC mail on my portable typewriter on my lap in bed or at a small table on the balcony. Few in wartime were as well cared for as I.

The FAU library in Cairo had the unabridged set of volumes of Arnold Toynbee's remarkable *Study of History* which came out just before the start of World War II. His comparative study of the rise and fall of civilizations aroused an understandable interest among anguished readers of the day. Only twenty years after the last war that had killed millions of men, disrupted states and destroyed cherished institutions, they had seen Europe descend once again into another war. Were European states doomed forever to such folly?

His study had a rather poetic theoretical structure. But his broad-brush historical generalizations were enriched by many examples and vivid anecdotes. This book offered my first encounter with much of Islamic history; the immediacy of Cairo gave it special meaning for me. Toynbee evoked great figures like the traveler and lawyer Ibn Battuta, whose life epitomized the once spacious Islamic world stretching from Moorish Spain all the way to Delhi in India. Later, in my scholarly incarnation as a South Asian specialist, I learned that Battuta's report of his fourteenth century stay in the Moghul court in Delhi remains one of the few detailed (if somewhat unreliable) eye-witness reports available to us. Then, too, there was Ibn Khaldun, former advisor to the rulers of Tlemcen and other kingdoms in North Africa. Toynbee gave him more attention, since Khaldun advanced a famous hypothesis attempting to explain the rise and decline of nomadic societies.

Toynbee's study is still known for his emphasis on challenge and response. He argued that societies challenged by external military or cultural threats, or by internal upheavals, can be either stimulated and renewed by such challenges or overwhelmed. Much depends upon the quality of their political, religious or cultural leadership and the resources at their command.

I also reread *Brothers Karamazov*. I was moved by the emotional intensity of Dostoyevsky's characters, though also impressed by how much tragedy their impulsive ways generated. The extraordinary passions of political life in the Europe I had known underlined the same reality. Virginia Woolf's *Mrs. Dalloway* captured so well the way a person's stream of consciousness carries along numerous simultaneous ideas and concerns, often competing for attention, sometimes leading to moments of sharp focus, more often resulting in a tangle of contradictory subjects and feelings. I later found that the Buddhists knew quite a bit about the often overly active "monkey of the mind." This is what Quakers must cope with when they try to "center down" in Friends Meeting. I also enjoyed Agatha Christie's mystery novels, laid in Middle East archeological settings.

It took three weeks beyond the month in hospital to recuperate in a spacious private home in Alexandria. Perhaps fifteen other guests were recovering from war wounds or various maladies. I had a small room of my own; we ate together, but I have no recollection of any of the others.

AFSC REGIONAL CONFERENCE AND DEPARTURE FOR ITALY

In early April, just as I was getting better, the AFSC scheduled a regional meeting in Cairo. AFSC had been asked to join the FAU Calcutta to monitor civilian food relief during the Bengal famine; on his way to Bengal James Vail was to chair our meeting. Eric Johnson came from Algiers en route to his new assignment as AFSC's representative in Calcutta. Ken Kimberland arrived from Algiers and Henry Scattergood, who had succeeded me, from Lisbon. In two days we each reviewed our own activities and considered possibilities for future activities in the region. James explored with Matthews possibilities for AFSC service in MERRA's area. By now there were 20,000 Yugoslavs and an additional 12,000 Greek refugees in El Shatt needing welfare attention. We also explored future plans for relief and reconstruction in Italy and the Balkans. All were favorable to the proposed unusual Quaker collaboration with the renewed IGCR in Italy. The upshot was that Eric went as planned with James to Bengal; Ken remained in Algiers and Henry in Lisbon. I was to stand by in Cairo until the IGCR post in Naples should open up.

Privately, James Vail was very reassuring to me. He and Elmore Jackson well understood my conscientious doubts when facing so directly the challenges of the refugees' dire circumstances and the harsh necessities of war.

Now it seemed only a matter of Sir Clifford arranging the permissions in Naples. While waiting, I was invited to Alexandria to have lunch with his wife. I assumed Sir Clifford wanted an advance briefing about the assistant he was to work with in Italy. Mrs. Heathcote Smith was a friendly person and the lunch went off well.

There was considerable delay before the Allied Control Commission in Italy was ready to have civilian staff from the IGCR on the ground, but permissions and travel orders were in hand in May 1944. For the flight to Italy I had been told to be at the motor pool at 4:30 a.m., so at 2:30 I loaded my stuff into a rickety victoria and had a cooling ride through Cairo's silent streets, to the clop clop clop of the old horse. It was a full moon night, and the shadows of minarets stood out sharply. Eventually I got down into the hubbub of a military motor pool. After long delays at the airport, we finally took off for Bari, in the south of Italy.

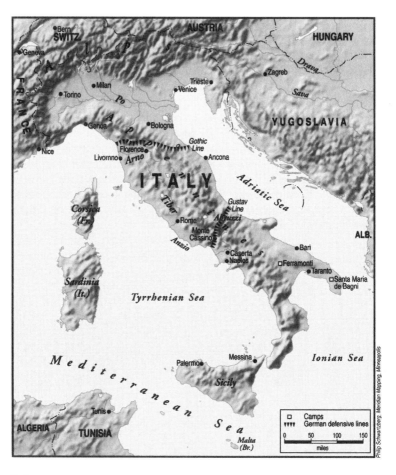

Italy

From September 1943 to April 1945, war up the spine of Italy between the allies and Germans left thousands of refugees and devastated countryside. Refugee relief and village reconstruction kept us busy while we wondered whether government leaders would be able to shape a peace that would endure.

PART III ITALY   1944-1945
Refugee Services and Rebuilding

All went wrong again. From September 1943 until the end of April 1945, Italy suffered the disaster of being occupied by two conquering armies at war with each other and the whole peninsula became a battleground.

Richard Lamb, *War in Italy 1943-1945*

CHAPTER EIGHT
START OF THE JOINT
IGCR/AFSC PROGRAM[1]

ITALY SWITCHES SIDES

In July 1943 the Allied forces in North Africa landed in Sicily. By September they had advanced far enough into Italy that the Governing Council and Italian King Victor Emanuel dared depose and arrest Prime Minister Benito Mussolini. An interim government promptly sued for peace. During six crucial weeks of indecisive negotiations with Washington and London, the Italian army disintegrated and the German army flowed virtually unopposed into the country to prevent an easy Allied advance. Italy was finally allowed to join the Allies. From September to December 1943, relentless warfare raged up the spine of southern Italy, from town to town and village to village, as the Allies sought to reach Rome and the Germans tried to stop them. There were military losses on both sides and huge civilian destruction. By December, the Allies and the Germans were dug in south of Rome, and there would be no effective movement until the spring of 1944. Hundreds of thousands of Italian civilians were made refugees by the fighting and there were an estimated 30,000 foreign refugees in the Allied-controlled areas.

These costly military efforts were reminders that our work in Italy depended on the success of Allied arms. Only their advance opened areas to the assistance we and others could give. This irony hung over Quaker and others' assistance. It troubled me, especially when I saw active troop units, that our good works depended directly on the risks that other men in my generation were taking.

In April 1944 the Allied Control Commission (ACC) finally gave the Intergovernmental Committee on Refugees (IGCR) and AFSC permission to set up joint efforts in Naples. In May Sir Clifford Heathcote-Smith and David Hartley flew in from Algiers to Bari. Once again I was in the midst of the hubbub of a Military Air Transport Service (MATS) headquarters. Planes were arriving from and departing to Gibraltar, Algiers, Oran, Palermo, Cairo and other Mediterranean posts, Madrid, Lisbon, Casablanca, and even London and Washington. I discovered that Sir Clifford and David Hartley, who was to become my closest colleague on this assignment, had rushed off to Taranto to help stateless refugees headed for Palestine.

I finally met Sir Clifford in Taranto. He was a tall, thin, well-tailored man, with grayish hair, blue eyes, a well-trimmed handlebar mustache. He was in his early sixties, in good physical shape and remarkably energetic. As a veteran of the British Foreign Service and a Middle East specialist, he had a wide network of buddies from the colonial and foreign service at various levels in the ACC (later called simply the Allied Commission [AC]). These he was ready to call upon on behalf of the IGCR program or when our AFSC activities needed a boost. He had sharp elbows and was prepared to use them when necessary to get his way with junior officers, Italian officials and senior British officials. He often eased his way with a fund of comic anecdotes that helped people feel good even though he was importuning them to do something that was not quite by the book. He had a certain zest for his mission as he understood it.

He dealt with Dave and me as colleagues and was ready to include us in social occasions—I recall one lunch with Anne O'Hare McCormack, of *the New York Times*, in the ornate dining room of one of Rome's grand hotels.[2] I found a delicious irony in the contrast between the talk of unduly short rations now available to the Italian people and the tasty four-star lunch.

Fortunately, Sir Herbert Emerson, Director of the IGCR,

supported the organizational anomaly that made me both Sir Clifford's assistant and AFSC's representative for Italy. It had the advantages of getting two free assistants for the IGCR and access to AFSC experience with refugees. As Sir Clifford described our relationship, the AFSC was in Italy "under the wing" of the IGCR.

The winter of 1943 was a time of bitter fighting between the Anglo-American Allies and the German army.   From September to December there was relentless warfare up the spine of southern Italy.

EMERGENCY DEPARTURE

Our first urgent task was to help move 600 Jews to Palestine. An opportunity for so many to go to Palestine at one time surprised and pleased us. Even before the war, the British had been reluctant to allow more Jews to enter Palestine for fear Arab opposition would inspire disturbances throughout the Arab world, in Egypt and among Muslims in India.

A British White Paper of 1939 had set strict limits on new entrants to Palestine, then under a League of Nations mandate. With the start of World War II, the British were even more determined to avoid possible disturbances. I suspected that it was President Roosevelt's War Refugee Board that induced London to now accept these 600 immigrants into Palestine.

A ship was standing by for the refugees. Sir Clifford had already visited with Jewish Agency people in Jerusalem and he felt able to take responsibility for revising the terms of reference for selection. By the time I got to the Taranto transit camp, lists had been filled out and selections made, and candidates for refuge in Palestine were already arriving in the camp.

Sir Clifford wanted the IGCR to have a visible role in this precedent-setting movement. Dave and I, on the other hand, accustomed to the Allied military way of handling civilian movements, favored only selective involvement, leaving routine emigration matters to the army staffs. The small IGCR staff would then be able to intervene wherever we might be needed. But Sir Clifford was the boss, so we were quickly enrolled in handling quotidian details, checking identity papers against names on the lists, accepting Italian money and giving receipts in return, accounting in detail for the cash.

At the last minute—there is always a last minute in emigration—we discovered that eleven people originally on the list could not travel. The night before the movement, Sir Clifford, Dave and I, and army Captain Lewis Korn (now part of the ACC Refugee and Displaced Persons Sub-Committee staff) met to choose replacements.

We were assisted by a Mr. Hermann, a thoughtful, apparently objective leader of the refugee community. Around a table in the middle of a large barrack, studying a list of eighty names illuminated by one kerosene lantern, we had to choose the eleven who would go. We depended heavily on Mr. Hermann's knowledge of the family circumstances of the refugees.

Outside the building, heads of families pressed against the windows. It was not a comfortable task, even though this was 1944 in Italy—not summer and fall of 1942 in France when those who could not embark on the departing boat risked being deported. To my surprise, there were no strong complaints when the names of the fortunate ones were read out. The ship for their transport was the *Batory*, the same one that I had sailed with Yugoslav refugees being moved to Egypt in 1943.

With the Allies established in southern Italy, Bari was the principal British contact point with Yugoslavia just across the Adriatic. Tito's *Partisanis* and Mihailovich's Croatian *Ustashis* were fighting each other as well as the Germans. People with mysterious missions appeared and disappeared. Our British messmates recognized Evelyn Waugh as he came and went, as well as Fitzroy McClean, both at the time rumored to have close links to Tito. We could only speculate about what help they were funneling to their favored elements of the Yugoslav resistance.

Bari was also a major air base for Allied raids deep behind German lines, particularly into the Ploesti oil fields in Rumania. Driving on a road north of Bari around dawn, I could see the remnants of flights from those raids trying to land. Some of the approaching planes were damaged by anti-aircraft fire. They often lurched on landing, as landing gear, stabilizers or rudders failed to respond predictably. Those that ran off the runway might crash and burst into flames. I saw one plane swerve and turn a virtual cartwheel before exploding in a fireball. I could not help thinking of the damaged airman I had seen in the French restaurant in Cairo. These limping planes were the closest thing to combat that I saw. I later learned from Mary Elmendorf that her brother Calvert Lindsey had been killed in one of those raids from Bari.

IGCR'S TASKS

Back in our Bari hotel after the ship's departure, where old dark green curtains shaded the windows for fear of air raids, Sir Clifford seemed somewhat at a loss as to what IGCR's next mission should be. Sir Clifford asked Dave and me for our thoughts on IGCR's program. As we saw it, the IGCR had three main tasks: to help refugees get out of Italy to wherever they wanted to go; to place within Italy those unlikely to be able to emigrate; and to improve the conditions of the refugees as they waited. These goals were simple to state. To move toward achieving them, the IGCR needed to know more about non-Italian refugees who had reasonable hopes of emigrating overseas. We also wanted to reunite separated refugee families wherever possible, which meant working closely with Italian social service agencies and the International Committee of the Red Cross (ICRC). For refugees remaining in camps, we wanted to help develop community activities. Finally, for the "unrepresented" refugees, those stateless or scattered outside the camps but without means, we should try to find some way to help them where they were, so they would not have to move to the camps.

As AFSC, we pressed for entry of displaced persons into the United States as a priority. Our immediate task would be to make life in the remaining camps more livable. Dave's collaboration with the wounded Spanish veterans in North Africa had shown us what could be done with ingenuity and close connections with military people, who could supply used blankets, wooden crates for lumber, and tools. Since our work would come under the IGCR, any refugee activities would have to be approved first by Sir Clifford and then by the ACC's Internees and Displaced Persons Sub-Committee. But our agenda looked like a good start.

Once Dave, Sir Clifford and I had resolved the IGCR's objectives, Dave remained in Bari to handle implementation in the south, while Sir Clifford and I went to Caserta outside of Naples. I found that he had already established the IGCR office at several desks in the headquarters of the ACC. A rambling eighteenth century palace had been taken over until Rome became accessible. Partitions of plaster-board stood higgledy-piggledy, in stark contrast to the lovely marble mosaics on the floors and elaborate murals of sylphs and heroic figures on the ceilings. Telephone cables ran everywhere and manual typewriters and teletype machines banged away. With luck and patience I could telephone Dave in Bari. I could also obtain local transport or travel orders, and gain authorizations to explore military dumps for "surplus."

The Refugee Division of the ACC at Caserta was headed by Colonel Findley, a large, friendly man who was a perfect replica of the British character actor, C. Aubrey Smith. Over 6 feet 6, with a big nose, bushy eyebrows and a hearty laugh, he wore remarkable flaring khaki shorts even in winter. He was seconded by rotund Colonel Fothergill, one of a number of British officers who were pleased to identify their Quaker ancestors or relatives. I was never sure whether these officers had much to do with what relief we eventually organized for the "unrepresented." Certainly, it did us no harm to have friendly men high in the Allied Commission's refugee division.

Occasionally I was able to get away from Caserta and the nearby refugee center of Cinecittà, a former movie studio, for a quick visit to Naples. It was a sorry sight. Many downtown buildings had been hit. Whole walls had fallen away, floors sagging and spilling out their desks or sofas and beds. A famous *galleria* of boutiques was a wreck of twisted girders and broken glass. The railroad station and port had been hit badly by air strikes; the harbor was clogged with half-sunken hulks of ships. Hundreds of street children in rags ran alongside army trucks, begging for candy or food rations. There were big signs warning troops about typhus or VD.

Dave and I wondered how AFSC might make a contribution to life in the camps? It was important for Dave and me to stay in close contact, and we managed to get together nearly every month. Sir Clifford urged me to pay periodic visits to the refugee camps in the south. Sometimes it was possible to fly to Bari, but often there were no seats. The alternative was an overnight train, sitting up in a crowded, soft-seat compartment. At a midnight stop lonely British troops served up coffee and a nourishing pot of Irish stew to all the passengers. British military passengers invariably began swapping stories of the London blitz or the North African campaign before settling down to a restless sleep.

One of the camps in the south was Ferramonti, which held British POWs during the later years of the war. Farther south, in the heel of Italy, there was most notably Santa Maria di Bagni, which sheltered several thousand Yugoslav civilian refugees and a number of other nationalities. In the port city of Taranto, a large transit camp was efficiently run by the British army. The system of refugee camps in southern Italy was far better than what we knew about the notorious internment camps in southern France.

On the fall of the Badoglio government and its replacement by a civilian-run government in late 1943, the gates of the camps had immediately been opened. Some internees had left to lodge with distant relatives or to return to communities where they had hidden from the Italian or later German police. The reduced camp population at Ferramonti was adequately cared for, although health services were pretty sketchy and available cash allowances were rapidly devalued by severe inflation. As the combat front had stabilized south of Rome during the winter, an informal supplementary assistance network emerged for the scattered Jewish communities. Vehicles from the Palestine Transport Corps, attached to the British Army, quietly brought help to the most needy, both in the camps and in scattered clusters.

At Sir Clifford's request, I became the IGCR's visiting inspector, checking up on the health care and sanitation, as well as on the morale and competency of camp administrators. My knowledge of health matters and camp administration was rudimentary, but eyes and ears for the IGCR were scarce, and helpful to Sir Clifford. Since

Ferramonti had housed British POWs, conditions were not bad. The principle of international reciprocity, at least among the European belligerents, meant that each cared for its prisoners of war with some minimum consideration.

Wooden "duck boards" throughout the camp suggested that the place was wet much of the time; indeed it had record occurrences of malaria. Santa Maria de Bagni was generally well run by the British army, but morale among the Yugoslav refugees was low; they were impatient to return to their homes on the Dalmatian Coast.

One afternoon I had tea with a French-speaking Yugoslav family. I wrote a note about their dilemma; impossibly hard choices then faced so many.

> As the Germans approached Belgrade we fled to the Dalmatian coast, where the independent state of Croatia had just been created. At first, the Croatians saw us only as Serbs. Later, when the Italians took control of the Dalmatian coast, we were interned as Jewish Serbs. As serious, what use will a furrier be in the new Titoist order? In Israel, though, I am quite unfitted for work on the land. What to do?

Should they return to Yugoslavia? The partisan leaders said that now was the time to go home: if they didn't take the opportunity they might never get back. But reports persisted that there was still no food in Dalmatia.

In addition to reminding me of the difficulties the refugees faced, these visits also gave me a chance to consult with Dave. I wanted his advice on how to deal with Sir Clifford's impulsiveness. I felt that Dave knew him better than I did, since the two of them had been stuck together for some weeks. They had been waiting in Algiers for permission to enter Italy.

I also wanted his thoughts on how the IGCR could better serve the refugees. I was impressed by how Dave came to focus on the reconstruction needs in the Abruzzi, a poverty-stricken mountainous district north of Bari. Our periodic consultations either in Bari or in Rome helped give shape to his thinking and helped me in working with Sir Clifford.

Sir Clifford showed his courage at the Taranto transit camp: before a group of refugees hoping to go to Palestine, he waved a pocket handkerchief to symbolize just how little land there was in Palestine. He urged them to avoid disappointment by considering where else they might go. All in all, he was a lively, helpful person. His connections among the British staffs helped him get many things done.

Sir Clifford was admirably impatient for some visible results, but I feared he might run with an idea further than it deserved. He did not share my American acceptance of people who were not Anglo-Saxon. He may not have been aware of his arrogance when he made Jews wait for appointments, or Italians put up with high handedness. Though we admired the job he was doing, Dave and I shared our disquiet with Philadelphia and together we wrote a letter to our home office expressing this view. We concluded that his discriminatory attitudes would be a liability for a resident representative of the IGCR.

In the summer the FAU contributed two more helpers to the IGCR. One was Dennis Mann, who had originally been part of the FAU anti-typhus team assigned to Naples. He was nearly six feet tall, with a high forehead, steel-rimmed glasses and a tight, disciplined smile. Always willing to do whatever he was asked, he had a scientific bent and a well-organized mind. He became a central figure in helping shape and operate the IGCR program for the "unrepresented," overseeing a growing staff who distributed monthly IGCR checks to scattered refugees.

The second FAU person, Sam Marriage, came to us from Cairo. He was a tall, lanky, loose-jointed lifetime British Friend, with a shock of hair that sometimes fell over his eyes. Sam proved to be highly ingenious and, like Dave, quietly persistent, focusing on community activities of all kinds. He had a gift for encouraging the refugees to see what they would be able to do for themselves if only they had a little outside help. Indeed, whenever I stopped long enough to reflect on it, I was impressed by how enterprising the needy were in bettering their own circumstances whenever they could.

MOVEMENT OF 1,000 STATELESS TO THE U.S.

During April and May the combat line began to move north toward Rome; the city was liberated on June 5th. The following day we heard the news of the assault on the beaches of Normandy. All of Caserta was delighted; Sir Clifford practically danced a jig. In July, in a miraculous reversal of the near total blockage of immigration visas earlier, the War Refugee Board in Washington obtained permission for 1,000 stateless refugees to go to the States. It was not until much later that I learned of the struggle behind the seeming bounty. Congress and the State Department were opposed to any immigration. By contrast, the War Refugee Board and voluntary agencies like AFSC, the Unitarian Service Committee and, of course, the JDC and its associates argued for a more humane exception. In the end, the President compromised, allowing 1,000 in as "guests" of the government, to be returned to their homeland after the war.[3]

We were presented with the major challenge of selecting these emigrants and gathering them in a transit camp near Naples. Len Ackerman, a staffer for the War Refugee Board, arrived from Washington, full of zeal. Before he and Captain Lewis Korn toured the southern camps to prepare a preliminary list we discussed selection criteria. Certainly slave laborers and those who had been in concentration camps, or slave laborers and their families, had first priority. Families with children, individuals who had multiple citizenship origins, and skilled professionals and craftspeople were also given precedence.

Selecting those who were to go was nerve-wracking. Some 3,000 heads of families applied for the 1,000 openings. Each had a terrible story; nearly all had lost family members; some had been in hiding during the German occupation of Rome; others had been in forced labor gangs. Max Perlman, a gentle, slightly stooped JDC social worker from Chicago (who later joined Dave Hartley's Bari office for the JDC), and Dave made preliminary lists in Bari, and Dave went to Potenza, a semi-rural area where a number of stateless had been living hidden in scattered communities. I came to Bari to collect names and details about candidates from the Bari area while Sir Clifford gathered names in Rome. We left specific decisions to Len Ackerman, though occasionally we intervened for a particular individual or family whose need seemed great or whose younger members appeared promisingly impatient to get on with their educations.

In Naples I worked one night with Len coordinating the lists. It was mid-summer and, holed up in our sweltering hotel room, we worked in nothing but our boxer shorts until 3 a.m., when we called it quits. I was impressed that someone fresh from Washington would expend such an effort. The next day I flew to Rome, and found that Sir Clifford and Lewis Korn had selected the 200 allocated for Rome. I was to escort them to the transit camp outside Naples in large army 4x4s with canvas covers to fend off the sun. Wooden seats ran along the sides and down the middle of the cargo area. Boxes acted as steps to help the less agile climb aboard. It was a rough ride on a pot-holed road, with numerous stops to deal with vehicles that had broken down in our path. Some of the older people grew very impatient. The younger ones were excited at the prospect of going to America; the parents hardly believed they were really leaving this accursed continent of Europe. On the convoy from Bari an Italian Red Cross nurse was accompanying a very pregnant young woman, who gave birth in the back of a Red Cross truck en route from Bari to Naples. Max Perlman became famous as her midwife assistant.

The transit camp had been a Catholic asylum for over a hundred years. The disheveled and anxious band of refugees waiting for the boat that was to take them to America must have seemed a familiar sight to the nuns. The heroes of the transit camp were the army medics who inspected the refugees for contagious diseases and supervised the showers and de-infestation stations with humor and humane care. Two leaders of the refugee community, Messrs Hermann and Rosenberg, managed the task of having groups ready at the right time for medical inspection, counter-intelligence interrogation, list checking by Len Ackerman, and the collection of Italian occupation currency. In the end, there were 983 emigrants. Among them 369 had been Yugoslavs, 237 Austrians, 146 Polish, 96 Germans, 41 Czechs; the remainder were stateless. Those more experienced must have wondered, with foreboding, why they had to sign an affidavit confirming their willingness to return to Europe after the war was over. Ignorant of this stipulation, I watched with satisfaction as they boarded the *Henry Gibbons* troop ship bound for New York and, for most, further internment in New York state.[4]

After the wild month was over, Max Perlman told me, "The hardest job I ever had was choosing among those harassed people. Playing God is not my thing."

While dealing with this transport, we received word that James Vail, head of AFSC's Foreign Service Section, would be stopping at Algiers in July on his way home to Philadelphia from Calcutta. I was asked to be there to report on the possibilities for wider AFSC service in Italy. I flew back to Rome, for the necessary air travel orders, then promptly flew to Algiers for a few days' consultation with him, Ken Kimberland, and our new man in Lisbon. James Vail reported on AFSC's collaboration with the FAU in the Bengal famine relief and heard reports on AFSC activities in Italy, North Africa and Portugal. We went over our program options. There was much work at hand.

Privately James and I also reviewed how my direct experience with the plight of refugees, the appalling civilian concentration camps and the positive effects of the Allied military presence in North Africa had persuaded me I was no longer a C.O. He was pleased with my report on our activities with the IGCR and Dave's work in the camps and hoped I would continue with the AFSC. I was much reassured by our conversation.

IGCR IN ROME

In July 1944 the IGCR office moved to Rome. Sir Clifford's energetic negotiation obtained two spacious offices in a building on the upscale Via Veneto. We found that although Rome had been spared from direct damage, it had a sullied, depressed air. Public transportation was very poor. Cars were rare, improvised trucks were filled to capacity, the few buses were jammed and most sputtered along on charcoal Gazogene. For civilians, gasoline was impossible to get except at huge cost on the thriving black market. People were cheered by the downfall of the old regime; but everything was scarce and public services barely worked. Rome had a long way to go.

Rome, a so-called "open city," had been quickly taken under control by special Nazi police after the Badoglio government had surrendered the previous September. Nazi police had arrested civilians freely, particularly healthy young Italian men who might be pressed into defense construction. The Nazis invaded the Ghetto and piled perhaps a thousand Jews into freight cars for deportation. Most of them never returned.[5] There were many stories of risky heroism by Catholics, that helped offset the Vatican's apparent passivity. Thousands of Jews were taken into hiding in monasteries and convents throughout the city and surrounding countryside. A Portuguese priest known as Brother X, who once had been an engraver, prepared false Portuguese passports as a way of helping. His first batch was not very good. A friendly Italian police officer collected several of them and showed the Brother where he had to improve. His next batch were passable, and gave the protection of neutral Portugal to hundreds for as long as necessary.

After several months of Allied advance, a new German defense line north of Rome and south of Bologna, the so-called Gothic Line, blocked further Allied movement north for the winter of 1944-45. During the previous winter food and fuel had been very scarce, electricity irregular and blackouts frequent and unpredictable in the cities. At the peak of summer 1944, food seemed adequate, but we began to fear shortages again in the coming winter, as Northern Italy had the best agriculture. Billeted in requisitioned hotels and eating army food, I and other members of the AFSC/IGCR crew did not suffer during that winter. However, it distressed Dave, Dennis and me, whenever we entered an overheated military office building, to see that there were even occasional open windows. To be fair, some rooms were deliberately overheated so that everyone in the buildings would get some warmth. But it still seemed an obscene contrast to the bitter cold of the winter streets.

REFUGEES IN THE SOUTH: CAMP WORKSHOPS

Sir Clifford and I worked on the broader IGCR agenda in Rome, reminding the Allied authorities that refugees of all kinds needed attention, and seeking ways to establish the IGCR's distinctive role. In Bari, Dave Hartley and Sam Marriage sought to improve the quality of life for refugees in nearby camps. The FAU truck that Sam brought with him proved indispensable. A large number of Yugoslav and other refugees were still housed in Santa Maria di Bagni. Dave and Sam prowled through military salvage depots, looking for army rejects that might be useful to the camp workshops.

Both men had a particular gift for scrounging. They took broken sewing machines from army tailor shops to be repaired so that refugees could improve the used clothing shipped to them from the States. Army surplus blankets could be recut and repaired and winter clothes made with the remnants. Idle refugees could be usefully employed in a woodworking shop equipped with tools from the army.

Into the fall, Sam concentrated on work in the camps. By November 1944, many refugees had found employment; the tailor shop was making sixty complete garments a week (trousers, jackets and coats) from salvage canvas and blankets. A shoe repair shop rebuilt salvaged army boots. A carpentry shop took used lumber from numerous shipping crates and turned it into beds, tent floors, chairs, tables, shoe soles, anything to get people off the ground for the winter. Sam's activities not only supplied goods but greatly improved the morale in the camp. His job was conceived as temporary and, once the organization had been set up and channels for supply had been established, he rejoined Dave in Bari. Max Perlman was also based in Bari, distributing JDC funds to needy Jewish refugees according to a program worked out with Sir Clifford.

In Rome, in a more modest effort than Sam's, Dennis Mann and I also promoted the self-help activities of refugees in the Cinecittà refugee camp.

FEAR OF DEPORTATIONS FROM NORTHERN ITALY

As a former intelligence officer in World War I, Sir Clifford was determined to obtain a full picture of all the refugees in all of Italy. Dave and I thought this rather hopeless because half the country was still under German control. Nevertheless, his urgent inquiries through the Vatican, Allied and Italian intelligence services and many other channels did lead to some heartening, if idiosyncratic, information. For example, a telegram sent from Rome in January 1943 to many towns in

Central Italy, ordering the deportation of both foreign and Italian Jews, was reported to have been received only in April of that year. This delay confirmed the impression that many Italian officials were sympathetic to the plight of the Jews, and dragged their feet if they could.

The investigations also gave us the significant disturbing news that in northern Italy convoys were picking up Jews and deporting them to Germany and Poland. By then we had well-confirmed information about extermination camps like Auschwitz and Treblinka. Sir Clifford sought to induce the Vatican to exert pressure on the Nuncio at Milan to persuade Northern Italian authorities to release into the safety of neighboring Switzerland these Jews and political dissidents. These efforts were followed up by his personal whirlwind visit to Switzerland, and interviews with the Nuncio there. He also consulted Ross McClelland, who had been AFSC's representative on refugee affairs in Italy before the war and who was then the War Refugee Board's representative in the U.S. Embassy in Berne.

Never one to be shy about trying to reach the top, Sir Clifford also attempted to have President Roosevelt and Winston Churchill personally warn officials in charge of the Italian camps through radio and leaflets. He felt that the two leaders should offer Italian officials mitigation of their future punishment if they ignored Nazi instructions to deport Jews and dissident civilians. His efforts were admirable and might have made a real difference if those he approached had responded. Precisely during the period Sir Clifford was most active, the Germans had been making heavy arrests in northern Italy with deportations to Auschwitz and other camps. Fewer than one eighth of the deportees ever returned.

In July, Sir Clifford—and all of us who visited the Ardeantine Catacombs in Rome—had been deeply moved by a horrific spectacle. In January, during the German occupation of the city, several German officers had been shot in a working class district of Rome. In retaliation, over three hundred men were arrested at random from the neighborhood by the Nazi police and summarily shot. Their bodies were stacked up in the catacombs like so much cordwood.

Operating on a more mundane level, Dave, Dennis and I thought the odds were poor that Sir Clifford would succeed, and we bent our efforts to mitigating the plight of those refugees who were already accessible to us. But Sir Clifford was right to try whatever he could. With his upper-level relationships he might have been able to achieve things we could not hope to accomplish. In retrospect, it is clear that his sense of priority was better attuned than ours to the realities of that awful period.

Occasionally I would go to the Vatican to consult with whoever was most concerned about the stateless and the "unrepresented" refugees. I was angry that the Vatican did so little to save the victims of the Nazis, and I supported Sir Clifford's efforts to encourage decisive action from the Vatican. I would walk through the endless corridors, my feet echoing on the marble floors, until I entered a spacious waiting room, the ceiling twenty-five feet high, with heavy tapestries on the wall. One of the tapestries would move aside and a black-robed Vatican functionary would take me down further corridors until I would meet, in a small office, another black-robed figure in Monsignor Montini's section. The nameless official would listen with apparent attention, take notes, promise to do what he could and thank me for my visit. I never received the kind of firm commitment I sought; but it was impossible to be within reach of this great establishment and not try to move it.

During nearly every visit I was able to steal a moment or two in one of the art galleries. My favorites were the Raphael rooms, where one could admire the great paintings, but also step out on the famous Raphael Loggia, which gives such a wonderful panoramic of the heart of Rome.

A salvage worker stands gazing at a small town in Italy destroyed in the bitter 1943 campaign that swept up the southern region of the country.

CHAPTER NINE
RECONSTRUCTION
AND AID TO THE
UNREPRESENTED

One of the most imaginative programs we developed was David Hartley's village reconstruction. During their drives between Rome and Bari, David and Max Perlman were appalled by the human effects of the bitter 1943 campaign up the spine of southern Italy. When Dave first took me to towns in the Abruzzi Mountains, in the Apennines east of Rome and north of Bari, I could not believe my eyes. Where the fighting had been stalled for the winter months, whole villages had been totally destroyed. As I contemplated the disaster brought to these villagers by the struggling armies, the pacifist argument once again seemed tempting. Roofs were gone; walls were now only heaps of rubble. Here and there a village was untouched, spared as if by a miracle. On the next hill, however, and the next and the next, and in the valley below, all others were piles of rubble. A narrow foot trail might lead to the sad remains of a house

with canvas stretched across the broken rocks as a roof sheltering a
rolled up mattress, the remains of a kitchen fireplace, a pot or two.

In the fall of 1944, Dave wrote of his surprise that

> such destruction remains virtually as it was when the
> troops moved on (six months ago) except for necessary
> military roads and installations. The people who fled to
> the hills seem to return when their villages are safe, push
> aside the worst of the debris and live in the remaining
> one or two rooms...They seem to have no energy or will
> to set things right. Spiritually there was an atmosphere of
> defeatism and despair.

In talking to a number of village leaders in the area, Dave
found that most of the villages in the mountains had communal
woodlots. The kilns that made the bricks and glazed roof tiles typical
of the region were in the lowlands, nearer the sea. The kilns were not
working—they could not get the charcoal they needed since all local
transport had been requisitioned by the military.

Dave introduced me to mayors for help. The older ones
helplessly shrugged their shoulders but a few younger ones, however,
saw possibilities. Some had been members of the Communist Party
and had gained a reputation for heroism during the resistance. They
became mayors during the chaos immediately following the German
retreat. Others made a point of differentiating themselves as
socialists. Whatever the party affiliation, they saw the urgent need
and were ready to act.

Lack of building material was the main problem. The key to
solving that was transport. Dave's proposal sounded simple and went
to the heart of the matter: to encourage a system of barter with the
help of some old army trucks, not to do something for the village but
to give them the means to do things for themselves. The vehicles,
with reliable drivers, would carry the wood from trees felled by the
villagers to the kilns below, and return to the villages loaded with
newly minted roof tiles.

We provided trucks and drivers so mountain villagers could swap timber for tiles from kilns in the valley.

Peter Gibson, now head of the FAU in Italy, set up his headquarters in Rome. He was a compact, lively, upbeat sort of man, full of stories about early FAU days in the western desert. He promptly sought us out. When he saw what Dave had started, he enthusiastically supported the concept, eventually assigning a dozen FAU drivers and vehicles to the project, which became a joint AFSC/FAU undertaking. To be sure, there were never enough working vehicles. Breakdowns were frequent. Maintenance was a never-ending problem. But wood and charcoal were moving down to the kilns and tiles and bricks were coming back up.

With the shortage of trucks and gasoline, Italian villagers were forced to work as their grandfathers had, with oxen and wagons.

Gradually village morale improved, more rubble was cleared away and damage repaired, even new houses began to be built. The work developed into a race against the winter and its snows which were creeping down the mountain sides, soon to make the transport of building materials impossible. A census in Montenerodomo showed that by the next winter 80 to 100 new rooms, housing 250 to 300 people, had been completed—all without the infusion of cash. The visible accomplishment by neighbors was inspiring.

As soon as the local villagers received the materials, they took the initiative and began their own rebuilding.

I strongly backed David's work in messages to Philadelphia. The FAU found it an ideally practical way of showing Friendly concern for individuals and families in dire straits. More important, this work became a model picked up and greatly expanded by UNRRA. Still later, the Italian government carried a similar program to other areas. Fifty years later, the Italian government held a ceremony of celebration, honoring the AFSC for its initiative. It had been Dave Hartley's idea from the beginning.[1]

Yet there are few accomplishments without a down side. I have often wondered what happened to the communal forests in the Abruzzi as a result of Dave's endeavors. Have the Italian Greens excoriated those foreigners who promoted the depletion of the village woodlots in their haste to get the returning people housed before the winter snows?

REFUGEE ASSISTANCE PROGRAM

While Dave and Sam were developing the idea of the Abruzzi building program, our priorities in Rome were quite different. We wanted IGCR to focus on the "unrepresented" refugees who were not in the camps and who did not have a homeland government to advocate for them. What a miscellaneous group of refugees they were! Many nationalities had consuls or military missions with quasi-official standing with the Allied Commission. But many refugees from central Europe—the Czechs, Bulgarians and Rumanians among others—had no such official standing. Delasem, the local Jewish organization backed by the JDC, was unofficially recognized as the good provider for Jewish refugees. But there was no recognized body able to deal with the twenty percent who were non-Jewish. I worked toward generating an assistance program for these stateless and other unrepresented refugees.

While visiting one of the Allied Commission offices, I met a man who epitomized the experience of European Jewry's lucky ones, those who had managed to survive. We met at a sidewalk café one evening, where he told me the following story.

> I'm now working as an interpreter for the Allied Commission. I was once a bank executive, assistant manager of a Berlin bank. Interned? Yes, I have been in for the best part of the past eight years. Dachau first. Clean it was, at least. But my arms have never been the same. After I was released on condition I would leave Germany right away, my wife and I made it to Paris in 1938. In Paris I worked as a photographer's assistant

until the start of the war in September 1939, when I was
arrested again, like all stateless foreigners in France. My
French cousin managed to get us out before the collapse,
and luckily we went south with the Exodus. We were
soon arrested again in the south—Gurs, le Vernet. You
know how they were—the hunger, the endless mud, the
awful sanitation. Thanks to one of the committees, we
managed to get out in the spring of 1942. We were able
to make our way to the Italian-occupied Alpes
Maritimes, where they assigned us fixed residence in
Hautes-Savoie, which wasn't too bad. And then, believe
it or not, when the Badoglio government was about to
capitulate, the Italians sent trucks up after us and
transported us out of France to Italy, where we were able
to go underground. We lived from house to house with
the help of a local relief committee. And when the
German army came into Rome, I was able to hide in a
monastery and my wife in a nunnery.

There were others who endured even greater difficulties
who nevertheless managed to survive and who were scattered in
small communities north of Rome.

As luck would have it, in the fall of 1944 I was asked to
comment on a draft proposal circulated by the Allied Financial
Agency of the ACC. It proposed providing cash relief to Polish,
Czech and other nationals of the numerous Allied military missions
then in Italy. The Allied Financial Agency would probably not want
to make such advances directly to a sectarian Italian agency, such as
Delasem. Even if it did, the non-Jewish twenty percent might well be
inadvertently left out.[2]

Here was an opportunity for the IGCR to administer basic
assistance and conceivably become the nucleus of representation for
the stateless (one role of the Nansen office). It would relieve the JDC
of part of the financial burden it carried for Jewish refugees, shifting
it to a public agency. It would also make public financial assistance
available to the twenty percent of non-Jewish refugees who were still
without regular assistance.

I lobbied hard for the proposal, first with Sir Clifford and
then with the members of the Internees and Displaced Persons
subcommittee of the Allied Commission. Others also supported the
idea. Luckily, we obtained approval in principle from Sir Clifford
before he went to England toward the end of September 1944. We
then had long and detailed discussions with the Finance Agency. As

for all such arrangements, an incredible amount of conferring and clearing was necessary before all were agreed.

On loan from the FAU, Dennis Mann organized and oversaw this highly selective short-term welfare scheme, drawing on good advice from experienced American social workers and the JDC. In the end we had a virtual League of Nations of our own—two Italian medical social workers on loan from the Italian Red Cross, one American T-5 Sergeant on loan from the ACC, one Egyptian clerk, one Austrian typist and office assistant, one Italian typist, one Polish accountant and three case workers, one of whom was Austrian, the other two German.

Our first payments were made in Rome around October 10, 1944; they eventually reached over forty towns in liberated Italy. Payments were made by the banks where the refugees lived. The costs were charged to the person's nationality or, if stateless, to the individual's last nationality. There were many complications. Payment through local banks was inflexible; it could hardly be responsive to the family's unpredictable needs. Introducing more cash into the Italian currency pool no doubt made a small contribution to inflation. However, we got something started that lifted a burden from voluntary organizations like the JDC and AFSC and was a real help to hard-pressed individuals. All the recipients were far from home, many did not know what their future held, and all had been interned for between eight months and five years. Later, UNRRA picked up the program and improved upon it.

FURTHER SEARCHES NORTH OF ROME

In late October, while the details of the cash relief system were being worked out in Rome, Art Greenleigh of the JDC, and I on behalf of the IGCR, visited a number of Jewish communities in the region recently abandoned by the Germans. We were seeking scattered clusters of unrepresented refugees who would be entitled to be included in the emerging refugee relief payments program. Some had been in hiding for some years, and others only during the threatening period just before the German troops withdrew.

One night I will never forget. In the darkness of that rainy night we were driving north toward Florence. Most of the city had been spared serious damage, though the railroad yards and all bridges, with the exception of the historic Ponte Vecchio, had been severely damaged. We were in a vehicle belonging to the Palestine Transport Corps, attached to the British army. The driver, a Major Frumkin, was a Palestinian *sabre* (one who had been born and raised in Palestine and was considered to be very English by way of education), articulate and witty. In addition, there was a Polish captain who had been taken prisoner by the Russians when they invaded Poland in 1940, was released via Iran, and joined Polish units organized by the British in Palestine. He was perhaps the most bitter man I ever met. In the back seat with me was Art Greenleigh, a JDC staffer. He had worked in the garment district of New York, which I knew from my buying trips for my father's store. There was a good deal of joshing back and forth, since I was the only goy in the crowd. But Quakers, too, were a small minority, and I was able to make a good deal out of that.

While we enjoyed our verbal games, we drove through terrible destruction. We were where the Gothic Line had been fought over for six months. Remains of buildings and great piles of rubble flashed past, brightly illuminated in the beams of our headlights; they were succeeded by deep black as we sped through the night. Suddenly Art and I saw dead ahead of us a great cement slab standing right in the middle of the road. A bridge had taken a direct hit and part of it was standing on end, just waiting for us. We felt bound for a final crash. In our shared fear, Art cried out, "Jesus Christ, look at that!" and at the same moment I cried out, "Holy Moses, look at that!" But the road dipped sharply to the left, down a steep slope and across a ford to rise safely on the other side. We all burst out laughing. We were pleased that, instinctively, at the last moment of life, we had called on each other's prophets. We completed our night drive safely, found an army billet for the night and spent the next two days talking to refugee spokesmen in Florence, Pisa and a number of smaller communities nearby.

Sir Clifford had gone back to London for consultation in September; he remained until the first of the year. During all the time he was away, Dennis and I were going ahead with the development of the IGCR individual relief system. By Sir Clifford's return in late January we were up and running. Fortunately for our work, he had originally come to Italy with a very able, and remarkably impersonal, Foreign Office secretary. While I do not recall thinking this at the time, I now believe she must have kept him pretty well informed as to what we were up to. When he returned, he did not seem surprised and was generally pleased with the service for the "unrepresented" that we had developed.

Howard and Art Greenleigh, while driving through a treacherous night in northern Italy, during a moment of fear, *in extremis* called upon each other's prophet.

NEGOTIATIONS WITH UNRRA

Dave and I watched with pleasure the gradual appearance of UNRRA people. Sam Keeny, head of the UNRRA mission, was a warm-hearted, friendly man. He quickly set up a relatively open, cooperative organization.[3] He was almost inseparable from his more austere General Counsel, who kept reminding him of the constraints imposed by legislation. One of his assistants had been with OFRRO in North Africa and knew of our work there. Keeny held the rather preposterous view that the staff of every UNRRA mission should be at least ten percent Quaker. He also hoped AFSC could reach a satisfactory working agreement for its activities in Italy. Under his management, the UNRRA mission handled emergency food and reconstruction assistance throughout the peninsula as it opened; and gradually UNRRA began to take over management of the refugee camps.

Sam Keeny and the IGCR agreed that the IGCR could help deal with the most intractable displaced-persons problems. We wanted to see UNRRA take over responsibility for financing the interim refugee assistance program. By mid-January, Sir Clifford was back from London and signed for IGCR the working agreement with UNRRA.

In the spring of 1944, Louise Tibbetts, whom I had known well in Chicago as an attractive, up-beat person, volunteered for overseas service with AFSC for work in Yugoslavia. She trained at the University of Maryland, specializing in Serbo-Croatian. It was great to see her again when we had a few days together in Rome before she went off to her UNRRA position in the Santa Maria di Bagni refugee camp, where her language skills were much admired.[4] Catholic Relief was also providing nurses for the British army-run camp.

VOYAGE HOME AND ASSESSMENT

After Sir Clifford came back from London, Dave Hartley took my place in Rome and I went home for leave after over three years away. In late January I sailed on a Liberty Ship in a substantial convoy bound from Naples. We traveled slowly, taking three weeks for the zigzag crossing by the southern route. It was a great period of rest, reading, and eating. The sea was tranquil for the most part, great slow rollers coming up the south Atlantic. The Merchant Marine served good meals to the officers, and I ate with them. I had a small but comfortable stateroom. For reading matter, we had a pile of paperbacks selected especially for the servicemen. I read Elizabeth Drinker Bowen's biography of Oliver Wendell Holmes, *Yankee from Olympus*; a biography of Paul Revere by Esther Forbes, Jack London's *The Call of the Wild*, and many others. As the only passenger, I felt pangs of conscience as everyone else was on a rigid watch schedule. Night time navigation was exhausting to the deck crew and bridge officers, who had to be alert at all times to avoid a collision course with another unlit ship in the convoy. Radar could not be used. By the time we entered Norfolk Harbor I had gained back some weight and was well-tanned from the sunny voyage.

On the slow trip I was able to prepare a long report, first in longhand and then on my trusty Underwood, and had a chance to assess what I had been up to as part of the AFSC. Did it make sense for the AFSC to maintain the close involvement with the Intergovernmental Committee on Refugees? Thanks to our relationship, AFSC entered Italy sooner than would otherwise have been possible. The AFSC in turn had helped steer the IGCR's programming. Moreover, as I put it in my report, not a little immodestly,

Since we were in on the formative stages of the IGCR in
Italy, and (while Sir Clifford was away) for four months,
we *were* the IGCR, the IGCR had more 'concern' for
individual refugee welfare and well-being and had less
of a 'racial consciousness' and sectarian perspective.

Being "under the wing" of the IGCR gave facilities and
status to us and the JDC which would not have been ours otherwise.
It permitted the AFSC to be among the first to establish itself as a
recognized agency, with the result that David Hartley's program in
the Abruzzi had been more easily accepted by Allied officials and
Italian authorities.   Sir Clifford left us much room for AFSC
initiatives, whether in direct help in the camps, in the Abruzzi, or in
starting services for the unrepresented. Had the IGCR been an
operating agency more like OFFRO, my evaluation might have been
different.

In any event, I urged that we continue with the IGCR, at
least until UNRRA took over the economic and welfare assistance
we had started for the refugees. Until UNRRA did so, we should
monitor how well the IGCR continued its representational activities
on behalf of the otherwise unrepresented.

While it was still early in our experience with UNRRA, I
concurred with James Vail's recommendation that we should accept
UNRRA's invitation to send one team to assist in the refugee camps
in southern Italy, at least for a trial period. There was useful work to
be done; there were good training opportunities for our first-time
overseas workers, and the camps were places for short term
assignments before other major opportunities might open up, either
in Italy itself or in the Balkans.

I reported on the high reputation held by the Quakers:

When you introduce yourself as a Quaker, especially
before refugees, there is a degree of confidence or
expectation that is often shaking...One often feels a sense
of inadequacy, of not being able to fulfill expectations.

A British passport control officer once said to me,

The great thing about you people [Quakers] is that you
are never disappointed in people. You expect them to be
decent, and even when they aren't, somehow you're not
embittered, but just keep on expecting the best and
you're seldom surprised either way.

I hoped he was right. Yet by then I had learned enough about the depths to which human beings could sink in their cruelty to others that I, at least, had lowered my expectations.

A particular satisfaction had been our close collaboration with the Friends Ambulance Unit. I greatly respected the FAU and the devotion, skill, and conscientiousness of its staff. In Italy, we were heavily dependent upon Dennis Mann's dedication in managing the welfare fund distribution, although he might have preferred a more collegial assignment. Sam Marriage's help to Dave was also notable. I urged AFSC to look closely at the way the FAU was able to place its members in many kinds of useful positions. Although the American Red Cross headquarters jealously protected its monopoly position on emergency civilian relief in combat areas and therefore may have helped delay our entry into Italy, I reported that its people in the field had always been helpful.

On arrival in Norfolk, I phoned my family in Germantown. My mother answered and when she heard my voice she immediately burst into tears. Foolishly, I was surprised at her response, and she soon recovered. On the sleeper train to Philadelphia, I was struck by the wonderful freshly ironed sheets and comfortable mattresses, after the all-night sit-ups on the Italian trains. It was great to be home and to find that, despite her loss, my mother seemed in good form, as my Service Committee friends had periodically reassured me. My father's absence left a huge hole, but we were also relieved that he was out of his misery.

I spent most of my days at the Service Committee debriefing and answering questions. I tried to evoke for staff the peculiarities of life in Italy, the plights of the different groups of refugees, and the stimulating and complicated lives that Dave and I were leading. There was also a brief ski weekend in Vermont, but it was a lonely affair since all my peers were away in either Civilian Public Service or the military.

On March 10, my sister Edith and Bob Atmore, who was back on leave from Red Cross service in the Pacific, were married in the Episcopal Church in Germantown. Bob had invited Rufus Jones, one of his Quaker professors at Haverford, to help the Reverend Aulenbach in the marriage service. Rufus Jones was a portly, cheerful man, with a round face, a well trimmed mustache and small wire-rimmed glasses. He radiated confidence in people. Yet, as the passport control officer put it, he would not be embittered if he discovered his confidence had been misplaced. He gave a good Quaker homily. It warmed my heart to be drawn back to my roots, to sense once more that radiating confidence in fundamentals. The following Sunday, the quiet of Germantown Friends Meeting brought refreshment of the spirit and a sense of hope that the follies of the European past might not be repeated this time.

In preparing for my return to Italy I was in New York to consult with the New York AFSC office. On the evening of April 12, 1945, an old friend and I were enjoying the spring air on one of my favorite outings— a ride on the Staten Island ferry. The bell was clanging, the ferry's engines were beginning to churn the water, when a newsboy came rushing onto the ferry at the last moment, calling out, "FDR is dead in Hot Springs." My date began to cry. I had an awful sinking feeling. So much still to be done! I grabbed a copy of the *New York Post* for confirmation. It must be so. The bottom dropped out of our world. Roosevelt had been president so long, it was hard to imagine how we could possibly do without him. Soon, however, the incredible view of New York harbor lay out behind us, with the towering city all alight in the early evening dusk. We both began to feel a little bit better.

By the end of April I was on my way back, again by convoy zigzagging its slow way across the south Atlantic. The voyage was similarly uneventful, except for one very exciting moment. In early May, about 10:30 one night, well into the lights-out drill, all the lights on all the ships suddenly went on, in front of, astern, and way out on the wings of the convoy. It was like Christmas tree lights going on, all at the same instant. The submarine threat was officially over and that meant the war in Europe, at least, was near its end. For most of us it was a time of cheer. But for some of the men on board the news was not unalloyed. It might mean a long and risky tour in the Pacific. For those of us interested in the politics of the near future, there was a big question: would our leaders be able to shape a peace that would endure?

ABRUPT CHANGES AT THE IGCR

On arriving in Naples, I had vowed to myself to sit quietly in Caserta, which was on the outskirts, catching up on mail and waiting for Barclay Jones, our Mediterranean commissioner, who was due in Naples shortly. But I could not resist the temptation to call Peter Gibson, the head of the FAU unit in Rome, to see what I might be missing. He was scheduled to leave in two days for a visit to the combined AFSC/FAU unit in the Aventino Valley; could I join him? I wanted to see the progress made while I was away, and Peter was always good company. I bummed a ride to Rome in a Red Cross truck the next day and on Sunday we headed off to Ortona and the Aventino valley.

The AFSC/FAU village reconstruction project was well launched. Four members of the FAU and Dave had a few vehicles. By August, when I left Italy for France, there were nine FAU and three AFSC staff with five three-ton trucks, a small truck, a personnel carrier and a salvaged motorcycle. I could see the promise of the project and understood why the chronicler of the FAU's wartime efforts, Tegla Davis, could later conclude, "No piece of work made more appeal to the imaginations of the Unit than the Aventino Valley Project."

On my return to Rome a few days later I learned that Sir Clifford had been abruptly fired by Sir Herbert Emerson! While Sir Clifford was a tough bird who no doubt had suffered some other knocks in the course of his long career, he was understandably hurt and angry. He shared with me Emerson's letter, which justified his decision by the reports he had received that the voluntary agencies working with him had lost confidence in him. I had a pang of conscience thinking that Dave's and my joint letter might have contributed. Fifty years later I discovered that at the request of one of my AFSC colleagues a JDC official had shared this letter with Emerson. But more influential, in all likelihood, was a comment to Sir Herbert by a senior official in the Allied Commission, that Sir Clifford's services "could be dispensed with."

I could honestly share Sir Clifford's indignation at the abrupt way he had been dismissed. He had been energetic and ingenious on behalf of persecuted stateless and other refugees, often with a zest not everyone with his Foreign Office background would have shown. In reviewing all his efforts, I reluctantly concluded that Dave and I had exaggerated his limitations for the short run immediately after the war. He certainly did not deserve to be fired like that. A British Colonel J. Tomlin, a colorless but more methodical executive officer in the Allied Commission, was appointed in his place.

During my consultation visit in Philadelphia, Julia Branson, the head of the Foreign Service Section, had asked me if I would be game to serve in France. I was all for it. My junior year experience at the *École libre des sciences politiques* and my bi-lingual capability would be useful. I believed the French needed all the support AFSC could manage. And just to live in Paris again would be a treat. Jack Waddington now had been appointed to replace me in Italy, but there were many delays until we were finally able to obtain his clearance.

In early July 1945, Col. Tomlin accepted my release from my IGCR appointment for work with AFSC in France. While waiting for Jack, I enjoyed Italian operas and, with a number of visitors, appreciated the ruins of ancient Rome.

In early August, Hiroshima and Nagasaki were bombed, and the Japanese surrendered. The war was now really over! Church bells rang out all over the city. Anyone with a car and gasoline took to the streets, honking their horns. Restaurants and bars were filled with cheerful crowds. We closed the shop and took to the streets with the rest of Rome.

The war in the Pacific was far away for most civilians in Europe. Certainly for the Italian people, the daily grind of feeding the family was far more immediate. For the thousands of men in uniform, however, a great burden was suddenly lifted. Instead of fearing a possible reassignment to the Pacific theater they could be nearly certain of soon returning home.

My own reaction was more subdued. I could not forget the stories I had read of the ecstatic celebrations of Armistice Day in 1918. Now came the test of making a wiser peace. Responsibility shifted back from the generals to civilian statesmen. President Roosevelt was gone. I prayed his successors would do better than the statesmen at Versailles.

France
The AFSC operation in France in 1945 was a million dollar matter--feeding programs, children's camps, visiting inmates and reconstructing Normandy towns were all parts of the ambitious agenda.

PART IV FRANCE 1945-1946
Refugees and Normandy
Reconstruction

We are afflicted in every way, but not crushed; perplexed but not driven to despair; persecuted but not forsaken; struck down but not destroyed.

Corinthians II, 4

CHAPTER TEN
THE PARIS HEADQUARTERS AND PROGRAMS

TRANSFER TO PARIS

Jack Waddington finally arrived. After I had introduced him to all the people we worked with, I obtained travel orders from the Allied Commission and took off for France in mid-August 1945.

As the plane flew northwest over the snowy crags of the Swiss Alps, I had in mind that the French program was the largest the AFSC then had, over a million dollars per year—a big budget in those days. There were three main components. In the south of France the four principal "*délégations*," or branch offices that we had serviced from Lisbon,[1] organized emergency feeding programs for undernourished children and provided supplies to "children's colonies" or orphanages. They also supplied clothing, medical stocks and other supports to refugees in internment camps.

The second component was centered in Paris, where the small Friends community had long "had a concern," as Friends say, for visiting prisoners of conscience and other inmates, offering food parcels, clothing and friendship to the isolated and lonely. Thirdly, Secours Quaker was assisting the people of Normandy in the aftermath of the Allied landings and the German efforts to block them. Urgent emergency assistance came early from London and continued in the form of vehicles, drivers and supplementary food and medical supplies.

Margaret Frawley was the first American appointed head of mission to Secours Quaker.

ARRIVAL

It was with mixed feelings of anticipation and some trepidation that I flew to Paris in late August. While I was still in Rome I had learned that I was to replace Margaret Frawley as head of the AFSC mission to Secours Quaker. At the time, this was a bit intimidating. Margaret Frawley was then the responsible American in Paris. To take her place looked to me like a tall order.

As we came in from the airport, the lines of tired and bedraggled people waiting outside food shops to pick up their rations for the week told me how far France still had to go. I phoned Secours Quaker and within half an hour a dilapidated jeep with the familiar black and red star showed up. We drove across the Champs Élysées to the Left Bank, up the Boulevard St. Germain to the rather elegant if time-worn offices at 17 rue Notre Dames des Champs, just west of the Luxembourg Gardens.

I was quickly surrounded by a welcoming group – French, American, Swiss and Scandinavian. The British Friends Relief Service, most American volunteers and some Swiss wore rumpled Quaker gray uniforms with the red and black Quaker star on their shoulders. "At last you have come!" Margaret Frawley said, with her welcoming smile. Originally from Syracuse, New York, she was a short, dynamic woman, with grey hair, a very straight back and friendly eyes.[2] She had returned to France in November 1944 to reopen AFSC's activities in support of Secours Quaker.

I was pleased to see Tom Bodine, who had been a friend of my sister Helen at Germantown Friends School and later was a fellow trainee at Pendle Hill. A handsome man with a well-ordered mind, he was the life of a party with a stock of anecdotes about the funny things that had happened to him. He was a whiz at numbers and worked in the finance office. Bill Fraser, my British counterpart, was the representative of the Friends Relief Service (FRS) to Secours Quaker. He was a short, compact, and laconic Scot. His French was impeccable, and while he said very little, his judgment was solid. Acutely sensitive to the nuances of our situation, he had a fine sense of humor, and the crinkle deepening around his eyes signaled when he was about to share a joke or amusing thought. I soon came to respect his good sense.

The key person in the whole operation was a Swiss-French Quaker, Marguerite Czarnecki, formerly in the import-export business. She was Executive Secretary of Secours Quaker and a pillar of the small French Quaker meeting. She was a tall woman, with high cheekbones and deep-set tired eyes. The one indispensable person, she had managerial talent and great human skills in three languages—French, English and German. Her office was the energizing heart of the organization. Her roll-top desk was filled to the brim with papers. She kept two secretaries busy, and she worked hugely long hours. Yet somehow she was patient, artfully welding the FRS team with the Americans, the other foreigners and the underfed French staff into a working team. Among her challenges: the Americans typically had little French; the FRS team was younger though more experienced in hardship; and the French staff was bone tired. She knew how to draw the best from all of us.

In a grand office down the hall was Henry Van Etten, the Secretary General, a thin, tense man we all took care not to ruffle.[3] At that time, there were at Secours Quaker headquarters some sixteen French Friends or "near Friends," twenty Friends War Releif (FRS) volunteers, six from AFSC, and a few from Swiss International Volunteer Service for Peace (IVSP). In addition there were nearly 200 French employees in these or other offices or nearby warehouses.

The building had once been an elegant private home owned by an American family. Indeed, in the well-appointed attic the family's elderly English nanny still lived in quiet seclusion. In some mysterious way that I never asked about, she had stayed there undisturbed throughout the war. Loyal friends of the family had somehow kept her provided with off-ration necessities. The offices had formerly been sitting rooms, a dining room, studies, perhaps even a ballroom, all well appointed. Tall French windows reached from floor to ceiling—fine in summer, but they turned out to be the devil's own invention in the two cold winters of 1944 and 1945. There was beautiful wallpaper everywhere, suggesting early grandeur.

Margueritge Czanicki was the one indispensable person, with real managerial skills in three languages.

The canteen, to which I soon went for lunch, was pretty bad. The carrot soup, I recall even now, was repulsive. Fresh from US/UK military messes in Italy, I found the food very spare. Since rations for everyone were still short, most of the French staff I worked with had to have their main meal at noon in this canteen. Other foreign staff members and I took our evening meals in two of our apartments where our simple imported fare relieved the hard pressed French ration system. The situation made me acutely uncomfortable, but there was nothing to be done about it immediately.

ANGLO-AMERICAN QUAKERS TO WORK WITHIN SECOURS QUAKER

Throughout the war, AFSC had been in close touch with the FRS in London. Organized as soon as the war began, its volunteers helped run hostels for those evacuated from London, and provided other civilian services.[4] In the early summer of 1944, when it looked as if the Continent might soon open to British and American Quaker relief efforts, AFSC and the Friends Relief Service agreed that any relief work in France would be channeled through Secours Quaker, with its headquarters in Paris.[5] Volunteers would be seconded as individuals. All supplies and vehicles would become part of Secours Quaker.

In November 1944, five months after the Normandy landings on D-Day, Supreme Headquarters Allied Europe Forces (SHAEF) had permitted Quaker committees to send representatives to France to see how they could be helpful. Roger Wilson, Executive Secretary of the London-based FRS, headed the British delegation with Edith Pye, a member of the French *Legion d'Honneur* for her medical social work in France after World War I. Bill Fraser came as the new coordinator for FRS's contribution to Secours Quaker whenever foreign Friends could join in. Clarence Picket and Margaret Frawley represented AFSC, Philadelphia. Leaders of the four southern delegations and their staffs were also there. This was the first meeting in five years. Altogether some 75 people gathered.

In the Paris meeting the southern delegations set out their needs for food, clothing, transport and fuel:

> Milk, sugar and fats are most urgently needed and of prime necessity, also clothes, underwear and shoes in all sizes, for babies, children, men and women...In view of the scarcity of fuel, we all agree we shall need a great deal of food which does not require cooking, such as chocolate, biscuits, sardines, corned beef, etc.[6]

Their warehouses were bare and relief needs were huge. They reminded their visitors of the years on short rations, scarcity of soap, of sugar, of fats of all kinds. Altogether their requests came to an estimated 10,000 tons, far more than the two committees could ever supply. French Friends in Paris laid out the more modest material needs for their aid to prisoners, refugees and indigent returnees. Helga

Holbeck, who had headed the Toulouse Delegations during the war, presented a vivid picture of the devastation in war's path in Normandy.

Fortunately, Philadelphia AFSC had already authorized the purchase of some milk, cheese, and baby foods in Switzerland, twenty tons of olive oil from North Africa, sardines, olive oil, and soap in Portugal. Ken Kimberland in Algeria had redirected a shipment of AFSC used clothing from North Africa to Marseille, and had acquired several decommissioned army trucks. FRS ordered used clothing to be shipped promptly and fifty tons of clothing were immediately ordered from AFSC warehouses. One half was for Marseille, to be distributed in the south, the other half destined for the bombed out people of Normandy and Brittany. In December 1944, Margaret Frawley reminded Philadelphia: "There is an urgent need for blankets and all the warm clothes you can put in your clothing shipments."

Roger Wilson captured the situation the Secours Quaker working staffs had to cope with:

> In Paris itself there was very little destruction. There was food shortage, and bitter cold and damp. "You've no idea how slow everything is here—partly a result of the perishing cold." Paris was the nerve center of a France crying out for rehabilitation. But nothing ever happened quickly for want of an adequacy of a hundred and one particular requirements, none of which except for food and fuel mattered much alone, but all of which together meant stagnation. And among the French there was the desolating feeling that the American and British military authorities, in their warm offices and their well-equipped messes, could do anything to prosecute the war while the French, excluded from the war, were frustrated in every project by lack of warmth, food and supplies of every sort.[7]

Staff members who had worked with Secours Quaker for a long time told me the French people were still deeply demoralized. The sudden French defeat in June 1940 and the harshness of the Occupation were hard enough. One never knew what new regulation would add fresh prohibitions; the midnight police knock on the door was never quite out of mind. It became well known that large shipments of food and other necessities were also being shipped to Germany while rations within France became progressively smaller. Food was so short in the cities that the ironic joke had it that it was better to have a cousin in the countryside than a brother in a ministry. Hitherto unthinkable steps taken by the Occupation authorities or the Laval/Pétain government in

Vichy, such as the deportation of Jews and French laborers, were even worse.[8]

THE PARIS PROGRAM

Working closely with Margaret Frawley and Marguerite Czarnecki, my first concern was to gain an understanding of the Paris program of Secours Quaker.

In an office near the front door Individual Services received several hundred visitors a day, seeking chits to get clothing or shoes at a *vestiaire* run out of a nearby warehouse. Staff were warm-hearted Ida Whitworth, an elderly English Quaker, Mary Elmendorf from the American South, cheerful Eleanore Candee and Eunice Clark, a New Englander who spoke precisely articulated French. They sought other answers if a chit was not enough. French women on the staff helped the lonely and confused refugees, disoriented French women and returning POWs. The Research Section helped reunite families who had been cast to the winds by the wartime hurricane. Networks provided by the French Protestant Church's charity CIMADE, the *Service Sociale d'Aide aux Immigrants* and Osé *(L'Oeuvre de secours aux enfants)* helped in these searches. Tom Bodine and a Russian émigré, Alexander Benzemann, helped keep track of the supplies the people needed, handled the Customs paper work and oversaw budgetary matters that the AFSC and FRS deemed essential. At the back, and in a much larger garage rented by Secours Quaker, young FRS volunteers kept an auto pool going.

Another office and warehouse sustained the concern for prison visiting, serving prisoners of all sorts. During the Occupation over 57,000 food parcels and nearly 30,000 pieces of clothing had been distributed to those jailed because they had been too openly opposed to the German occupation. After the end of the war, when these prisoners were released, visits and parcels continued being sent to their replacements, those accused of having collaborated with the Germans.

Whenever they could, visitors made repeat visits to specific prisoners and sought to keep them in touch with their families in the provinces. Mary Elmendorf recalls interviewing at the notorious camp of Drancy, through which so many deportees had passed on their way to Dachau and the extermination camps in Poland. Food was short, fuel unobtainable, sanitation abysmal. In a period of bitter accusations after Liberation, many people were imprisoned there for allegedly having collaborated with the Germans. Mary and Quaker colleagues interviewed Czechs, Poles, Russians, Spaniards and AWOL German soldiers, all dumped in together. They helped these people get in touch with their embassies or locate relatives and friends as a first step in possibly getting out. It was part of the Quaker witness to assist all we could reach, regardless of their political affiliations or their past. Mary recalls it was the hardest work she ever did.

Secours Quaker was managed through a committee structure like those of AFSC or Friends House in London. There was a *Comité d'Action*, an executive committee with AFSC and FRS representatives. There were a number of more specialized committees. At first, I took this as natural in a Quaker organization; later I concluded that it was also one way to ensure that decisions, once taken, had a legitimacy that quicker, more individual decisions might not have had. When meetings were called, one of Marguerite Czarnecki's aides would pass through the building, ringing a small bell, calling *"Comité, Comité..* Committee members would drop what they were doing and go to the largest room we had, where we would "center down" in the Quaker fashion, silently and , it was hoped, prayerfully.

This provided a useful way to help us reach a perspective beyond our own.   Each of us approached organizational and administrative issues in our own "natural," largely national, style. Achieving consensus was not as fast as it would have been with a less democratic approach. But it was a method Friends had found effective for many years.

Marguerite Czarnecki had studied at the devout École Vinet in Lausanne, a strongly Protestant school, so the search for spiritual nourishment came naturally to her. She also had a genius at interpreting from English to French and back, always choosing words to soothe rather than inflame. Where she saw real differences, she could go to the heart of the problem and suggest a mutually acceptable way through.

Administratively, Secours Quaker was receiving a subsidy from *Entr'aide Francaise* (the French government's welfare organization), to cover its administrative expenses. This was not a special favor to the Quakers but represented the French Government's way of assisting charitable Catholic and Protestant Non-Governmental Organizations performing useful welfare activities. Accordingly, Secours Quaker was answerable to the French authorities. We also reported to the FRS Overseas Committee in London and AFSC in Philadelphia on the activities of their volunteers and what happened to the supplies they provided. In effect, we in Secours Quaker were accountable to three different entities.

The offices at 17 Notre Dame des Champs were crowded, with five or six desks to each room and at least two noisy manual typewriters going at the same time. That many of the women were still wearing shoes with wooden soles added to the din. All the rooms were connected but there was no central hall, and there were few inter-office phones. I often had to pass through at least three other offices to get to the person I wanted. Luckily Micheline Salmon, a witty, sharp observer and enormously helpful secretary to Margaret Frawley, came to work with me when Margaret went home.

After some months, I concluded that generally the British preferred informal, apparently casual ways, while the Americans seemed to pay more attention to organizational structures. The French had been through such stressful times together, they knew each other very well and understood exactly where each stood. It was hard for us to imagine the fatigue they had to struggle against, and sometimes their frustrations unexpectedly broke through their hard-earned stoicism. I found it wiser to let Marguerite massage people in exactly the best way than to raise delicate points directly in our more blunt "Anglo-Saxon" way.

Combining such diverse people, drawn from many nationalities, contrasting organizational practices and diverse historical experiences, was a challenge peculiar to the period. At the same time, most of us found working together in Secours Quaker stimulating and even exhilarating. There were daily surprises and satisfactions from working with young people of so many different nationalities. Even our language difficulties were cause for laughter, as we struggled with French, English and that peculiar Franglais that became our own argot. We shared a sense of relevance from knowing that our efforts could make a real difference to people in deep difficulties. As I thought back on that experience, it became clear we were pioneers in creating a multinational NGO.

The four long-established delegations in Toulouse, Montauban, Perpignan and Marseille in the south of France had done yeoman service during the war, the Occupation and deportations. In addition, two new delegations were working on reconstruction in Normandy, at Caen and Le Havre. I wanted to be sure that before Margaret went home we should visit these delegations together.

CHAPTER ELEVEN
VISITS TO FRENCH
QUAKER DELEGATIONS

ESCAPE FROM PARIS

By mid-September 1945 I had a good grasp of the Paris operation, but winter was coming and I needed to know how the field operations were set for the problems of the cold weather. I asked Bill Fraser, my British counterpart, and Margaret Frawley of the Paris office to help assess the programs. We urged Marguerite Czarnecki to join us to see how the FRS and the American volunteers were fitting into these delegations. For our trip south we decided to go by car. It might have been more sensible to take the train but we knew we would see more of the countryside and be less trouble for the delegations. We had an old army command car and coupons for gasoline. The car had no doors, only loosely fitting curtains, but the weather was fine. In the countryside everything had an air of dilapidation. We drove straight through to Toulouse, then to Montauban and finally to Perpignan.

TOULOUSE

The Secours Quaker office right across from the Toulouse railroad station looked as if it might once have been the house of a well-to-do provincial doctor. In a later incarnation, it had been a factory making knitted goods; there were large workrooms on each floor. As I entered the building I had the strange feeling that I had known it before, so much had the refugees in Portugal told me of the welcome they had received there. It was exciting at last to see one of the delegations Phil Conard and I in Portugal had struggled so hard to support by gaining exceptions to the Allied blockade.[1]

Hélène Rotte de Neufville, an ample woman of great self-confidence, greeted us warmly and showed us around. She always had a cigarette in a simple cigarette holder, which she waved for emphasis. "What a relief it was to see your supplies arriving from Portugal, Switzerland and the States!" she told us. "You have no idea how near despair we were as we watched our stocks dwindle. Now we have reopened and the children and destitute are coming back, but they are all still so thin." We were cheered to know that Toulouse was back at its traditional service and that the scattered AFSC and FRS supply offices had moved so promptly to renew their stocks.

A canteen at one end of the building could seat up to 300 people. Some 125 college and high school students received a special meal to help ward off tuberculosis. In the afternoon, here and at two other places, some 350 children who had been identified by the delegation's clinic as undernourished received a special afternoon snack, including milk or cocoa and cheese or sardines. Most times, the children had to bring their own bread ration. Hélène told me that, given the undernourishment of these scrawny children, marked by their small bones and the vitamin-deficiency sores on their legs, the visits made a real difference. Noticeable improvements were almost immediate.

I was delighted to see Marnie Schauffler, my former mentor in Philadelphia. With her usual warmth and zest undiminished, she was helping Hélène manage the delegation. "What a relief it is to be dealing directly with real human beings," she cheerily remarked, "back home I could be working with endless and often fruitless paper."

In 1945 some 100-150 people of every nationality came to the office each day, seeking information, references to other agencies, or immediate help. Mondays were for old people needing food, clothing or money. Most of them had only a government pension of forty cents per day. Tuesdays were for pregnant women. Wednesdays were for general requests, Thursdays for school children needing clothing, Fridays for sick people, particularly in the afternoon. The visitors were destitute stateless people from all over Europe, each without a passport or a place to call home. Another part of Secours Quaker's task was to provide food supplements, particularly imported milk and fats, to children's colonies and to undernourished French school children.

Hélène recalled that even though the French state at its center had collapsed and leading government figures had fled to Vichy, it was remarkable how quickly the *préfets* and *sous préfets* regrouped and began to follow orders from the new Pétain government. *Indésirables* to be interned in the camps included all communists and foreigners, especially stateless foreign Jews; but also French Jews began to be arrested. She could not forget her outrage and sense of helplessness in the summer of 1942, when French prefects began delivering Jews to the Gestapo. French police trucks came to the camps, names were called out, and people were loaded pell-mell to meet the quotas designated by the Laval government.[2]

She recalled how, for a short period, Secours Quaker had been the sole NGO allowed to supply rice soup and milk to the children on the trains; they had to work surrounded by Gestapo police pointing guns at them. Even this service was soon forbidden.[3]

At the time, Helga Holbek, the intrepid head of the delegation, had written to AFSC's Geneva representative:

> We have just spent the most terrible days of our life,
> in seeing the people that we have cared for a year and
> a half depart toward new sufferings...I beg of you,
> continue to protest. It is a thing so inhuman that has
> been done! Protest! Protest! Protest![4]

Hélène recalled that, as their supplies dwindled, Helga had been able to obtain a trickle of powdered milk and cash from friends in Sweden and Switzerland in addition to what came in from Portugal. During the few days between the Allied landings in North Africa and the German occupation of the rest of France, Joe Schwartz of the Joint Distribution Committee happened to be in Toulouse. He quickly drew out all the JDC funds from the local bank and distributed the cash to people he trusted. For some weeks Helga, Hélène, Alice Synestvedt and the others were able to give extra funds to Jews then in hiding, some of whom managed later to reach the relative safety of areas of France the Italians had just occupied. They kept in touch with the quietly heroic Pastor Trocmé in LeChambon who hid children from the Gestapo and helped some pass to Switzerland.

The delegations continued to visit the prisons that were now filled with people accused of collaboration. Some German POWs were held in former internment camps and needed attention: medicines and food supplements were short, and books in German were almost non-existent.

The Toulouse staff was also appalled by the condition of the few returnees who managed to make their way back after their years of hard labor in Germany and Poland. Many were totally destitute and their health broken. The delegation did what it could to help.

MONTAUBAN

Marguerite Czarnecki joined us before we went off to Montauban, where, as in Toulouse, the team had regularly visited other internment camps, and ran a number of *goûters*. These were usually afternoon gatherings where undernourished children could drink milk prepared under carefully supervised conditions and be given a protein-rich biscuit, many of which had come in from Portugal. Before each *goûter*, the spindly children kicked off their sandals as they stepped onto the scales, their progress carefully noted in a big ledger. The Dutchman Fred Cornelissen, head of the Montauban office, and his handsome Norwegian wife, Nora, were now distributing supplementary food to pregnant and nursing mothers and to some 250 pre-tubercular children five days a week through school canteens.

During the Vichy period and the later German occupation, they had lived through hugely tense days following the French defeat and then the occupation. They and the Secours Quaker Montauban staff provided blankets and supplementary food, as well as advice to individual internees on how to deal with the maze of paperwork that might lead to release. During the 1942 and 1943 deportations, they saw many of their refugee friends and some of their own staff loaded onto trains and sent off.

More than the other delegations, Montauban had developed unusually sophisticated workshops for some forty-five wounded Spaniards who were eking out a kind of living from the products of their workshops. An orthopedic shop produced prostheses for the severely wounded; cobbler shops repaired shoes for the refugees; tailoring shops helped repair clothing donated for the needy. The Cornelissons had also been ingenious in tapping their fellow nationals in Holland and Scandinavia to help with milk powder and animal fats they needed to keep their programs going, though these supplies were severely depleted during the later war years.

As if Fred and Nora Cornelissen had not had enough to worry about during the Vichy period, suddenly several trainloads of Ukrainians and Russians arrived, deported from Alsace without advance notice. Since no one government ministry was immediately ready to take responsibility for them, the desperate Prefect had turned to Secours Quaker and other French charities to help him cope until the decision could be made on the responsible ministry.

Since the end of the war, a number of pathetic individuals just returning from forced labor in Germany or Poland had come to the Cornelissens' door. They needed extra food, clothes to replace their rags, and sometimes money to help them on their way home. Of some 800,000 reported French deportees, perhaps 200,000 never returned.[5] Many who did come back were mere scarecrows, dull eyed, half starved from their years of hard labor and short rations. We were impressed by how exhausted both Fred and Nora were. Luckily an experienced FRS volunteer was already helping them, and soon others would be there from AFSC.

PERPIGNAN

At Perpignan, Mary Elmes, an Irish national considered a neutral, had been working with Spaniards for over a decade. Soft-spoken, reserved but determined, she had excellent Spanish and French and a certain presence.[6] She thanked us warmly for the fresh supplies that had helped her delegation get through the previous winter and resume some of the former child feeding programs. The delegation provided supplementary food to over 2,000 undernourished school children and 180 expectant mothers, and sent over 1,200 food parcels to prisoners and 450 pounds of food supplies to a nearby children's colony.

Working in the nearby camps in 1942-43, Mary had handled paperwork to help individuals get out of the camps, and then perhaps make the risky journey to Spain or Portugal. She helped some obtain a transfer of funds from a family abroad, or sent letters abroad for others. During the deportations, she argued that particular individual internees were neutrals and therefore should be spared. While stocks lasted, she could bring some medicines to ease the shortage in the camps' clinics. Three thousand blankets and 43,000 pieces of clothing helped the inmates who wore only rags. At a number of colonies established for the refugees' children, she saw to it that extra milk supplemented the meager ration.

We knew that she had been particularly courageous during the German occupation of southern France. Her regular visits to a nearby camp were suddenly interrupted when she was arrested and held for six months in a German jail. When questioned later about that period, Mary replied simply, "Well, we all experienced inconveniences in those days, didn't we?" Like others (except Hélène) who had lived through that time, Mary was reluctant to talk about it. Margaret and I resisted the temptation to ask questions. We were glad that two volunteers from FRS were in Perpignan already and that an AFSC volunteer would soon arrive.[7]

After a much too quick visit, we drove back to Paris. One of Marguerite's great assets was her ability to be blunt, with a smile, sometimes with a quip. On that drive, she more than once reminded us of how much more comfortable we would have been had we taken the train. Whenever I think back to that journey, I can still see Marguerite's image in the driver's mirror, unaware as she fell asleep that her face revealed her extreme fatigue.

NEW DELEGATIONS IN NORMANDY

The successful Allied landings in Normandy in June 1944 had been a great military achievement, but for civilian life in the region they had been a disaster. Whole towns were rubble; fields were churned up, spring crops were ruined. Mines were everywhere. Nearly all bridges were destroyed, and whatever bridging the armies had laid down, they had taken up as they rushed forward. Normandy naturally was a rich province, but there were pockets of destitution as whole areas were totally isolated. There were no trucks or buses. The cities of Le Havre and Caen were unimaginably ravaged. In Le Havre, of 19,000 prewar houses, some 12,000 had been destroyed.[8]

Roger Whiting of FRS first visited Normandy in April 1945, ten months after the landings. He wrote in his diary:

> There is appalling destruction and almost complete lack of transport. Whilst some villages have almost no food at all, in others one can have great omelettes made from fresh eggs and fried in butter. Nearly every other bridge has been demolished by bombing, sabotage or the retreating Germans...The center of one village pays tribute to the handiwork of the medieval builders—the church is the only building of which anything is left; the tower, though wrecked from top to bottom, still stands and part of the decorated nave and chancel still remain, roofless of course. Around the ruins lie heaps of rubble with here and there bits of a wall, whilst a cart track ploughs its way through, a miserable pretense of a road.

In late October, I was able to visit the Secours Quaker

delegations at Caen and Le Havre in Normandy. As I gazed at the destruction my mind went back to the villages of southern Italy or near Florence, where the Gothic Line had held out for a full winter. That Le Havre and Caen had been major cities before the campaign was all the more disheartening. No doubt thousands of civilians had lost their lives; the labor of generations and centuries now lay in rubble.

The Secours Quaker team, with fifteen FRS men and women and six from AFSC, stressed the urgent need for transport. As Roger Wilson put it, they tried to provide

> an honest [trucking] service, prepared to work for cost on jobs whose priority was determined by the public authorities, and whose integrity could not be diverted by the colossal earnings to be made on the black market—such a road service was invaluable in freeing the indigenous French forces of healing and construction.[9]

When trucks broke down, parts could not be had. To keep vehicles running, whole engines had to be lifted from vehicles declared surplus in army depots.

In Caen, the FRS team's trucks were used to clear rubble and deliver building materials to destroyed villages. They also moved families who had fled from the air raids back to their land or into temporary barracks while their homes were rebuilt. They made emergency repairs to damaged homes and improvised shelters. The team opened a community center in a barrack brought from Sweden, and a *vestiaire* to provide much-needed clothing. Charlotte Brooks, an AFSC member of the team, reported that eighty tons of clothing were distributed directly from the Secours Quaker barracks and to some 140 villages and 40 institutions and schools.[10] Along the route taken by the advancing Allied armies, hundreds of returning deportees were to discover their homes flattened. They found temporary shelter in hospitals or in whatever public buildings still stood. Sometimes parts of the Secours Quaker community centers served as temporary shelters for these returnees.

In Le Havre, where John Kay of FRS was in charge, Secours Quaker had provided a barrack to serve as a community center until established municipal buildings could be repaired. The FRS team made emergency structural repairs to severely damaged homes, propped up unreliable walls, nailed temporary boards over gaping windows in efforts to keep out the interminable rain. Harvey Buchanan of the AFSC team encouraged the captain of a repair ship standing in the harbor to supply loads of scrap lumber from old shipping crates to help the repair crews.

Local social workers helped identify needy French families, pregnant and nursing mothers and those who were particularly undernourished; these people received supplementary food packages of pasta, figs, malt, cocoa and sardines from Secours Quaker. All these precious foods, as well as soap, were still severely rationed. This was dramatized for me when one of our volunteers was offered 300 pounds of potatoes in exchange for one bar of soap! Secours Quaker scrounged sheets and blankets from the military for the Babies Hospital in Le Havre. Like every hospital at the end of the war, it was short of everything. Diapers could be changed only once a day; only cold water ran through the taps. So much of the hospital had been damaged by bombs and fire that only a small space was left for beds.

The Secours Quaker teams in Normandy lived in a small corner of their community center, or wherever they could find a place. Their food rations were meager and many of them seemed very tired. I was impressed by the amount of rubble that they told me had been cleared since the 1944 landings and by the rebuilding already under way, but they still had so very far to go.

BACK IN PARIS

Once back in Paris, I discussed with Margaret Frawley my impressions from the five delegations. It was a source of satisfaction finally to have seen the work of the southern delegations helped from Lisbon. These had obviously been important to the stateless, the Jews and other so-called *indésirables* in the camps, or even more, to those we had helped get away, as well as to the thousands in the children's colonies.

The delegations had experienced leaders and staffs who looked back to a heroic past that they were glad to have behind them. They were cheered to find stocks again arriving from abroad to give renewed life to well-established programs. Leaders who had carried responsibility through the war were bone-tired and deserved a rest. Some of the newer volunteers whose French was still rudimentary wished they could have greater responsibility, with more direct contact with the needy. But so long as AFSC's advance language preparation remained so sketchy, volunteers would have to take their chances until they knew the language better.

By contrast, the newer delegations in Normandy were finding down-to-earth ways to be useful in the more dramatic immediacy of destruction. What needed to be done to clear away rubble and rebuild was obvious here. Volunteer muscle, carpentry skills and transport were unambiguously needed.

The southern delegations had been used to receiving and dispersing supplies from abroad during wartime when careful reporting to Philadelphia and London could not be expected. Margaret and I wondered how we could tighten reporting requirements to meet the demanding standards of the American IRS. The French Fisc had reviewed Secours Quaker's accounts only once in the past five years! If we pressed our over-stretched French colleagues too hard, they might feel we were doubting their sense of responsibility, let alone their integrity.

As a result of the trip, I was all the more persuaded we should import as much as we could to help meet the challenge of the next two winters. Where everything was scarce, particularly food and fuel, people's wellbeing depended directly on the weather. The winter of 1944-45 had been brutal. Supplies of coal and food had been short. The food we had seen in the markets on our trip we thought was largely seasonal and the coming 1945-46 winter could well be as difficult as the last one. If the AFSC and FRS could induce the Intergovernmental Committee on Refugees (IGCR) to reimburse us for our expenditures in France on behalf of assisting Spanish refugees, all of AFSC funds could then properly go for imports of scarce food and other relief supplies. So long as supplementary food supplies for our volunteers kept coming from FRS and AFSC we figured that each American or Britisher would cost only about $100 a month from our budget.[11]

We doubted that the French government would continue indefinitely to cover the administrative costs of Secours Quaker. French organizations could now deal directly with suppliers in the US, UK and Scandinavia. We would be watching for signs of slackening government enthusiasm for our activities, since many in the Friends community were dependent on Secours Quaker. They and the loyal non-Friends staff would need time to find alternatives if we had to reduce the number of jobs.

Margaret, Bill Fraser and I reflected on the impact on the small French Quaker community of such quantities of relief supplies and so many foreign volunteers. Margaret and Bill feared we might be inadvertently swamping them. The very size of Secours Quaker and the quantities of supplies it handled had changed the direct relationships that had always distinguished French Friends' efforts. Too many members had become warehouse keepers and supply people. Clarence Pickett was the first to bring this up, and the concern persisted in both head offices. While the concern was very real, I was more moved by the utility of the supplies and the contribution of the energetic, optimistic people we provided.

About mid-October 1945, two months after my arrival from Rome, Margaret left for Philadelphia. Trained as a journalist, with a few deft strokes she could capture what was really going on. She loved France and cared for the staff at all levels. Alas, she was a compulsive smoker and could not resist smoking even during a good French meal. Her neighbors at Notre Dame des Champs could hear her weeping at night with frustration at the state of her health. She died in 1947, of lung cancer.

I was more pessimistic than Margaret and doubted that the Germans and French could ever bury the hatchet. But she was alert to hopeful signs that this time they would not repeat the errors of the past even before Jean Monnet's ideas about the Coal and Steel Community had become policy, when Adenauer's and de Gaulle's leadership had not yet been tested, and the political and economic collaboration to be induced by the Marshall Plan was not even imagined.

Back in Paris in 1945, I had seen the efforts of French Friends succeed because of their energy and perseverance. Replacing Margaret Frawley as head of AFSC mission to Secours Quaker seemed a tall order.

CHAPTER TWELVE
LIFE IN PARIS:
THE DAY-TO-DAY
PERSPECTIVE

Once I was on my own in Paris, I could see that my role was to be more a coordinator than a Head of Mission. Working day-to-day with the Secours Quaker organization that Marguerite Czarnecki was managing so well in Paris, I connected our activities with those of the Philadelphia and London committees. I was no longer directly involved in the programs that aided individuals and families. Instead, I conveyed to AFSC headquarters in Philadelphia what we were doing with the resources they provided, and what we would be needing in the coming months. Much could be done if we were willing to improvise. We made mistakes, to be sure, but we managed to care for people, save lives and deliver goods to those who needed them. And, despite the demoralized soldiery, the lethargy of hungry people, and the slow pace of recovery, Paris remained always Paris.

FEEDING AND HOUSING THE FRS AND AFSC TEAM

Once the Occupation was over, French people returned to their capital city along with thousands of American and British military in the Supreme Headquarters Allied Europe Forces (SHAEF), so the town was now full. We needed to make sure our forty-five expatriate team members—twelve Americans and some thirty FRS volunteers—had places to stay. The impeccably dressed John Judkyn, a British Quaker and New York antique dealer, and Ida Whitworth, a gray haired British Quaker lady, had two different approaches to finding apartments. John, personnel secretary to the AFSC in Paris, knew wealthy English owners, whereas Ida's network was among less affluent longtime British expatriates in Paris. The scouts found housing that enabled some team members to live in outrageous style. One apartment on Quai St. Michel directly faced Notre Dame and the Isle de la Cité, a coveted location. I recall the marvelous view from the roof, with Notre Dame in the foreground and all of the Right Bank stretching back to Sacré Coeur on Montmartre. Another apartment was at 98 rue du Bac, owned by Couve de Murville, the French ambassador to Rome and later foreign minister for de Gaulle. The ambassador had offered his flat to the Quakers, retaining one bedroom for himself as a *pied à terre* in the event he had to return from Rome for consultations.

Despite the grand surroundings, these were temporary digs. Most of us had to move several times as people who had lent us their apartments returned. My own room in an apartment at 27 Avenue d'Éylau in the Passy section of Paris had no pretensions. I and three other Quaker volunteers shared the kitchen and the bathroom with the owners, a White Russian refugee couple whose silk-screened scarves were sold in the fancy boutiques on the Rue St. Honoré. Four in our part of the apartment had only enough wood for one small fire each evening, but we were lucky to have that. The apartment at St. Michel might have had a wonderful view, but wood for its fireplace had to be carried up seven flights from the Metro. Gas for tiny heaters was strictly rationed.

The winters of 1944-45 and 1945-46 were cruel in Paris as they were all across Europe. Normally, Paris' coal was supplied by canal boat from the northern mines, but they were not yet working. Coal shipped from the States could not be brought to Paris since, for the first time in living memory, the Seine froze and the barges were locked in the ice. We attended staff meetings bundled in coats and scarves. The secretaries typed in gloves with the fingertips cut off. Nearly all of them suffered from chilblains.

Electricity was often on only half a day. We would not know in advance which half of the day it would be on, in which part of the city. All illuminated signs were forbidden, shop windows were left unlighted; streetlights were turned off unexpectedly. By the spring of 1946, however, power was more available and the streets and shops more cheerfully lit and colorful.

The primary problem was protein. Every team member had ration tickets for at least a taste of the delicious fresh *baguettes*. To ensure minimum protein, the early FRS team had been given a daily ration of one or two sardines on a small triangle of cheese from Switzerland. Margaret Frawley ended each letter and report from that period with a "please send us a food parcel."

Many staff members lost weight; a number quickly came down with flu. In staff diaries the lack of food and the consequences of not getting enough was reported a constant worry.

Secours Quaker staff meetings were held at unheated headquarters, a building that had been the private home of an American family. Bundled up in coats and scarves are Tom Bodine, Howard Wriggins, Libby Morris and John Judkyn.

The cook at the de Murville apartment, always trying to feed the mixed FRS/AFSC team, encouraged the transport teams headed for the countryside to bring back food whenever they could. One tale widely told amongst us had FRS volunteer Bernard Walker and Tom Bodine returning to Paris with a live pig provided in a friendly gesture by the team in Toulouse.[1] There wasn't any salt to preserve pork, so the pig had to be delivered live. Bernard and Tom, arriving in Paris near midnight, couldn't take the live pig directly to the de Murville flat. An ever resourceful neighbor, *Tante* Elise Conklin, who had in a sense adopted the young Quakers, roused her butcher. He quickly dispatched and partitioned the pig and in return kept some of the finer cuts for his own business. The remaining parts of the pig, dripping blood, were rushed up the stairs at Rue du Bac, and placed in the one receptacle large enough—Ambassador de Murville's bathtub.

As luck would have it, for the first time in six months, at about 3 a.m., the Ambassador returned, after a very tiring trip from Rome. The unused bedroom was in perfect shape, but prior to getting into bed to catch up on some sleep, he naturally went into the bathroom. His shriek was heard all over the building. Years later, at a diplomatic reception in Washington, Tom reintroduced himself to de Murville as one of the Quakers who had enjoyed his hospitality, and thanked him for it. The experienced civil servant paused for a moment and then burst out laughing, "*Ah, mais bien sûr, le cochon!*"

This was no way to run an operation the size of ours. While the committees in London and Philadelphia sent basic staples, we were short on meats and vegetables. Yet supplementing our meager rations without drawing down scarce supplies on the local market was becoming increasingly difficult. I decided to approach the American army for access to their mess for our people. From my experience with military messes in Algeria, Egypt and Italy, I was aware how wasteful Allied systems could be. If we could draw on the PX for basic food requirements and also improve the diet of the French staff, it would make sense to try. Mary Elmendorf, Tom Bodine and I went to a central American army mess on the Right Bank, hard by the Opera, to see if they would issue cards for American relief workers.

Luckily, Mary ran into a friend of her brother Lindsey who alas, had recently been killed in a bombing raid against the Rumanian oil fields. In a long talk we learned that Lindsey's friend was the very officer we had hoped to find. He authorized mess cards for our American relief workers. We could also use the PX for basic necessities for the American staff and supplement the Secours Quaker canteen for our French staff. Mary was the heroine of that expedition.

Her triumph at the PX reduced the burden we imposed on our French friends. While we were uncomfortable eating there, and did it rarely, the mess was in fact a convenient place to meet American and British civilians and officers who could be helpful to the relief effort.

OPPORTUNITIES AND NEEDS

Secours Quaker always welcomed the occasional windfall of fats or protein for the people we were helping. For example, it was asked by a Danish newspaper, *Berlingske Tidende,* to distribute some bacon they had raised by subscription for the starving children of Paris. The Quakers expected a truckload from Copenhagen, but it turned out to be five trailer-truck loads! As one after another of these vehicles arrived, the *cul de sac* that led to the small Quaker warehouse was totally jammed. A symbolic portion from one truck was unloaded so the Danish Embassy, the French Public Welfare Department and a representative of the newspaper could be photographed for the press and the newsreels. The Catholic Sisters of St. Vincent de Paul offered space in their large warehouse. But first the Quakers had to uncork the narrow street as, one by one, the trailer trucks were maneuvered back onto the nearby boulevard. At that time there were still relatively few vehicles in Paris, and the nearly three hours of maneuvering were accomplished without incident. The Danish bonanza was shared with the Catholic sisters, and passed on to the numerous children's colonies that the Friends, the Catholic sisters, the Protestant CIMADE or OSE were supporting.

Once the war was over, obtaining blankets, food and clothing was difficult, but delivering them to people who needed them was often the toughest part of all. Just before my arrival the Quakers had finally been able to rent a garage of their own. The new security from vehicular theft and disappearing spare parts gave the FRS transport team a fresh lease on life. Head mechanic was Roger Whiting, who later replaced Bill Fraser as coordinator of the FRS team.

A bit stooped, Roger was tall and lean, with thick horn-rimmed glasses. He had a resonating guffaw, slapping his knees while enjoying a hearty laugh. His sense of humor served him well as, in one awful period, six of nine vehicles in the Paris pool were off the road at the same time. He and the other mechanics had to work late into the night to have the trucks or jeeps ready for use in the morning. The whole team cheered when a vehicle that was not too ancient arrived from England. Gradually we replaced our original fleet of battered British civilian vehicles with serviceable GMC, Chevrolet or Bedford trucks. One of our mechanics would visit a British or American army depot, raise the hoods (or bonnets) of several vehicles, look at the belts, try the starters, kick the tires. They were sold to us as "surplus" so we had to be wary.

Roger Whiting, head of the auto shop, became FRS coordinator after Bill Fraser went home.

OPERATIONAL PROBLEMS

Language got in the way of clear communication, as many of the Americans arrived with very little French. As we all recalled from "My Fair Lady," the French "didn't mind what you said, so long as you pronounced it properly." But our vocabularies were as limited as our pronunciation was excruciating to our French colleagues. Tortured French had many possibilities. Once Tom Bodine returned late from lunch, explaining that he had walked all the way to the PX. He said, *"j'ai fait le trottoir jusqu'au PX."* In French slang, *"faire le trottoir"* is what a working prostitute does when looking for business. Everyone burst out laughing.

Funny twists were not limited to French; our own language was subject to cross-cultural misinterpretation. Henry J. Cadbury, chairman of the board of the AFSC at the time, disarmingly wrote ahead of a planned visit, asking for a simple "cot" on which to rest his head. Roger Whiting toyed with the idea that he might be a dwarf, since a "cot" in Britain is exclusively for babies. Some of the FRS had a nice appreciation for exactness in the use of our mother tongue.

As already made clear, Secours Quaker was highly decentralized, with the well-established southern delegations not used to following instructions from Paris. Marguerite handled each delegation with full respect for the remarkable individuals who had borne such heavy responsibilities before and during the German occupation. As the London and Philadelphia committees came to deal more and more directly with the Paris headquarters, the staff naturally felt an increased sense of responsibility, but as will be seen, we never managed the detailed reporting as it should have been.

In early January 1946, Lois Jessup arrived from the New York office to assist me with reports that the Philadelphia headquarters required and that the French delegations were simply too preoccupied to prepare. Although to the French, the endless accounting seemed like a pointless American obsession, detailed reports were indispensable to those back home who were trying to motivate donors and prepare reports for the IRS.

Getting good statistics on the refugees we were helping proved difficult. To the regional offices, the nationalities or countries of origin of the stateless did not matter all that much. In principle, of course, we agreed with this. But to Secours Quaker as an organization, outside financial support came from different sources often targeted for specific groups of refugees. As I look back on it, we clearly should have insisted on more precise statistical reports from our field offices. This possible cost of lack of precise information came home to me in a very direct way.

In 1945, the Intergovernmental Committee on Refugees asked us for a budget to cover Secours Quaker's assistance to the Spanish who were left stateless. One Tuesday afternoon, three weeks earlier than we had expected, the IGCR office called to inform us that Sir Herbert Emerson was in Paris. He expected to review our budget with us at 10 a.m. on Thursday. We were nowhere near ready for that; inclusive data had not yet been received, let alone collated. Material from the southern delegations was always sketchy. We were not even sure how many Spanish refugees there were in France, let alone how many we were assisting.

All day Wednesday and late into the night, Mary Elmendorf and I scrambled to draw together what data we had from our reports and budget estimates, searching onion skin flimsies, carbon copies, smudged corrections—well before the day of white-out and xeroxes, not to mention word processing and computerized data banks. It was not until 11 a.m. on Thursday that we had assembled a legible report, dashed across Paris and finally saw Sir Herbert. To keep him and IGCR, the principal source of funding for Spanish refugees, waiting for an hour was a serious breach of good sense and Sir Herbert was clearly annoyed.

We sought 350,000 francs per month to change the Spanish assistance from conventional welfare handouts to a craftsman training program. We hoped the Spanish refugees could become economically independent in a southern France that was short on skilled craftsmen. The southern delegations already had been ingenious in developing training programs, so we left actual design of the programs in their hands. The IGCR ultimately approved our grant request, thanks in part to the persuasive explanations offered in further negotiations by Hugh Jenkins and Mary Elmendorf. Secours Quaker was one of only three organizations in France to receive direct IGCR support for needy refugees.

The years of work under great stress took their toll on different people at different times. In the spring of 1946 Fred Cornelissen appealed to me to drive down to Montauban and bring his exhausted wife, Nora, to Paris to enter a nearby rest clinic. Woody Emlen of the Montauban team came with us to help in case of need. The change in the countryside from the previous November was marked. That spring in France buoyed people's hopes that much would come right after all. People were at work in the fields, crops were being planted, farm machinery was being reactivated, there were more cars on the road. France was stirring.

THE VICHY/OCCUPATION HANGOVER

Whatever our preoccupations with supplies, shortages, or bureaucracies, we could not escape the shadow of the recent occupation.

From my Quaker friends I learned that, like much of France, the Quaker community faced difficulties during the years of war and Occupation. Like everyone else, they too faced acute shortages of food, heat and electricity and anxieties about arbitrary arrest.

Hard and often divisive decisions faced them. At personal risk, some Friends hid Jews and others designated by the regime as *indésirables,* sometimes for substantial periods. Some who could, withdrew to the countryside. Others, in order to continue their traditional work of visiting the enlarged number of prisoners, had to negotiate with individual German officials who controlled access to Fresnes and other major prisons, risking gaining a greater than necessary reputation of collaborating. Some managed to keep their small businesses going while others found useful work in Secours Quaker.

With such diverse responses to recent events, uncovering consensus in the small community was not easy. The leadership of Marguerite Czarnecki was all the more important as she sought to soften the sharp differences. Nevertheless, by the end of the war Secours Quaker in Paris and the southern delegations won widespread respect for humanitarian relief.

Suspicion of foreigners, arbitrary arrests and a lethargic military justice system were illustrated for us in Paris by the difficulties that beset a Franco-Polish couple. The wife, Madeline Maas, was a small, delicate but stalwart French woman who worked in our clothing center. Her husband Walter, a Polish economist, had, like so many others, sought security in France in the 1930s. He was fluent in Polish, German and French. When the Germans occupied Paris in 1940, the Gestapo arrested him and offered him a choice: "Be an interpreter for us or be deported." Shortly after the Allies entered Paris he, still in a German uniform, was arrested as a collaborator. Madeline too was arrested. When she was released some months later, her papers were stamped *indignité nationale* (deprived of civic rights), and the only job she could get was with Secours Quakers, who worked, unsuccessfully, to have her husband freed.

Madeline did not give up. Periodically, she asked for time off to knock on the doors of officials—the Prefecture of Police, the Ministry of Justice, *le Garde des Sceaux*—to seek his release. She badgered the military courts until they finally declared, "We have nothing against this man; he should be released." Because he too had been marked as *indignité nationale,* the French police sought to deport him and the Quakers obtained a temporary delay. But without real security in France, he emigrated to the new Germany and became a schoolteacher. When Madeline tried to join him there, it took another two years for the French authorities to grant her an exit visa.[2]

Those of us in the local delegations and in Paris were unable to forget the miseries inflicted on so many refugees and French men and women. Nonetheless, there were moments when the magic of Paris distracted us and we could enjoy that wonderful city.

THE LIGHTER SIDE

Margaret Frawley had advised me to make the most of my time in Paris. I heeded her advice. Walks were always a pleasure—though sometimes mixed with sad reminders. The glorious stained glass of Sainte Chapelle and Notre Dame had been removed to safety during the war; they were not yet back in place when I first visited the chapel. The incredibly delicate stone work of the Sainte Chapelle stood out even more starkly without the vivid lights and shadows of the glass.

By the time I arrived, bookstalls along the Seine had reopened, but their stocks were badly depleted. I was relieved to see that the model sailboats were again plying the waters of the main fountain in the Luxembourg Gardens. In the summer of 1946, a doctor lent me a room in an apartment on the Boulevard St. Michel while his family was out of town. Every morning I walked to the office by crossing the gardens. This gave me a daily immersion in the Paris of leisure: children playing, old people feeding pigeons, artists trying to capture the play of light and shadow under the plane trees. On the Seine the barges, with their tattered canopies but bright geraniums enlivening the family's quarters, again moved their cargoes. Sometimes I would take friends or perhaps a visiting delegation member for an inexpensive but delicious serving of *crêpes* in a tiny Breton restaurant nearby.

Annick Roche, whom I had known briefly in Algiers, returned to Paris to rejoin the main office of the Ministry of Public Health. We and other members of the team enjoyed wonderful plays at the Athenée theater, including Anouilh's *Antigone*, which resonated now that the tyrants of the occupation were gone. I particularly recall a walk in a January snow to the oldest church in Paris, St. Julien le Pauvre. There was a great exhibition of the Impressionists, and I found them more exciting than ever before, my eyes more responsive to Mediterranean light and color since my time in Algiers, Egypt and Italy. Another continuity brought Mme. Thierry, in whose apartment I had lived as a student, to Secours Quaker as a language teacher. She added her zest and French *esprit* to our company. Her readiness to encourage easy conversation talked a number of our shyer members to some fluency.

One of our satisfactions was getting to know members of the French Quaker community. As one would expect, they were markedly individual. From my student days I recalled Ernest LeRoi, who was indelibly etched in my mind because he cultivated a large white beard and even on the coldest winter days he wore on his feet only heavy woolen socks and sandals! Other members I came to know during my Secours Quaker period included Pierre Échard, a schoolteacher with a wide-ranging mind and unusually specific interest in the United States. I visited his modest farm in Brittany one weekend. He shared his worries about the demoralization and pessimism of so many of his countrymen.

Joseph Kreutz was a gregarious wine merchant, who occasionally invited us to a delicious dinner party prepared by his wife. These were always cheerful occasions, with serious talk about Quaker ideas, as well as many amusing anecdotes about the *comédie humaine.* His large table came from a monastery, and so did the uncomfortable narrow bench on which we perched. We thought this a rather painful gesture toward the simple, austere life as we enjoyed the best culinary and wine products of France. In moments of acute difference within this small Quaker group, Joe Kreutz's warmth and wit often relaxed the more severe.

Marius Grout was the intellectual leading light, a recipient of the prestigious literary Goncourt Prize for his moving novel, Passage de l'homme. It was a quiet evocation of experiencing the presence of God, as Friends have long believed. He also wrote a thoughtful paper on meditation that I still retain.

Henri Schultz was of a totally different character. He was not a thinker but a dedicated humanitarian. With Henry van Etten, he was deep in the wok of prison visiting. Later he took over a run-down castle of some sort and turned it into a home for homeless, troubled boys. Marcelle Fournier was the secretary of France Yearly Meeting, a quiet, sensible, basically cheerful person who helped keep together the small group in Paris as well as Friends scattered throughout the Provinces.

British, French and Americans I worked with became lifelong friends. By 1946 some of the early-comers began to go home. In March 1946 Bill Fraser, who had guided the British team during the first harsh winter, went back to Britain to finish his studies, and Roger Whiting became the FRS coordinator. I greatly appreciated Roger's sense of the comic and his ready wit. Several years later, after I was married and again working for the AFSC in Geneva, my wife Sally and I went to Paris with our three-months-old baby especially to meet up with Roger. Roger and little Diana were off quietly in a corner. When asked how they were doing, Roger replied, "Just engaging in small talk, Sally."

In the mid-50s, on our way for scholarly work in Ceylon as it then was, Bill Fraser and his Nancy arranged a house for us to rent in Welwyn Garden City, and the local Friends community cleaned out the jungle garden for our three months research stay. Every time we visited Paris from 1949 on, we had evenings with Micheline Salmon (now Sriber) and sometimes stayed with her family. I saw Marguerite Czarnecki when I could, and sometimes dropped by the Quaker Center to see other friends I had worked with.

CHAPTER THIRTEEN
CHANGING PRIORITIES

France had been at the center of AFSC attention from 1942 until 1945, with Philadelphia committing whatever resources it could raise to meet emergency needs. With the end of the war in June 1945 AFSC became vividly aware of the utter devastation of Poland, Germany and Austria. Gradually, investigators for the AFSC gained permission from the military to visit the worst hit areas. All returned from the wreckage of these places to impress us with the still more urgent needs to the east. Armies had grappled all the way across the three countries; cities had been bombed from the air for months. Entire cities had been destroyed; rail and road systems were shattered. Hundreds of thousands of people were homeless wanderers; families were scattered; food distribution was totally disrupted where bridges were down and vehicles disabled.

As early as January 1946 Margaret Frawley, now back in Philadelphia, was sensitive to changing priorities. She warned us that we had to foresee a reduced program well before the next winter. Newly arrived Lois Jessup, an experienced volunteer from the New York office where most of our fund raising occurred, explained the increasing difficulties in raising for France the kinds of money we had been able to find while France was still occupied by the German armies.[1]

In view of what we in the French team saw around us in Normandy and in the southwest, we thought this shift premature. At the same time, we could not help agreeing that many of the shortages in France now resulted more from internal administrative and political problems. Emergency supplies brought in by a small organization were now less likely to make a critical difference. More important, Entre'Aide Française now sought to strengthen permanent French service organizations instead of covering administrative costs of temporary emergency organizations like Secours Quaker.

Changes in the FRS in London also affected our program. For six years the FRS staff had been hard at it. They had to deal with emergencies in Britain itself from the start of the war in 1939. Since early 1945 they had been active in France, staffing transport and other services. Many of their most experienced members were understandably impatient to get on with their lives. FRS had always been seen as a temporary wartime expedient, while the AFSC was an organization active in peacetime as well as in war.

A number of those who had labored so hard during the war in the southern delegations were beginning to depart. Helga Holbek went back to Denmark in June 1945 and later joined a UNICEF mission to Poland. The cumulative effect of the years of occupation had exhausted others and home responsibilities could no longer be put off. Toot van Ordt needed to visit Holland to see her family; Ima Lieven from Latvia asked to be relieved so she could try to track down those of her family who might have survived the war's disasters. FRS and AFSC volunteers took up some of the slack.

Roger Whiting and I had to explain to Marguerite Czarnecki and her closest colleagues the likely decline in Anglo-American support. Marguerite, at least, was not surprised. She had known all along that the British and American committees were here only for the immediate postwar emergency. At the end of one of our consultations, she laid down her pencil and said quietly, "This has come sooner than we would have wished. But we knew it was bound to come. Now let's plan how best to pass on our activities to others."

At the January 1946 meeting of the *Comité d'Action* of Secours Quaker, I had the unpleasant task of reporting these hard conclusions to all the staff. I explained the decline in our financial support from the French government and from foreign private sources, and the greater urgency of the needs to the east. Philadelphia and London now had to reduce their overall support for Secours Quaker in its present form, but they both wanted me to express the deep thanks all of us felt for the unusual opportunities Secours Quaker had given so many from FRS and AFSC.

Because of the Philadelphia and London committees' longstanding concern for the plight of the remaining Spanish refugees, they were not prepared to retire completely from the southern field. They hoped to replace our relief programs with a more focused training program, designed to help more Spanish and stateless refugees gain the skills necessary to settle into constructive lives in France. Training would not be as easy as distributing relief supplies but in the end would be more useful. If the Paris Friends wanted to continue their prison visiting, the committees hoped to be able to continue some support.

REDUCING SECOURS QUAKER AND STRESS ON OTHER PRIORITIES

For a good part of 1946, my main preoccupation was to help reshape Secours Quaker into a more modest but still useful organization. No one wants to have a hand in hastening the demise of a constructive enterprise, and I believed that winding down our supportive presence unduly rapidly might be felt by our French associates as abandonment. Marguerite Czarnecki and I took some comfort from the knowledge that a number of French Friends would be relieved if Secours Quaker demanded less of their time and energies. She and others recognized that major responsibilities for AFSC and FRS lay ahead in Poland, Germany and Austria.

Fortunately, the three principal southern delegations had inherited skilled and devoted French and Spanish staffs. Moreover, during the hard years of the occupation, Secours Quaker had worked closely with local social service agencies. It was relatively easy for the delegations to transfer by June the relief supplies remaining in our warehouses to programs in which they had confidence. However the three delegations might set about assisting the Spanish and stateless refugees, they were likely to collaborate closely with these knowledgeable and congenial people in the other agencies. The remaining joint activities of AFSC and FRS on behalf of Spanish refugees and stateless would be designated as "Quaker Service." I must own that in the fifty-odd years between these events and my review of them, I had forgotten how rapidly we pushed for downsizing Secours Quaker.

Two new programs showed AFSC's continuing concern for assisting Europeans in addition to work in Poland, Germany and Austria. In early 1946, the European Transport Unit (ETU) was started. Young men released from Civilian Public Service camps sought a period of overseas civilian service before taking up their careers.[2] Under the energetic Winslow Ames, they established a modest headquarters in a garage in the Sixteenth Arrondissement in Paris and later moved farther out to larger quarters. AFSC bought fifteen trucks released from an army depot at Rheims. ETU teams of driver-mechanics were mobile and ready to go anywhere they were needed. In March, ETU dispatched a team of half a dozen trucks and ten men to Saint-Nazaire, where Secours Quaker had a third community center, smaller than those in Caen and Le Havre. The drivers helped families displaced by the Allied bombing move back to their homes or into temporary barracks until their homes could be made habitable. ETU soon began to send teams to Germany and Poland and eventually moved their headquarters from Paris to Germany.

The committee also began a School Affiliation Program, designed to encourage selected schools in America to develop links with schools in France, Italy and the Low Countries. Louise Wood, former head of a school, was the principal proponent of this new direction. Although these new efforts did not come under my direct responsibility, they were part of the AFSC's continuing presence in France during the last months of my stay.

In the spring of 1946 I visited Friends House on Euston Road in London. We wanted to shape the work in Paris, and the joint Anglo-American Quaker Service program for training Spanish refugees, in a way congenial to Paris Friends and to the London and Philadelphia committees. This impressive building recalled the notably affluent days of the great Quaker banking and chocolate families.

Roger Wilson played a key role in the discussions. His periodic visits to the FRS team in Paris had been brief, but were a tonic for all of us. He invited discussion of hard choices, listened carefully and was sensitive to the concerns of everyone involved. I was impressed by the sensitivity he and other British Quakers showed toward the needs and perplexities of the French Friends. As Bill Fraser once put it, "he helped FRS to find a vocation in listening to what he saw as the corruption of the human spirit in a world at war." Another time Roger Whiting and I went to Friends House together for joint consultations. I greatly appreciated his company.

Knowing of my interest in international relations, Roger Wilson introduced me to his younger brother, Geoffrey. He had been an aide to Sir Stafford Cripps on his failed mission to India to find common ground between Gandhi, Nehru and Jinnah, and was now working in the Foreign Office. I was impressed that a British Quaker could find his way through the thickets of international affairs without running into impossible dilemmas. (In 1961, when I agreed to accept a position on the Department of State's Policy Planning Council in the Kennedy administration, I thought of Geoffrey's example.) Whenever I could, I haunted the bookshops near the British Museum, relished the exhibitions at the Royal Academy and the National Gallery off Trafalgar Square, and enjoyed London's great parks.

In April 1946 we organized a committee at Secours Quaker with the daunting title of the *Comité de Liquidation* to minimize the disruptions of the coming six months' transition. Each delegation had already prepared a plan for passing to some other local or national organization those relief functions it hoped could continue for the French. Each would focus its remaining efforts on behalf of the Spanish refugees, the stateless, civilian prisoners and POWs. It was very important that individual members of the French staff be fully informed of our plans and given recommendations to help in their search for jobs elsewhere. Mary Elmendorf went to Toulouse to help plan the more sophisticated training program. I visited the southern delegations to discuss how the remaining work for Spanish and stateless refugees, prisoners and POWs might be carried forward.

During these visits we saw many signs of improvement. Electricity was becoming more reliable, roads were being repaired. The telephones worked more easily. Food was better, of course, as this was the growing season. There seemed to be fewer people walking in dejection; their clothes looked better, the women were looking smarter. People in the streets were more animated. The pace of everything seemed to be picking up. Perhaps it was just the season, but we hoped it was more than that.

FRANCE YEARLY MEETING, EARLY JUNE 1946

Each national grouping of the Society of Friends holds a Yearly Meeting where issues of major concern are discussed and plans worked out for the coming year. France Yearly Meeting met in early June at Henry van Etten's suburban home in Montmorency. Friends carefully discussed the decisions about Secours Quaker. Some members of the Paris Meeting had not been close enough to our work to understand why the previous system could not continue indefinitely.

As spokesman for AFSC, I explained AFSC's changing priorities, its diminishing financial support for work in France, and why we could not continue as we had been. Roger Wilson made many of the same points for FRS, with his usual grace and sense of Friends' purpose. Edith Pye came with him, and I was glad that Julia Branson and Stephen Cary, the new European commissioner, were there from Philadelphia.

We also discussed retirement arrangements for Henry van Etten, who had been Clerk of France Yearly Meeting for many years, a central figure for French Friends and a major link with British Friends. He personified the persisting Quaker commitment to prison visiting and reform. He was a familiar sight at Fresnes, Cherche-Midi, and la Santé prisons. He wrote a number of Quaker tracts and the only chronicle of French Quakerism that reached to the eighteenth century Protestant mystics in Languedoc.[3] By then in his fifty-third year, he deserved an honorable way to wind up his productive life as a professional Friend. The committees jointly financed an annuity for him and his wife. As one note put it, "that would free our Friend to find his own avenue of usefulness." Not entirely incidentally, it freed French Friends to choose a new clerk. Louise Schmitt, a capable member of the Paris Meeting, was chosen.

REVISED SPANISH REFUGEE PROGRAM
Shortly after France Yearly Meeting, we held an important consultation in Toulouse on how best to retrain as many Spanish refugees as possible so they could become fully earning members of the French community. Roger Whiting and Hugh Jenkins for FRS and Mary Elmendorf and I for AFSC met with key members of the three southern delegations for a day and a half. Hugh, a seasoned Spanish-speaking FRS volunteer, had worked with the FRS Team 100 in Germany, and had entered Bergen-Belsen camp only four days after it had been liberated by British forces. For four exhausting weeks they helped bury the dead and got that pestilential place ready for burning.[4] Later, FRS appointed him to Toulouse as executive secretary of the Quaker Service Refugee Program to coordinate the work of these delegations. His Spanish-speaking wife, Juanita, was a key member of the team.

These consultations were difficult. The staff knew that decisions had already been made, but to honor their wartime and postwar achievements they were impelled once more to reargue the case for continuing. Respect for them and their work required Roger Whiting and me to listen intently to their arguments and quietly make the case once again for change. Looking back, I better understood their need to go down with all flags flying. But at the time I found it called on quite a bit of Quaker patience. The veterans were persuaded that French young people still needed their help. The newer staff were less experienced. Inherently the new effort toward retraining would be more difficult and the results harder to measure than those of child feeding programs and clothing distributions.

By the end of these discussions, I was so obviously tired that Hélène Rott shunted me off to a nunnery that took in guests for short stays. After a quick appraisal the Mother Superior insisted that there would be no lunch until I went immediately to bed. Following a delicious peasant soup and country bread with slathers of butter and honey, I happily fell fast asleep. Supper came early in the long spring evening, brought by a shy nun who kept her eyes lowered and never said a word. After three days of sleeping, eating, and reading books I had borrowed I felt more human. On leaving, I shared a tea with the Mother Superior. In answer to my query, she explained, "Oh no, Monsieur, the novice has not taken a vow of silence. Poor dear, she has always been a deaf mute!"

In his unpublished memoir, Hugh Jenkins recalls the challenge of becoming accepted as the coordinator of a Spanish refugee training program already designed by others and operated by offices with a long tradition of virtual autonomy. After consulting with the Ministry of Labor, the three delegations organized training and apprenticeship programs and workshops in practical skills then in short supply. Electrician, radio repair, automobile mechanic, tanning and tailoring— all skills were needed. The three delegations, building on their reputations and somewhat different experiences, each attacked their problems in a slightly different way.

Fortunately, the Intergovernmental Committee on Refugees agreed to support these efforts. Mary Elmendorf and Hugh Jenkins both remembered well their first visit to Governor Valentin Smith, resident representative of the IGCR for France. He was surprised by the request for support for a training program, rather than simple emergency hand-outs. Nevertheless, they were able to persuade him to approve our request.

In addition, each delegation developed a community center to provide a place of warm fellowship for these wanderers. Here they could meet, develop together programs of mutual support, and bring cheer to one another. Perhaps the high point was in Perpignan. The cellist Pablo Casals, who had spent most of the years after the Spanish Republic's defeat near Perpignan, all along had been close to the

Secours Quaker center. He returned from Barcelona to celebrate the opening of the Perpignan Catalan center, where he gave a great performance.

Back in Paris there were difficult choices. Many French Friends wanted to get back to their quieter corner at rue Guy de la Brosse. They felt they could be more themselves there and not buffeted so much by pressures from the British and American committees. There were others, however, who wanted to keep strong links with the Friends International Center, which the sponsoring Friends World Committee for Consultation hoped would remain at the more prominent and accessible Notre Dame des Champs. Louise Schmitt, clerk of the Paris Meeting, Madeline Grout and Frank Revoyre were among those who helped the International Center remain in touch with the community of French Friends. The treasurer of Secours Quaker went back to the business he had worked with before the war. Others quietly adjusted to changing circumstances, as they had done so often through the war years,.

When Roger Whiting went home to continue his engineering studies, Jo Noble replaced him for FRS.[5] Marguerite Czarnecki helped with the transition to the reduced Secours Quaker program. She never intruded but was always ready with sensible suggestions. She provided names of people and organizations that might be helpful in the new directions. Later, she took a long, well-deserved vacation in Switzerland and was invited by Clarence Pickett to visit Philadelphia in the autumn.

CHARLES READ ARRIVES AND I RETURN HOME

I was delighted in mid-summer to learn that Charles Read had been chosen as my successor. He was a good six feet tall, with a relaxed air, and wore tortoiseshell glasses that sometimes slid down his nose. Well-organized and serious about the tasks in hand, he nevertheless had an off-beat sense of humor that quickly relaxed those around him and reassured us that he would not be likely to take himself too seriously. He had been a professor of history at Juniata College in Pennsylvania, and was able to use his knowledge to good effect.

In September we went together to Friends House in London, for I wanted him to know the principal Friends who were jointly concerned for continuing Quaker Service work in France. He went back to Paris to take charge and I stayed to visit with FRS friends—the Roger Wilsons, Bill and Nancy Fraser, and several others. Working together in Paris had given me a further respect for the way British Friends responded to the challenges of wartime. FRS was managed with less bureaucracy than AFSC; and they were fully sensitive to the paradoxical situations we found ourselves in as we worked in military areas or drew resources from military depots. When I returned to Paris, I realized how much Secours Quaker and its close-knit, unusual company meant to me. Part of me was greatly relieved that Charles Read had taken over. But part of me hated the idea of leaving while so much still needed to be done.

I was touched toward the end, when on a surprise occasion my friends in the Paris office gave me a lovely book, *Les Peintures du Moyen Age,* with hundreds of black and white reproductions and many in color. I could hardly believe that a work of this kind could have been produced in 1942, in the midst of the war. The signatures of some thirty-five members of the office were appended, with a citation from II Corinthians 4 as the New Standard Revised Version of the Bible has it:

> We are afflicted in every way, but not crushed; perplexed but not driven to despair; persecuted but not forsaken; struck down but not destroyed.

> —signed by Louise Schmitt,
> Clerk of the Paris Meeting

The verse admirably captures the response to the challenge the French people had faced.

Now I was impatient to get home, but returning troops and those whose citizenship needed to be renewed had priority for shipping space. I tried to get space for Julia Branson, who had been in Europe for some time, and me on the troop ship *Ericson,* but without success. In late October Julia was finally able to fly off. I read a lot about the parlous state of Europe and while I waited, I helped my *Sciences Po* tutor with whom I had studied European diplomatic history in 1938-39. Professor André Tolédano was a bright gnome of a man, a descendant, as he pointed out, of a Sephardic refugee family from Spain's Inquisition. He was working on a statistical survey of France's economy and needed some clerical assistance.

Paris once again had become the focus of diplomatic activity, as foreign ministers of the victorious powers struggled over peace treaties with the defeated countries and relations with each other. Professor Tolédano and I followed as best we could the generally stalled Paris peace negotiations. Of course we were, in fact, far from all that, though we often saw the shiny black limousines parked outside the Luxembourg Palace or the Quai d'Orsay foreign office. By the time I left to go home, they were not finished. We didn't know that the difficulties they faced, particularly over Poland and eastern Europe, would lead to what became the Cold War.

I also attended a number of political rallies of the moderate conservative MRP and the Gaullists. I recall a meeting of the French Communist Party, in a large smoke-filled theater. A band warmed up the crowd. Maurice Thorez, the party's general secretary, was among the speakers. The cheers and boos seemed well orchestrated; the very large crowd was well marshaled by muscular fellows strategically placed. It was an impressive show of strength compared to the meetings of the MRP and the Gaullists, where policy and ideological differences were vigorously argued.

Finally, late in November 1946, I was assigned space to fly home. We landed briefly at Shannon in Ireland to refuel for the Atlantic leap. Compared to the France I then knew, Ireland—or Shannon airport at least—seemed to flaunt its overflowing milk and honey. There were tubs of butter and cheese for sale; the snack bar had bowls piled high with fresh eggs. On the luncheon table were slices of peasant bread or croissants and all the butter you could want. Here was a sense of plenty the like of which I had not seen since New York. After another refueling stop at Gander in Newfoundland we were over New York by about 11 p.m. We circled the still lighted towers of New York and landed at Idlewild Airport, which later became JFK. To my astonishment and pleasure, Lois Jessup met me at the airport, even though by the time I had cleared customs it was nearly midnight. She drove me back to the Jessup apartment on Morningside Heights, hard by Columbia University. The next morning I took the train to Philadelphia and was soon home.

On the flight home I had had time to review my wartime experience. We had been living in terrible times. Thanks to the special niche the Quakers had carved out over the years, I had been in a position to help many different kinds of people in distress. While thousands of my cohorts were serving under military orders, often in harsh combat, many never to return, I had been privileged to concentrate on humane, constructive effort, with a good deal of independence. I had worked shoulder to shoulder with wonderful people. I hoped I had avoided playing God while nevertheless helping people in deep trouble.

From my first days in Portugal more than four and a half years before, I had been dealing with refugees, victims of tyranny and the side effects of war. Now that the atrocious Nazi ambitions had been blocked, Europe's peoples were going home. One evening in Paris, while I was walking along the Seine on the Quai Voltaire toward the team's apartment, near St. Michelle, one of the FRS men recalled how, early in his stay, the roar of a flight of bombers overhead made them flinch and look for cover;. "Then I remembered that the French, British and American air forces were ferrying forced laborers, deportees and French POWs back to France. The fighting was at an end and that awful scattering of people was now over." As I flew home, I thought that an end to the forced flight of refugees from Germany, Austria and Poland, and the return of deportees to France were fitting ways to mark *finis* to my AFSC service.

Now I had to think ahead to what should be next. Some months earlier Julia Branson had asked me if I would accept a contract for further work with the committee, probably overseas. Well before that I knew I was not a long-term relief worker. Picking up the pieces of tyranny and war for the five years' emergency had been enough. It was time to try to go more deeply. Surely one could understand more about the roots of war. What drove international rivalries? The unintended by-products of wars were so horrendous there must be better ways, short of war, for resolving serious differences. My conscientious objector position had not proved sufficient for me in the face of the moral challenge of the Hitlerian assault. Graduate school was clearly the next step. I was confident that I would be able to find a program of studies that would help me see more clearly why such regimes and such terrible conflicts arise.

PART V GENEVA and GAZA
1948-1949
PALESTINE REFUGEES

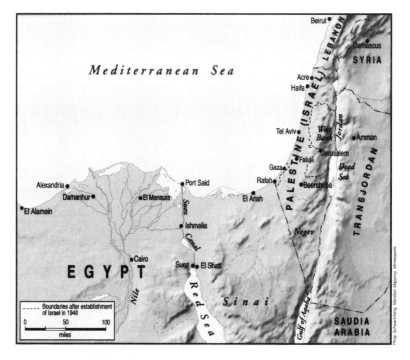

Israel, Egypt and Palestine

My graduate studies were interrupted a second time in 1948 when war broke out between the new state of Israel and Palestine. I was recruited to help jumpstart an emergency relief program that, alas, turned out to be a rather long haul.

In all the camps I saw the utter despair of people living in tents or on the ground with only elementary nourishment and meager health facilities. They asked why they could not go home. In many cases they could see their farms across the barbed wire. Whoever had been responsible, it had not been these poor people.

George McGhee, *Envoy to the Middle World*

CHAPTER FOURTEEN
PALESTINE REFUGEES IN GAZA

By 1948 I was back in the United States, studying international relations as a graduate student at Yale. After my stint with AFSC I wanted to study alternative ways of understanding and affecting this conflicted world. Persuaded that my early pacifism was an inadequate response, I had seen the consequences when a government with outlandish ambitions turns its power against its neighbors and parts of its own people.

The aftermath of the war was on the front pages of every newspaper every day. The Marshall Plan was a high priority; a coup in Czechoslovakia had given full powers to the local communist party; Washington and Moscow were arguing over Berlin. What became known as the Cold War had begun. I did not know then the extent to which these would distract Washington's attention from events in the Middle East that were to preoccupy me.

As a result of work with Jewish and other refugees in Portugal and Italy and briefly in Egypt, I was following the United Nations' effort to shape a mutually acceptable division of Palestine. The Palestine Partition Plan, passed by the Assembly on November 29, 1947 despite universal Arab protest, provided for a Jewish state all along the Palestinian coast, including the Negev and the Palestinian shore of Lake Tiberius. The bulk of the West Bank and Galilee was to be the prospective Arab state. Jerusalem was to be internationally administered. The optimists had hoped that the plan would prove acceptable to both Palestinians and Jews as a way to end the British Mandate, due in May 1948 when British troops and officials would withdraw. No one was pleased with the scheme, but the Jewish leaders accepted it for a starter while the Arab leaders rejected it out of hand.[1]

War broke out immediately after the Israeli declaration of independence on May 14, 1948 followed by President Truman's prompt recognition of Israel. Neighboring Arab states immediately invaded the territory allotted to Israel. Overly optimistic and preoccupied with security problems at home, the Arab states devoted only a small proportion of their armies to the campaign, and they did not coordinate their efforts. They failed to overwhelm the new state.[2] Hundreds of thousands of Arab civilians fled their homes for areas designated in the partition plan as Arab. Invading Palestine from the east, Jordanian troops gained control of much of the West Bank area assigned to the Arabs, as well as a part of Jerusalem. The Egyptians, entering from the south, were generally thrown back although they retained control of the Gaza strip and a small enclave in the Negev, the "al Faluja pocket." The Israelis made better use of a month's truce in June and further consolidated their position during a break in the second truce in December.

I closely followed the efforts of Count Bernadotte of Sweden to mediate a cease-fire and implement the UN Partition Plan. He was assassinated for his pains at an Israeli checkpoint by an Israeli guerilla band, the Stern Gang. Ralph Bunche, who succeeded him, with great difficulty negotiated terms of armistices. Apart from a new conflict that erupted in an effort by Great Britain, France and Israel to overthrow Egypt's President Nasser following his nationalization of the Suez Canal, these armistices provided the framework for whatever peace there was to be until the war of 1967.

THE QUAKER CALL-UP

On December 6, 1948, in my second year of study, to my surprise, Elmore Jackson of the AFSC called from Paris. As I recorded, he said:

> Howard, the Secretary General Trygve Lie has just asked the AFSC to organize an emergency relief program for some 250,000 Palestinian refugees now concentrated in Gaza. The AFSC board has agreed. There are 500,000 additional refugees, some in areas now in Israel, others in Lebanon and Jordan. The International Red Cross has agreed to take responsibility for those in Israel and the League of Red Cross Societies will work with the Arab states. Colin Bell and I are in Paris, observing the General Assembly and now working with Andrew Cordier [Secretary General Trygve Lie's deputy] to get us started. It is an emergency program, from now until August. We urgently need your help in Gaza. Won't you please join us? It's very urgent. The need is great. It would only be for a short period, to get relief work going.

My first reaction was no, not again. I quickly said, "But Elmore, I am in the midst of graduate studies at Yale; it's just what I had been looking for. I can't interrupt now."

He answered, "Yes, I'm glad you've found what you've been looking for. But the need is urgent. You spent time in Cairo during the war; you worked with refugees for five years. We really need you to help us get started..."

The previous year had been a very important one for me. I had fallen hard for Sally Hovey, a delightful, positive-minded young woman I had met at a Quaker wedding in Germantown. A Reed College graduate, she had been part of the AFSC's Relief and Reconstruction training program at Haverford College that prepared a small band of women for overseas relief work. A medical problem prevented her from going to Germany, but that was lucky for us, since we might never have met had she gone. She was working in the Washington office of UNRRA, researching the millions of refugees then wandering across Europe. We quickly hit it off. On December 22, 1947 we were married in Seattle. She brought me a joy I had never expected to find.

"Furthermore," I said, "Sally's pregnant, so I'm not a free agent. Let me discuss it with her and sleep on it and I'll call you back tomorrow morning." He gave me a number in Paris to call the next day. We were torn. I did not want to be disturbed from the academic track and I feared any deviation might lead to challenging offers of administrative positions that would tempt me from academia, where I wanted to make my career.

On the other hand, especially for one with some experience of the Middle East, the plight of the Palestinian refugees could well be imagined. The victory of Israeli armies could not conceal the human cost to those who had fled the fighting. To many of Hitler's victims and those of us working with them in the early 1940s, Palestine had seemed a place of refuge. Now the Palestinian refugees were, in one sense, the victims' victims and deserved our attention. The human need was so obvious, how could I deny the AFSC the Quaker humanitarian concern that had inspired me during World War II? For Sally, Elmore's call offered a chance to get closer to the world of relief work she had prepared for. She was enthusiastic about the offer.

I consulted two of my professors, Arnold Wolfers and William T. R. Fox, who agreed that if it was a short-term assignment, the experience of working in an international organization at this formative time would be too good to turn down. They warned me, however, that many people with experience behind them who once interrupt their graduate study never complete it. The more Sally and I talked about it late into the night, the more we were sure that this was the right thing to do next. I told Elmore that I would do it if I could return to Yale the following September. He said, "That's great! We will need someone in Geneva who knows the UN and Egypt. Let me know when you will arrive; come as soon as possible, please!"

Then began six hectic days. The high idealism of changing course on such short notice quickly dragged us down to the nitty-gritty matter of practicality as I arranged leave from the Yale program, found student tenants to carry our apartment lease, applied for passports and checked at AFSC headquarters. Clarence Pickett, the Executive Secretary of the Service Committee, greeted me warmly in Philadelphia and thanked me for dropping everything for this new challenge.

We took off from New York the evening of December 11, stopping at Gander in Newfoundland and Shannon for refueling. The next morning Sally and I watched with some anxiety as the TWA plane circled above the clouds that typically overhang Geneva before plunging down to the airport. Neither of us will forget the look of astonishment on Elmore Jackson's and Colin Bell's faces as two of us descended from the plane. In everyone's haste, no one had thought to tell them that Sally was coming. They greeted us warmly and hustled us off for a continental breakfast.

Elmore and I had worked together before. He had invited me to join the experimental training program at Pendle Hill six full years before. In the spring of 1947, before I started at Yale, he and I had laid the groundwork for the Friends World Committee for Consultation to obtain consultative status at the United Nations. The UN headquarters were still at Lake Success on Long Island, temporarily using the Norden Bombsight Company's wartime factory. Many with a Biblical bent appreciated the irony that the fledgling United Nations was, as Isaiah had commanded, turning swords into ploughshares. Elmore was an inconspicuous person, very discreet, blue-eyed, with a youthful, friendly face. He was a trusted helper for Clarence Pickett on diverse special projects. [3] Colin Bell, a Britisher who had been with the Friends Ambulance Unit in China, was now head of AFSC's Foreign Service section (and later became executive secretary). He had had considerable business experience in England before going to China. He had an expressive face, and was a joy to work with, having great good sense and a sharp, dry sense of humor.

FIRST WEEK IN GENEVA

That first week was intense as we hastened to organize AFSC's part of the refugee effort. On November 19, 1948 the General Assembly had resolved to establish the United Nations Relief for Palestine Refugees (UNRPR), the UN agency we would work with in this emergency, and President Truman had recommended Stanton Griffis as its director. He was an excellent choice. As Truman's ambassador to Egypt, he had championed the cause of the Palestinian refugees. [4] Griffis was a big man with a large head, balding in front. He wore wire-rimmed glasses, had a loud voice and an appealing chuckle. He managed to be driving and impatient but also a good listener, decisive but willing to take into account what others said.

Griffis's task was to generate support for the three distributing agencies—the International Red Cross assigned to northern Palestine, the League of Red Cross Societies in the Arab states, and the AFSC in the Gaza strip. He established an operations office in Beirut but retained his headquarters in Geneva. As he described his job in a letter to a friend:

> I have two jobs, one to shake the tambourine for international contributions, and the other...to play grocer boy for Arab refugees. I am charged with raising $32,000,000, which as it comes in I am spending for food, tents, blankets and medical supplies for the distributing agencies. I have an elemental job and that is to keep these

refugees alive, sheltered and in reasonable health until Allah or the United Nations settles their future and the question of their absorption back into their homeland and/or into other Arab nations. I buy and distribute for them each month 7,500 tons of flour, about a thousand tons of pulses (dried vegetables to you), and thousands of other tons of dates, sugar, edible oils and such other delicacies as we receive as gifts in kind from foreign nations.[5]

In our consultations with Griffis we emphasized the AFSC's need for full autonomy. We would have to count on the UNRPR to cover our administrative costs and provide the relief supplies. We would also depend on the Egyptian army for transport of our goods. It was crucial that our field staff should not become mere cogs in the UNRPR structure. We were determined to retain the Quaker quality of our operation. Colin Bell drafted what became known as the Nineteen Points, which clearly confirmed the autonomy of the AFSC team, the responsibility of the UNRPR to provide supplies, and the cooperation of the Egyptian government in allowing duty-free entry and military transport.[6] Colin and Clarence stood firm in pressing these points, and they were incorporated into the working agreements with the UNRPR and the Egyptian government. They were referred to whenever over-zealous Egyptian officials sought to intrude on the field operations in Gaza, or when the team needed more cooperative help from the UNRPR officers or the officials in Cairo.

Important for AFSC, too, was an underlying assumption that this was truly an emergency effort. Point 8 put it this way: "We would not be prepared to undertake this minimum of relief unless we could be assured that a solution to the vital problem of resettlement is being vigorously sought by U.N. and all others vitally concerned."

Why had this small organization, the AFSC, been asked by the Secretary General of the United Nations to take on this large emergency responsibility? Quakers were then seen as advocates by both parties. The aid they had given to desperate Jewish refugees was still vividly recalled by Israeli leaders, while Quaker support for Palestinian schools brought trust from the Arabs. Early in the spring, Rufus Jones, the founder of the AFSC, had urged Christian, Jewish and Muslim religious leaders to unite in calling for a Truce of God to insulate Jerusalem from the conflict that then seemed likely.[7] Finally, in December 1947, the Friends Service Council of Great Britain and the AFSC received the Nobel Peace Prize for Friends' years of civilian service during international conflicts and their tireless efforts to promote peace and reconciliation.

Almost in desperation, I imagined, the Secretary General's office had appealed to us, to the International Committee of the Red Cross and the League of Red Cross Societies. As so often happens in international relief, rapid improvisation had to take the place of careful planning. In this case, there were no other bodies readily available to be called upon.

During July of 1948 some 100,000 Palestinians poured into Gaza. Resources became scarce; hundreds of families had to get their water from a single hydrant.

Gaza was then under Egyptian political and military control. When the war started almost immediately after Israel's declaration of independence, Palestine refugees began to flow south from Lydda, Jaffa and Haifa and west from Beersheba into the Gaza strip; and the Egyptian army quickly took control of the area. As the war intensified, more and more refugees fled to Arab-designated areas.

Within a week of our arrival in Geneva, Colin and Elmore went back to Philadelphia AFSC. Griffis headed for Cairo to oversee the emerging UNRPR operation, confirming in his stead a retired British officer, Brigadier Reginald H. Parminter. Sharp minded and skilled with numbers, he was a short, ample man with a monocle that he could toss in the air and catch in his right eye, and a store of anecdotes for charming his way through the UN bureaucracy. I set up a small office in the Palais des Nations, the old League of Nations Building high on a hill overlooking Lake Geneva; it was grand in a prewar modern way, simple and spacious. I could imagine the portly Stresseman, foreign minister of Weimar Germany or the dapper Anthony Eden striding down the halls. My secretary was Joan Ryder, a capable and intelligent woman, whose response to people and ready sense of humor carried us both through moments of discouragement. She had another great asset: whenever the telephone rang, her "Howard Wriggins' office," in a strong BBC accent, enhanced my standing among my UN colleagues.[8]

THE HUMAN PROBLEM

From the distance of Geneva, I tried to understand the problems facing the refugees in the Gaza strip. Gaza city, the largest town near the north end, was close to Israeli positions. Villages were scattered beside the rail line from the Egyptian border north along the coast. The Gaza strip, a sandy land twenty-five miles long and seven miles wide, had been home to a scant 80,000 people before the refugee flood. A few permanent residents owned citrus groves and formed the local elite; most others worked for them or were small farmers. Imagine two surges of refugees who fled to Gaza: some 100,000 during July 1948. and another large flow three months later. The population trebled in only a few months, with nearly all of the arrivals destitute! The Palestinians called it *El Nakbe*, the catastrophe.

There was bitter disagreement over why so many Palestinian Arabs had fled. Zionist supporters of Israel argued that the exodus resulted mainly from exhortations to leave home made by Arab League spokesmen over the radio and in mosques, in order to give the invading Arab armies room to "drive the Jews into the sea." But it seemed reasonable to me that civilian Arabs would flee an imminent armed conflict, much as millions of Europeans fled advancing German armies, especially after over a hundred residents of the Arab village of Deir Yassin had been mowed down by one of Israel's guerrilla forces. All the refugees I talked with knew about it, a story that lent wings to people's feet.[9] Being still organized around extended families who found it difficult to cooperate with one another, Arab society lacked cohesion. Once the British Mandate administrators departed and middle class Arab leaders sought safety however they could, many towns and villages were left without their normal leaders.[10] Refugee flight becomes infectious when leaders are scarce.

Members of the Quaker team had a vivid view of one other reason why refugees fled. In December and January, the team delivered emergency food and medical supplies to some 3,000 civilian Palestinians who, along with an Egyptian brigade, were entirely encircled by the Israeli army in the town of al Faluja. A nurse and a supply man stayed in Faluja between convoys to ensure that the food and medicines were properly delivered to the civilians. Many of the Palestinians were concerned for their safety once the Egyptian troops withdrew as had been agreed between Israel and the government of Egypt. Moshe Shertock, the Israeli prime minister, assured the AFSC representative that his government would protect the Arab residents of Faluja and their property if they elected to stay—reassurances the AFSC passed on to the residents.

Soon after the Egyptian army marched home, new Israeli recruits celebrated their occupation of al Faluja, firing their guns at all hours. Some broke into houses, forcibly robbing and stealing. Four days later, when the Quaker convoys came to Faluja to pick up the AFSC nurse and supply man, Palestinian civilians had been so intimidated that the entire village opted to flee. Some went to Jordan-controlled Hebron, the remainder joined the convoy back to Gaza.[11]

All these refugees had left their homes, often on foot, without warning, without advance planning. They sometimes carried a few clothes, more often nothing but what they were wearing. They lost their land (over sixty percent of the refugees in Gaza had been farmers), often in their families for generations. Some families could see from their wretched camp the very earth they had once owned.

> The misery in these camps is indescribable: feet covered with sores tell of many miles walked barefoot, spontaneous infections and others proclaim malnutrition, scabies, lack of hygiene; cases of vitamin deficiency are numerous. It sometimes occurs that we go to see patients at home. But can one speak of a home when it consists of 2 or 3 square meters per family, in a hut without a window and often without a roof, bed, blankets or furniture or any kind?[12]

As one witness put it: "The situation in Gaza was explosive, as thousands of refugees crowded into a tiny area with nothing to occupy their minds except the memory of what they had left behind and how they were going to return"[13]

AFSC's TASK

Our task was to help the quarter of a million who were crowded into the Gaza strip. AFSC worked to establish its field team as

soon as possible in order to start distributing UNRPR supplies. We
wanted to provide tents, blankets and minimal medical attention. We
planned rations to give a minimum of 1500 calories; UNICEF pledged
to supply most of the milk. The UNRPR could purchase the bulk of the
other provisions in the Middle Eastern markets. From Geneva I
watched over the U.N.'s budget assumptions that roughly $250,000 per
quarter was to be for Gaza. I also monitored allocations to the
distribution agencies; one-fourth of all UNRPR commodities were to
go to Gaza. I tried to ensure that the principal donor countries kept to
their preliminary commitments. Parminter and I watched closely as
U.N. members responded (or didn't) to Griffis's urgent requests for
funds. Some contributed surplus grain, or vehicles, tents or blankets. A
proportionate share of what became available to the UNRPR was sent
to Port Saïd, the supply point for Gaza. The Egyptian army was to pass
our supplies without delay to the southern end of the Gaza strip,
without the usual customs charges. AFSC's success would depend in
part on how effectively we could cope with the phlegmatic Egyptian
bureaucracy.

New arrivals to Palestine had to improvise, creating shelter with blankets and
rope. Only later did we begin to receive regular army tents, sometimes already
well-used.

SEARCH FOR RECRUITS

In Geneva I was in a position to use the U.N. and Quaker networks to recruit staff for Gaza, including supply, distribution and medical personnel. For medical staff my first stop was Dr. Brock Chisholm, a gentle, white-haired man who was head of the World Health Organization (WHO). His staff provided a list of nurses who had experience with displaced persons. We sent them letters, enclosing clippings from Swiss papers about the condition of refugees in Palestine. I spoke with the responding nurses on the phone, describing skills, pay scales, and Quakers and our involvement. Three or four volunteered and, after interviews with me in Geneva, left for Cairo.

A doctor working with the WHO also offered his assistance, stopping by the office out of the blue. Dr. Jerome Peterson was an energetic black American who wanted to help get the medical service going. The WHO agreed to lend him to the UNRPR and late in December he and his wife, a nurse, went out to Gaza. He eventually became the key figure in the medical service for the International Red Cross, the League of Red Cross Societies and the Quakers, operating out of Beirut. A number of Swiss readily joined in. One of these was Bernard Klausner, who knew about Friends and brought experience from a youth work camp in Yugoslavia. A number of French Quakers volunteered. But it was the Philadelphia office that miraculously managed the principal recruitment. As a result, one of my immediate functions was to meet the planes, usually in the middle of the night, carrying tired AFSC people bound for Cairo the next day. Sally provided a warm welcome and, as promptly, a welcoming bed. By mid-February we already had thirty people on the job in Cairo, Port Saïd and Gaza.

For the early arrivals, before the truce between Israel and the Arab states was declared, traveling was especially difficult. From Cairo to Gaza alone took sixteen hours, or more with delays. One volunteer recalled, "We arrived with no food, no heat, semi-frozen at Gaza in the middle of the night, blacked out and under bombing attack." It took Josina Berger, a nurse recruited from Holland, two days to get from Cairo to Gaza. Her car got stuck in sand and had to be dug out five times. In an oral history collected by the AFSC:

> The one boy who spoke English said, "Doctor will come today because he hasn't been here in two days." When the doctor came, people came in slowly, one behind the other, but that was a mistake. We tried to push them to where they could go because there were so many. They had hardly time to talk to the doctor. Well, the doctor didn't have anything

to work with except five bottles of solutions...After half an hour the doctor had seen 75 patients. He was exhausted. He said "I can't stand it any more...I'll be back tomorrow"...This was just at the beginning. There was nothing yet.[14]

The doctor was from the sixty-bed hospital of the British Church Missionary Society (CMS) in Gaza and had a small but qualified nursing staff. They were nearly overwhelmed by the numbers. Lee Dinsmore, lent us by the Cairo YMCA and one of the two Arabic speakers on the team, recalled the anguish of a village woman who bared her empty breast while crying, "I can't feed my child!" Her lifelong habit of keeping herself covered in public was overcome by her frantic search for milk to feed her baby. [15]

Within three weeks, a rudimentary medical team was in place. But it took much longer before we could provide even minimum service to all camps and centers.

QUAKERS IN GENEVA

Among the Quakers in Geneva that Sally and I came to know, two ladies, Irene Pickard and Rosalie Stack, became especially close to us. Irene was a confident and well-read woman who for years had been active in the Geneva Quaker Center. She drew around her a circle of intelligent, caring women and quickly included Sally among them. Rosalie Stack was gentle, wise and very funny. These women were able to help us find an obstetrician who would see Sally through delivery. They became like two devoted grandmothers as she carried our first baby, far from her own mother half a world away in Seattle. Thanks to the warmth and security provided by these Quaker ladies and Sally's obstetrician, I had full confidence that Sally would be well cared for in my absence.

FIRST VISIT TO CAIRO AND GAZA

As useful as we were in Geneva, I needed to visit Cairo, Gaza, and Beirut, in order to understand how the organizations effectively operated together—or where they failed—and in February I went off to visit the teams in Cairo and Gaza.

I found Cairo the same crowded, noisy, exciting place I had known five years before. AFSC's modest office was with the UNRPR, with Delbert Replogle in charge. He was a round, restless man, with a troubled frown; back home he had owned and managed a successful electronics company. Cassius Fenton was his finance man. A thin blond man of middle height, somewhat humorless, he prepared budget documents and expenditure reports that came to be well received in Beirut, Geneva and Philadelphia. Both men seemed very tired. James Keen, the UNRPR purchasing agent for Gaza, was a retired regular British army man, with a proud posture and sardonic blue eyes. He was a first class administrator, but his distant manner and intolerance of muddle won him respect rather than affection. As I got to know him better, I discovered he had a scholarly side not frequently found in able administrators. He was troubled by AFSC's "amateurish" ways, but sympathetic to our efforts. Stanton Griffis, who was temporarily in Cairo, greeted me warmly with, "This is the best damn relief job I've ever seen!"

Delbert had the critical role of coaxing assistance from all levels of the Egyptian bureaucracy. Top officials readily offered assistance and were called upon in emergencies and for new projects. However, mid-level staff moved at a slow pace, preferring to exercise control over, rather than expedite, a task. To ensure the free flow of imported goods, Delbert periodically had to renegotiate with customs officials and sometimes go back to the top, a fatiguing and time-consuming exercise.

He described the chaos that met the team when they began distribution in Gaza. Desperate refugees swarmed onto the trucks, each trying to take as much as he could carry. There was no proper census and no way to know how many members were in each family; fair distribution would have been nearly impossible even under more controlled conditions. After the initial free-for-all, the AFSC began to gather numbers village by village. In a preliminary census, each headman (*mukhtar*) confirmed the number of wives and children each man had before he could be registered to draw blankets and food rations. Later, tent-by-tent head counts improved the accuracy of the record. The count was not exact since, understandably, deaths were not always reported, and because during the head counts, children scooted from tent to tent to inflate the number for neighbors. But with time, the AFSC workers believed they were close to a reliable count of the refugees in Gaza at about 220,000.

To sustain this many people, large quantities of supplies were needed. By mid-February over 100 tons of food were being handled, and 100,000 blankets and 1,000 tents had been distributed. More supplies were needed, and the team had to greatly expand its warehouse space.

To assist Gaza Strip refugees, AFSC distributed
UNRPR supplies. Flour, blankets, and UNICEF
milk were among the crucial provisions.

After five days in Cairo, impatient to see the distribution
process, I took a train to Port Saïd, where most of the supplies were
received. Bernie Klausner, a Swiss volunteer, received goods provided
by the UNRPR and UNICEF, assuring proper records. He cleared the
goods through Egyptian customs and oversaw their loading from
dockside into railroad cars with a minimum of pilferage. Then he
confirmed that they went on their way to Rafah, AFSC's major supply
depot. Bernie was energetic yet meticulous. He had the patience to deal
day by day with customs officials, stevedore bosses and train
dispatchers. To accelerate delivery of goods, all UNRPR supply
contracts included a provision that charges would not be reimbursed
until UNRPR had confirmation that the goods had been received in
Raffah. The distribution process grew more complicated as the AFSC
added to its supply list, but it was straightforward. As I wrote after
visiting Gaza:

> An individual would show his ration card at one table, have
> it punched and his name checked off. He would go on to
> the next table where a ration of flour would be poured into
> a used milk tin and the top leveled off by a stick. 2.5 kilos

per week. Depending on how many there were in his family, he would receive a number of rations and they would all be poured into a cloth sack.

Distributing flour is relatively simple, but blankets are difficult, for their quality varies greatly, some being excellent ex-US army green wool, others somewhat soiled and some even tattered surplus. Should they be given their choice? Or should each take what chance gives them? If it is to be by chance, how endless is the jockeying of each gambling on reaching the blanket desk just when the good ones are being given out! And if not by chance, how endless are the arguments.

When items like oil, beans, meat and dates were added, the complexity of the task threatened chaos.

From Port Saïd I went on to Gaza. The drive should have taken six hours, but we left at 5 a.m., got stuck in a sandstorm and didn't reach the AFSC team's headquarters until six that evening. The team had obtained a number of two-story houses in compounds near one another. The houses were relatively secure but cramped. Everyone had at least a camp bed but only rare moments of privacy. Although the team members were tired from working near their limits, their morale was high.

Emmett Gulley, the team leader, was a tall, heavy-set man, an Oregon farmer, slow-spoken and thoughtful. I was particularly struck by the size and strength of his hands. He was beset in his duties by an overwhelming number of unpredictable details. He had a good way of interpreting AFSC's relationships and aims, and of describing in general terms the work and our problems. He was "a mountain of patience," as one member put it.

Having studied the field reports to UNRPR and the UN references to "camps," I expected serried rows of carefully aligned, nearly identical dwellings, similar to the British Army-run camps I had known in Italy and El Shatt four years earlier. But as I wrote in a letter home,

'Camps' is hardly the right word. They are groups or clumps of tents, widely scattered over the sand and along the coast, stretching almost unbrokenly from Raffah at the Egyptian frontier up to Gaza. There are army tents, bedouin tents low to the ground, long and rangy, old camel's hair blankets, some tiny pup tents improvised from blankets we have distributed, some pathetic attempts to use rags on strings to give some protection from the February rains.

Nights and even days are cold. I slept with several blankets,
flannel pajamas, a sweater and socks.

Relations between AFSC people in Gaza and the Egyptian army were
uncertain. Egypt was the recognized sovereign power in Gaza but had
suffered a humiliating defeat at the hands of the untried Israeli army.
The officers had to look on the areas as terrain for military action
should the truce break down. Our warehouses and the refugees would
be impediments to the maneuvers they had to anticipate. The rail line
that had supplied the army during the conflict had become
indispensable for the relief effort. And officers who had been active in
the nationalist independence movement must have hated to see
Westerners supply aid to the refugees, eliciting their gratitude. On
AFSC's side, some of the men who had served years in Civilian Public
Service camps as conscientious objectors were troubled by the heavy
presence of Egyptian army and police. It was important to demonstrate
that relief workers and refugees could manage complex affairs without
resorting to force. I tried to counter complaints about the Egyptian
military with stories about the American and British military in North
Africa and Italy, who took our lack of understanding of their well-
established procedures as willful ignorance. In spite of the pacifist
principles of AFSC and many team members, I agreed with many
members that the police presence was indispensable.

AFSC team members and Egyptian officials had to work
together to get anything done. The Egyptian forces were able to
administer justice and impose stability in a highly volatile situation.
The army moved and delivered our supplies to the central warehouse
and often on to each distribution center. Tank trucks delivered water.
Their engineers helped the refugees erect the tents we issued and built
latrines and the milk-feeding stations where UNICEF milk was
distributed to 100,000 pregnant and nursing mothers and to children
under fifteen.

Sometimes difficulties were compounded because only a few
of the team understood Arabic. Lee Dinsmore, a youth director from the
Cairo YMCA, and Alan Horton, then studying and teaching at the
American University of Cairo, were indispensable go-betweens. They
could deal directly with aggrieved Palestinians or army officers. Even
without the language barriers, communications between Gaza and
Cairo, a distance of about 100 miles, were painfully slow and
unreliable. A wire took two days. A phone call could be made from the
frontier on an army phone, but messages had to be relayed from the
police station to us, invariably getting garbled on the way. Griffis

eventually hired a courier. He took the train twice a week; riding thirteen hours to Gaza, staying a day, then returning for another thirteen hours by train.

Tent schools served less than one-third of the school-aged Palestinian children. Funds and teachers were scarce; books even scarcer.

Early on it was clear that schools of some kind had to be organized. The dean of the Cairo School of Social Work, Dr. "Mido" Zaki, planned a simple school system. Teachers were found and hired among the Palestinians, chalk and slates were ordered. Books presented a problem, as some of the teachers balked at using Egyptian textbooks, which were filled with praise for King Farouk.[16]

The team's day of rest became Friday, which to most seemed an appropriate conformity to local practice. And how welcome that day was!

POLICY DISCUSSIONS

In the evenings, the AFSC team held meetings on policy. In one they considered developing a grievance procedure for the refugees to register complaints or report a suspected irregularity to AFSC staff. The discussion then turned to ways our efforts might carry a Quaker message. One member with long field experience in Madagascar felt that the distribution itself, with ways for refugees to express complaints and to have them responded to, would demonstrate Quaker respect for all regardless of their poverty or circumstances. Nothing like this would have happened to these people before. Having seen food distributions on this scale elsewhere, I was impressed that the team placed so much emphasis on providing a complaint mechanism.

The evening meetings were open discussions where alternative ways of solving problems were considered. Emmett chaired the meetings, patiently keeping the team focused on one bothersome subject until it was settled. At this early stage, it wasn't surprising that ways to deal with particular situations were still under debate. Despite the physical and mental strain, everyone paid full attention to each subject.

In less than two months the team set up a regularized food distribution system, an at least minimal health service, rudimentary sanitation, and a few schools. This fell far short of what would be tolerable for a longer run. As I saw it, the achievement was a near miracle but one accomplished with a heavy cost to members of the team. Would they have to continue at this pace? Or would their jobs become easier as routines were set in place? Of course it was the refugees who were paying a higher price by far, having lost their land and ancestral ways of life.

After spending an enlightening week with the Gaza team I flew to Beirut with James Keen, who had stopped briefly in Gaza. Once in the air, I found Keen still worried about the thoroughness and efficiency of our record keeping, but otherwise impressed by AFSC's dedication and accomplishments in such a short time.

Beirut, set by the sea with lovely mountains rising behind it, was a heaven compared to Gaza. I reported to the UNRPR staff on the visible progress in the Gaza program, and pressed the urgent need for fuel. It was hoped that one of the local oil companies would donate kerosene for the primus stoves many of the refugees owned. No wood remained in Gaza; orange groves had been cut down, even their roots unearthed. I also had substantial consultations with Dr. Jerome Peterson about the medical program. I flew back to Cairo to review my findings with Delbert and then took Swissair to Geneva. On the flight, I thought again of the pressures on the hard-working staff in insalubrious Gaza compared to the pleasures of Beirut or the comforts of Geneva. I therefore felt a special responsibility to the Gaza team to make the maximum use of my remaining months in Europe and the Middle East.

A FAMILY AFFAIR

It was wonderful to be back with Sally again. As I had hoped, she had been absorbed into Irene's and Rosalie's entourage. She was well and in good spirits. We found an austere but sunny apartment within a quick bike ride or pleasant walk to the Palais des Nations, where the UNRPR and AFSC offices were.

Within a few weeks of my return, on April 21 our first child was born at the *Clinique Bois Gentil*. The obstetrician allowed me to serve as Sally's interpreter, even though in those days fathers were not usually present at delivery. Sally had trained for natural childbirth and managed beautifully, breathing wisely. With the mid-wife's encouraging *"plus fort*, Madame," first a little bit of head appeared, then the whole head, then the shoulders and torso and arms, and finally the whole baby, all parts in order! Our daughter's arrival was so moving for me it seemed as near a miracle as I have experienced, even today. As Rosalie Stack put it to Sally later, "It's one of the few times in your life when you feel you are great. And you really are!" We named her Diana and quickly dubbed her Dinny. Even our Swiss neighbors upstairs, whom we rarely saw, cheered as we brought Dinny home.

CHAPTER FIFTEEN
RETURN TO GAZA

THE PALESTINE CONCILIATION COMMISSION

My happy family situation did not distract me very long from the AFSC/UNRPR commitment to relief of the Palestinian refugees. My attention shifted from recruitment of medical staff and the allocation of supplies as I became more involved in the United Nations diplomatic process. The UN General Assembly had set up a Conciliation Commission on Palestine at the end of the first Arab-Israeli war. The commission was to find solutions to the intractable conflicts between the new Israeli government and its Arab neighbors, and the conundrum of the future of the refugees. In early May they held consultations in Lausanne with representatives of Israel and of Egypt, Jordan, Lebanon and Syria.

It may have seemed plausible to the commissioners to bring together representatives of Israel and the Arab states. But the Arabs refused to meet directly with the Israelis since all the governments lacked reliable popular support at home and could not risk recognizing the legitimacy of the new Israeli state. So they insisted on meeting as a group with the staff of the commission, which acted as an intermediary for the exchange of proposals.[1]

In the late spring, I went to Lausanne with Delbert Replogle, who was on his way home from Cairo, to meet with the commission. It was headed by Mark Ethridge, editor of the *Louisville Journal*, a tall, dignified man who asked good questions. Delbert and I described the condition of the refugees. We stressed the explosive pressures building up in the camps if no solution could be found. We urged the return of at least some refugees to their homes and the assisted resettlement in various Arab lands for the remainder. The commission members went on to consult in Tel Aviv, Cairo and Beirut. Delbert urged me to represent AFSC at their mid-May meeting with the relief agencies in Cairo. At that time we still had faith in the commission, so I dropped everything and hastened to Cairo.

SECOND VISIT TO CAIRO AND GAZA: SHORT-RUN CAMP IMPORVEMENT, LONG RUN POLITICAL STALEMATE

When I arrived in Cairo we had a full day of meetings, first among the AFSC, the International Red Cross and League of Red Cross Societies, UNICEF and the UNRPR staff. Later we met with the Conciliation Commission staff for a preliminary exchange of views. By this point we had a better understanding of the apparently irreconcilable political views of the principal states. When the Arabs met as a body, they strengthened each other's inflexibility in the name of outrage and Arab solidarity. They were matched only by the heady new self-confidence of the Israeli spokesmen. The Israelis were not ready to discuss refugees or other issues until the new frontiers resulting from their military success were recognized. The Arab statesmen refused to discuss anything until Israel accepted the right of the refugees to return.

For our part, those of us from the relief agencies pressed the commission not to forget the immediate needs of the refugees. I reminded them (though they knew it quite well) that the original appropriation would run out in the middle of the next General Assembly in September. We stressed the urgency of the refugees' plight. I argued that the cost to the international community would be very great without the return of at least a few refugees and a resettlement of nearly all the others. The commission staff listened sympathetically. Whether they could persuade the relevant statesmen was another matter, and far more important.

Over the next several days our Cairo accountant, Cassius Fenton, and I went over the project's cash outlook for the rest of the year. As we neared negotiations with the UNRPR on extending our program beyond August 31 we needed to be sure we had solid numbers reflecting our needs.

After this review, Dick Rhoades, the AFSC supply manager based in Rafah, and I drove to Gaza across the Nile Delta, passing scenes that might have been unchanged since Biblical days: men pulling plows, women in black with bundles or water jars on their heads, camels, donkeys. We saw ships in the river, sometimes towed by teams of men. On the other side was the desert, empty except for graveyards of wrecked cars and tanks from the recent war.

When we arrived I found the team in much better shape. Many of the difficulties that seemed dramatic at the outset were now managed routinely by the staff. Alvin Holtz had emerged as an imaginative, driving assistant to Emmett Gulley. Al's wife, Edele, inspired a high degree of efficient and friendly service from the staff, helping make delicious Arab/American meals; morale was much improved.[2]

MORE THAN FOOD

At our Cairo discussions with the commissioners the three agencies had agreed that, after food, the next needs in order of priority were shelter, sanitation, fuel, blankets, clothing and soap. I discussed these priorities with the AFSC camp directors. First, they urged me to seek 10,000 additional tents. Many of the old ones were very small; most of the second-hand ones had deteriorated and would be in shreds by winter. A supply of tents had arrived from Scandinavia, and created great excitement. However, they proved to be arctic tents for use in deep winter! Each had a tunnel entrance four feet long and eighteen inches in diameter. Everyone burst into laughter. Nights could be quite chilly in the desert, but snow was not a problem. The tunnel material was soon transformed into patches for leaking tents.

A part of the UNRPR medical budget was already going toward sanitation, but that was still inadequate. The hard labor of digging latrines had to be paid for. Pumps were so important that diesel oil was also included in the medical budget. Luckily, there were no major outbreaks of serious disease.

The third matter, fuel, was critical for cooking. In Cairo, we had been clear that fuel was more urgent than blankets. But in the field,

AFSC staff insisted that blankets, too, were indispensable. They wanted 250,000.

By April some 16,000 refugee children and 6,000 Gaza resident children were in school. That sounds impressive, but the 16,000 represented only a fraction of the 70,000 school-aged among the refugees. There simply was not enough in the UNRPR budget to educate all the children. Mido Zaki believed it was better to educate few children well than to double or treble the numbers, until he could double or treble the number of teachers; and teachers were scarce.

SHOULD WE CONTINUE?

Colin Bell, head of AFSC's Foreign Service Section, wanted me to explore with the team whether we should continue beyond the original August 31, 1949 deadline. We were all worried by the lack of progress toward agreement on the future of the refugees. AFSC could not take long-term responsibility for those in Gaza. On the other hand, we could not just walk away from obvious need. Much would depend on what would replace our emergency effort. But the immediate question remained: should we continue beyond August 31, 1949?

For many, the very idea of quitting at the end of August was a kind of folly unheard of among Friends. Recollections of the horrendous first three months made stopping now seem inconceivable; the team had brought about much constructive change in a short time. The human need remained urgent and obvious and even those who were to go home in the summer hoped we would continue. But the volunteers were unsure if there would be enough money to sustain what they saw as a minimal program. We needed more tents and blankets. There were too many children without schools. Medical service was still rudimentary. Could I reassure them that the budget would be retained at least at the present level after August?

I had to respond that the answer lay not in the hands of AFSC or UNRPR, but with members of the next United Nations General Assembly in September. None of us was happy with being beholden to such political uncertainties. Quarterly hand-to-mouth financing was both unreliable and inhumane. In the end we concluded that we should continue at least to the end of the year. Replacements for those who had to go home by August would be needed early in the summer. Whether we went beyond the first of the year would depend on financing from the UN General Assembly and on AFSC's administrative support in Philadelphia.

ON TO BEIRUT AND ISRAEL

Cassius Fenton and I flew in the UN plane to Beirut for consultations with the UNRPR on budget requirements. Dr. Peterson, Cassius and I coordinated the Gaza medical budget with those of the ICRC and the League of Red Cross Societies. We reviewed AFSC's needs with James Keen and the UNRPR field staff. They listened respectfully. Since it all depended on what the next General Assembly decided, we knew that only so much could be resolved. The UNRPR staff was as committed as we were to doing the best that could be done with the resources provided. We met with UNICEF, which had been supplying milk to the Gaza team, and much admired our operation. We thanked them urging them to continue their indispensable contribution.

Cassius and I then flew to Haifa to visit the small program that had been working in nearby Acre since AFSC had undertaken the Gaza project.[3] While most Arabs had fled from Haifa, some remained in picturesque Acre. The AFSC's hope that an effort on both sides might bring about a modest reconciliation, proved unrealistic. Passions were still high and the inhabitants of Acre were too exhausted just surviving to reach out across the ethno-religious-linguistic division. We visited an Arab village in western Galilee where the Acre team was distributing food and clothing to refugees who had fled the major towns. The village was small and primitive and the refugees appeared beaten and confused. Their leaders had departed, everything was dilapidated.

After thirty-six hours in Acre, we drove two old jeeps along the coast to Tel Aviv en route to the AFSC Gaza car pool. In the throbbing energy of Tel Aviv everyone seemed to be in a hurry with important things to do. I found that the Major Frumkin I had known in Italy was now quartermaster for the Israeli police. He took us to a fine hotel and quietly talked about his problems as we looked out at the cobalt blue ocean. Each day a thousand Jews arrived; they couldn't be turned away even though there was no place to put them in the already overcrowded city and there was no clear way to feed and clothe them. He concluded with, "Thanks only to New York can we survive." I did not then realize how important New York and Washington would become for Israel's survival.

Frumkin did not need to tell me that each of these early arrivals had a story to tell—of a blighted profession, expropriated assets, a police knock on the door, of arbitrary arrests, of relatives deported or killed, of internment or hiding under the most bleak conditions. I had heard it all in Lisbon and Italy years before, an unforgettable collection of tales of woe.

Israel's vulnerability to civic problems was counterbalanced by the great feeling of confidence inspired by survival in the face of the Arab invasion. Jews had gained a new security in the knowledge that they were free from religious discrimination and persecution and could now protect themselves.

We left Tel Aviv and drove south. The rich green land was dotted with abandoned and demolished villages and uncared-for orange groves. Gaza seemed very crowded after the no man's land that was southern Israel. We told the Gaza team about Beirut and Tel Aviv that night, and returned to Cairo where we finished our budget drafts, UNRPR requests, and reports to the Philadelphia office on our discussions with the Gaza team.

THE CONCILIATION COMMISSION AGAIN

In late May I returned to Geneva to further talks between the AFSC and UNRPR on whether to continue beyond August 31. Parminter made it clear that the U.N.'s funding for the refugees was sufficient only to carry the two million dollar monthly budget for Gaza through October, "with luck" through November. In early June, the Conciliation Commission met in Lausanne with the UNRPR, ostensibly to gather information on the refugee situation. Parminter had asked the commission to prepare a census. Unless steps were taken promptly, the UNRPR's money would run out in the middle of the upcoming General Assembly. June was hardly a propitious time, Parminter noted, to expect new monies to be forthcoming.

Ethridge reported on the status of the negotiations between the Arabs and Israelis. His mood in June was far more pessimistic than it had been in May. Unfortunately, he told us, peace was not at hand. The Israelis were not prepared to discuss the refugee problem until territorial questions had been settled and the newly expanded frontiers of Israel confirmed. The Arabs demanded a solution of the refugee problem first. Each side tried to put the onus for the stalemate on the other. Ethridge also informed us that he would soon be leaving the commission for personal reasons.

Altogether, the meeting was discouraging. I circulated among the Commission's staff and knowledgeable observers to learn the story behind the talk. The threat of future military action had been lifted by armistice agreements—which had the unfortunate consequence of removing the impetus for compromise. Fear of security threats from a hostile Arab population hardened Israel's reluctance to accept back Palestinian refugees, as did the Arabs' stridency. The Arabs were still enraged by the establishment of the Jewish state over their strong protests, and perceiving themselves as the weaker party, they used the plight of the refugees to arouse international sympathy, hoping this would lead to pressure on Israel. At the same time, much of the Arab states' shrill anger was more to impress embittered Arab citizens than to reflect a readiness to risk war anew.

It was hard for us on the spot to realize that our concern for the refugees was a small matter to the major powers beginning to be embroiled in the Cold War. To understand the caution of Washington and London, we had to remember the larger picture. The reconstruction of Europe was beginning under the Marshall Plan. Relations were tense with Russia as an American and British airlift breached the Soviet blockade of Berlin, carrying urgently needed food and supplies to the beleaguered city. In China, Mao's armies were advancing on key cities. Washington was ready to tolerate an impasse in Palestine rather than take on painstaking and possibly futile negotiations between Israel and its Arab neighbors. Avoiding anything that might encourage the presence of the Soviet Union in the Middle East would be an overriding United States concern. This would continue so long as the Cold War persisted. Moreover, domestic political pressures brought to bear on members of Congress and on the White House worked against undue direct pressure on Israel.[4]

Despite the lack of progress in finding a home for the refugees, AFSC agreed to continue beyond the August 31 deadline. In a letter confirming this decision, I reminded Griffis that the UNRPR was not able to meet the needs of the refugees at the current levels of funding. According to our team's requirements, the UNRPR was in a position to supply only two-fifths of the blankets, less than one-third of the fuel, and one-third of the textiles our staff needed.

In early July, after apparently no interest from representatives of the principal states, I observed a substantial shift. A number of U.N. officials and diplomats from Britain, France and the US found their way to the AFSC office. First, several key members of the Secretariat responsible for shaping the start of the September assembly dropped by before heading for New York. They were relieved that AFSC would continue, and asked about our priorities for the next period. I told them that tents, fuel, and blankets were in short supply and that schools and sanitation were being neglected.

A bit later, a bright young man from the British Foreign Office knocked on my door and sat down for a leisurely chat. "Surely," he ruminated, "the Quakers would not walk out at the end of the year on such an unfinished program." "Probably not," I replied, but we needed to see evidence that key members of the Assembly would provide necessary funding through the end of the year and beyond. Until recently, we had assumed this to be an emergency program. Alas, the Commission's lack of progress suggested that the refugees might well be in for a long haul. Major governments had to take the refugees' need for resettlement more seriously. My hopes that these displays of interest signified official concern on behalf of the refugees were ultimately disappointed.

In Geneva we began to receive a number of Gaza staff on their way home and fresh recruits heading into the field, which preoccupied us for the remainder of our stay.

HOMEWARD BOUND

During the first week of August, our ship reservations were ready. The AFSC no longer needed a full-time liaison in Geneva; the UNRPR operation was now coordinated in Beirut. Recruitment was in Philadelphia's hands. Hospitality for team members passing through Geneva was delegated to the UNRPR and our friends at the Geneva Quaker center. We said good-bye to our many friends, including Parminter and the small UNRPR staff, and took the train to Cherbourg where we boarded the *Queen Mary.* Our most indelible recollection of that quiet crossing is of the railings that led to our little stateroom draped with drying diapers.

As I sat watching the wake stretch back toward Europe, I had time to reflect more deeply on the painful irony of our Gaza effort. In Lisbon, since the United States had not then been willing to receive them in large numbers, Palestine had seemed an answer for Jewish refugees. They were finding space, however constricted, in which to shape their futures; but this was occurring at the expense of Palestinian Arabs, who became newly destitute refugees in turn. In a real sense, Europe and the United States had salved their bad consciences toward the Jewish victims of Hitler's madness by encouraging the insertion into Palestine of what devout Jews had always called for, a return to Jerusalem. After harrowing centuries of victimization, Jews migrating to Israel now had in their grasp a future full of promise.

On the other side of the truce line, three quarters of a million Palestinian refugees had become victims. As human beings, they deserved the right to go home as much as did the millions of displaced persons in Europe. We all hoped that at least a few refugees could go home and that the international community and the Arab states would find ways to resettle the others. We did not know then that the Arab states would continue to refuse to recognize the existence of Israel until Tel Aviv agreed to the right of return. Nor did we know that the Israelis would use the time of diplomatic stalemate to vigorously build settlements for Jews in so many areas already designated by the United Nations as part of the Arab state.

After arriving home I had long discussions at AFSC with those who were trying to keep up the flow of new recruits to replace those coming home. AFSC's collaboration with the UNRPR continued until 1950. It became obvious that an improvised organization like ours that had worked well for the emergency period would not be good enough for a long haul. The UN General Assembly established the United Nations Relief and Works Administration (UNRWA) to take over responsibility for the refugees. Few of us imagined that fifty years later the situation would be so unchanged except that the area once designated for the Arab population was now marked by settlements housing over 200,000 Israelis.

For our part, we returned to Yale to prepare our own futures.

AFTERWORD

Europe during the late 1930s was a place of hatreds and despair; the war years brought the land and people to desolation. The transformation of that wretched continent to a prosperous, peaceful one was a major achievement of the 20th century. Within a single generation, Europe was led by its statesmen to become a model of how such hostilities can be overcome. The hellish concentration camps that scarred European nations are long gone. Because of my service with the Quakers I had a close look at forms of human suffering that have virtually disappeared from Western Europe.

Costly military efforts were necessary to eliminate the Nazi scourge. Arrival of Allied forces in North Africa brought a sense of safety and of hope to millions.   Treatment of minorities quickly improved. In Italy, once Allied forces established themselves there was an immediate end to arbitrary arrests and deportations. After liberation, the French government restored electoral choice, a system of justice, and local administration restrained by the rule of law.

However, it is essential to recall that it took far more than military force for the Europeans and Americans to overcome intense hatred and state rivalries. Generous non-military American and European policies were also indispensable. Without civilian innovations such as UNRRA, the Coal and Steel Community, the Marshall Plan and the Adenauer-Schuman partnership, economic rebirth would not have been achieved.   Moreover, these innovations that rebuilt Europe did not come about spontaneously. Brave individual political leaders, such as Harry Truman, Jean Monnet, and Ernest Bevin deviated from the conventional behavior of victors in order to bring home the fruits of peace.

The Quakers' role in this complex drama was unusual. We were symbols of support for the harried and the persecuted. We became more than symbols as we eased supplies through troubled ports during periods of acute shortage. We did our best to help people in refugee centers, internment camps and prisons. At a time of intense discrimination, we were able to help needy people regardless of nationality, religion or ethnic origin. We brought encouragement across barriers of language and nationality at a time of despair. We were among those trying to ease the burdens on the stateless wanderers in Europe. At home in Washington we spoke against the restrictive immigration policy that denied Europeans a safe haven. Through it all, however, was the nagging awareness that whatever we might achieve was small compared to what needed to be done.

My experience during those years left a number of indelible impressions. The easy, often arbitrary and accidental destructiveness of war devastated the lives of civilians as well as soldiers. The flight of masses of people in advance of modern armies - in the exodus from northern France, from the battlefields of Italy and of Israel/Palestine - showed me how hapless citizens needed to search for temporary safety. Later, whenever would-be statesmen in the Academy or corridors of power pondered "military options," or "demonstrative signals," I was unable to forget the likely human wreckage their abstract visions might inspire.

In each country where I worked, there was a distinct tradition. No two countries shared the same government structures, images of history, ideas about their neighbors or even religious beliefs. It was indispensable for Americans to understand the diversity of the world outside the United States. Typically, statesmen's conceptions of their own interests paid insufficient attention to the interests of their neighbors. This early encounter with the variety of the international reality from one Mediterranean country to another made me wary. The beguiling abstractions of Wilsonian idealistic politics or the simplicities of the grand strategists usually concealed more than they revealed. Unlike idealistic perfectionists or enthusiastic chauvinists, I doubted that everyone's problems had answers made in America.

As I headed for Geneva in 1948 for work with AFSC's service in Gaza, I lamented to myself that once again innocent civilians had to flee war's path. Part of me was glad a homeland for Jews was coming into being. Hitler's mad Holocaust had added an understandable desperation; the traditional Jewish prayer for Jerusalem seemed within reach. On the other hand, having followed the impassioned debates at United Nations headquarters, I knew it would be painfully hard for Arab leaders and their peoples to understand why they had to be displaced because the Europeans and United States were unwilling to accommodate Hitler's victims.

To those of us who had spent the war years helping Jewish and non-Jewish victims of Hitler's insane schemes, the plight of the Palestinian refugees came as a woeful consequence. Despite the barriers to understanding between the contending parties, I hoped at the time that the more sophisticated Jewish and Arab leaders would understand the advantage of seeking a mutually tolerable peace. Looking back we can see that, unfortunately, both communities in

Palestine/Israel shared the fate of being held hostage by their respective zealots who sought maximalist goals rather than mutual compromise.

Few of us then imagined that in the next millennium Israeli and Palestinian leaders and their foreign sponsors would not have found a way for them to at least co-exist. There has been plenty of blame to be shared. Palestinian leaders did little to encourage their people to accept the new state of Israel. Systematically implanting ever more Jewish settlements in land allocated to the Arabs was bound to embitter the weaker occupied party. It makes finding an agreement more difficult as a new constituency grows more prominent. That this state-sponsored encroachment was abetted by unstinting American support surely had something to do with Arab resentment against Washington

Their tragic inability to resolve their differences has made life a misery for them both. Their conflict still burdens the whole region. Nor did we foresee that beyond Europe, where the signs of warfare have all but disappeared, millions more human beings have since become refugees seeking to escape the hounds of war, tyrannical governments, or desperate poverty. The work we hoped was nearing completion alas must still go on.

I hope this memoir, a good deal more personal than my other writings, communicates something of my gratitude to those farsighted men and women who first organized the American Friends Service Committee during World War I. While I was young, energetic and idealistic, their successors gave me an unusual opportunity to serve humanely during and after World War II.

HISTORICAL BACKGROUND TO CHAPTER 14

A Brief Political Background Note:

Following the end of World War II, the British were having grave difficulties managing Palestine. A near civil war broke out between Arabs and Jews; both of them also fighting against the British.

The intense strife resulted from the incompatible goals of the leaders of two peoples. Palestinian Arabs, residents for centuries in an area the size of Vermont, were seeking to replace Ottoman rule with their own independent state. European Zionists hoped to realize in the same area a biblical vision of a home for persecuted Jews. Each group's aspirations were encouraged by conflicting promises made to Arab and Jewish leaders and to Britain's wartime ally France during the desperate days of World War I.

In October 1915 the British High Commissioner in Egypt, Sir Arthur McMahon, wrote what later became a famous letter to the leading Arab official, Hussein ibn Ami, the Sherif of Mecca. Though somewhat ambiguous about the exact frontiers, McMahon's letter promised that if the Arabs would rise against the Ottoman Turks, who then ruled over much of the Arab Middle East, Britain would recognize the "independence of the Arabs." At the time most officials thought the Arabs would be unlikely to rise and the letter seemed of little policy import. Though Palestine was never explicitly mentioned in this correspondence, Arab leaders who knew about the exchange expected that Palestine would be part of the independent Arab world.

Three months later, in the Sykes-Picot agreement, the British and French allies agreed between themselves that Syria and Lebanon should become French-ruled territory and Palestine and Jordan should be under British control.

Later, as Britain continued to face the ghastly stalemate on the Western front, with Lloyd George now Prime Minister, London sought to secure Zionist organizational and financial resources in support of Britain's position in the region. In October 1917 Lord Balfour, Britain's Foreign Secretary, issued the famous Balfour Declaration. It committed Britain to facilitating the development of a Jewish "national home" in Palestine, "it being clearly understood that nothing shall be done which may prejudice the civil and religious rights of existing non-Jewish communities in Palestine."

Since the end of the first World War, Palestine had been under British rule. A League of Nations Mandate granted to Britain confirmed the 1917 Balfour Declaration, in effect giving international sanction to the establishment of the Jewish national home, whatever that was to mean.

During the 1930s the British had been unable to find a way to implement the contradictory promises made by the wartime London Government. It might well have been foreseen that, as part of the widespread rise of nationalism, Arab leaders considered Palestine to be among Arab areas that had been promised independence. Understandably, they rejected both British Mandatory rule and, more particularly, the intrusion of a Jewish "homeland" in Arab Palestine. Arabs feared that, however defined, a "homeland" for Jews in Palestine would mean their own eventual displacement and an end to the dream of an independent Arab state of Palestine.

For many years Zionists had been developing a shadow government, the Jewish Agency, which gave shape to the Jewish community, provided essential services to their community and generated support in London, New York, Paris and Geneva. By comparison, the Arab community remained fragmented. Clan rivalries, confessional and well-established ethnic differences were not encompassed within a national Arab organization; there was a far smaller educated and cosmopolitan Arab elite than among the Zionists. Moreover, the periodic eruption of violent Arab protests against the British had led to the exile of a number of Arab nationalist political leaders. This left Muslim religious figures as the most prominent remaining Arab leaders, not the most effective candidates to shape a political consensus between Muslims and Christian, Orthodox and other Arab minorities.

In the meantime, the rise of Nazism in Europe and its vicious anti-Semitism increased the flow of Jewish immigrants into Palestine. In 1936, to dramatize Arab opposition to the increase in Jewish immigration, Arab nationalists called a major protest strike, and guerrilla groups rapidly formed. Violent attacks were made against Jewish businesses and settlements, and some British officials were assassinated. The revolt was quashed but bitterness between Arabs and Jews increased, and a large British military presence was required to contain the disorder.

As war clouds gathered in the late 1930s, London's efforts to ensure quiet in the strategic Middle East led it in 1939 to mollify aroused Arab opinion by issuing a White Paper that set limits to Jewish immigration and land acquisition. This came at the very worst time for the harassed Jews. Any steps to deal with Arab worries angered the now well-organized Jewish community; any moves to meet Jewish interests infuriated Arab leaders. Successive British plans to partition Palestine met with vigorous opposition by leaders of both communities. Moreover, both sides had engaged in armed opposition to the British authorities; both had guerrilla action groups that assassinated the other's leaders and British officials. It became increasingly costly to enforce public order.

By 1947 the British Labor Government was at its wits' end. The British were exhausted by their enormous exertions during World War II. They were opposed by both these diametrically antagonistic communities. Moreover, the United States was clearly unprepared to help London maintain its traditional imperial position. In April 1947 London asked the Secretary General of the United Nations to call a Special Session of the UN General Assembly to consider the Problem of Palestine. The resulting Palestine Partition Plan led to the war that produced the refugees AFSC and other agencies were called to assist.

ORGANIZATIONS AND ACRONYMS

AFSC American Friends Service Committee, with headquarters in Philadelphia. A Quaker organization begun during World War I to provide service opportunities to Conscientious Objectors in aiding European civilian victims of the war. British Friends and AFSC organized the *Quakerspeisung* in 1920 for 500,000 hungry children in Germany and Austria. An Anglo-American Friends child feeding program on both sides of the Spanish Civil War in the 1930's led in 1936 to relief work in southern France supported from Portugal in the 1940's. In the late 1930's.British and American Friends worked in Berlin, Rome, and Geneva to assist emigration of Jews subject to Nazi persecution

FRS Friends Relief Service The British Quaker relief organization, with headquarters at Friends House in London. It was developed by the Friends Service Council to deal with the emergency of World War II and designed to be laid down following the end of the immediate post-war emergency. In addition to emergency civilian relief efforts in Britain during the war, FRS provided the majority of foreign volunteers working with Secours Quaker and had units in Germany, Poland, Greece, Palestine and the Netherlands.

FAU Friends Ambulance Unit with headquarters in London. Independent of the British Quaker religious establishment, the FAU provided service opportunities overseas for nearly 1500 conscientious objectors. The FAU worked with British civilian authorities and medical services attached to British armies. They were active in Greece and the Middle East during the war and in post-war Germany. With the AFSC, they organized a unit in China delivering medical supplies to civilians.

JDC The American Jewish Joint Distribution Committee with headquarters in New York, the principal organization providing assistance to Jewish refugees and hard pressed Jewish communities throughout the world, sometimes called simply "The Joint". AFSC and JDC worked closely together on aid to refugee families and emigration from Lisbon, and in Algiers Spain and Italy. I greatly admired Dr. Joseph Schwartz, JDC European Director based in Lisbon.

SECOURS QUAKER organized in Marseille in 1942 as southern France was occupied by German forces. For the remaining war years a largely French staff carried on in Marseille, Toulouse, Montauban and Perpignan, serviced by AFSC in Lisbon. In Occupied France, Paris Secours Quaker continued prison visiting. Following the Liberation of France in 1944, Paris became the principal headquarters of Secours Quaker. British and American aid was channeled through this office.

IMPORTANT MORE GENERALLY

ACC Allied Control Commission, Italy (later Allied Commission (AC) After the Allied forces entered Italy they controlled political and economic life in areas of Italy liberated from the Germans. We needed permission for IGCR and AFSC to enter Italy and to function. AFSC was attached to the Refugee and Displaced Person's Division of the ACC.

AFA Allied Financial Agency, Rome. The AFA was the financial arm of the ACC and responsible for financial matters, including issuing Occupation Lire. We dealt with the AFA for our safety net cash relief for "unrepresented" refugees.

AFHQ Allied Forces Headquarters, Algiers. Military Headquarters for the Allied Command during and after the North African landings in November 1942. AFHQ was transferred to Caserta near Naples and then Rome. It became designated as the MTO or Mediterranean Theater of Operations in December 1943.

HIAS Hebrew Sheltering and Immigrant Aid Society One of the oldest Jewish organizations helping immigrants arriving in the United States, renowned for its services at Ellis Island, allied with HICEM, a European coalition of Jewish aid agencies, including HIAS. Headquartered in Lisbon from the occupation of France to the end of the war, together they provided case workers for JDC-supported programs and assisted emigration of refugees.

ICRC International Committee of the Red Cross, headquartered in Geneva. In the early 1940s the ICRC in Portugal traced divided families, handled exchange of civilians and officials and shipped relief supplies to France. Our French delegations worked closely with the

ICRC in French internment camps and assisted prisoners of war. From 1948 to 1950 we were co-workers in aid to Palestinian refugees.

IRC International Rescue Committee Founded in the 1930s, during WW II IRC rescued endangered intellectuals, artists and political opposition figures from Nazi Germany in France. Varian Fry and Albert Hirschman were two important operatives in France in 1940/41.

MERRA Middle East Relief and Refugee Organization Organized by the British Middle East Command and based in Cairo, a civilian organization to care for refugees who fled to the Middle East from Poland, Greece and Yugoslavia. It was the British equivalent to the American OFFRO we knew in North Africa. It coordinated all volunteer organizations in the area. The Friends Ambulance Unit worked under MERRA and provided the chairman of the Cairo Council of Voluntary Agencies, a model of Government-NGO collaboration. MERRA was later absorbed into UNRRA, the United Nations Relief and Rehabilitation Organization, established in late 1944 by the American and British governments.

MEW Ministry of Economic Warfare Originally based in London, MEW administered the Allied naval and economic blockade of German-held territories. Any shipments we succeeded in sending from Portugal to France or Spain had to receive permission from the MEW as exceptions, before they could be shipped either directly or with the help of the International Red Cross.

MSC Mennonite Service Committee The Mennonites also engaged in overseas relief and refugee assistance and participated in the Cairo Council of Voluntary Agencies.

OFRRO Office of Foreign Relief and Rehabilitation United States Government overseas relief organization first active in North Africa became the predecessor to UNRRA and provided official sponsorship for AFSC and other American NGO's in North Africa and later in Italy.

PENDLE HILL A Quaker study and retreat center near Swarthmore, outside Philadelphia, providing training for AFSC overseas volunteers that began there in the fall of 1941.

PWRCB President's War Relief Control Board A World War II board established by President Roosevelt to coordinate activities of NGOs working in relief abroad, and to ensure they fulfilled their promises to donors.

PVDE <u>Portuguese Vigilance and Sate Defense Police</u> Policed the citizens and foreigners, including refugees. They were not as lethal as the Gestapo but people were afraid of them and assumed they were watching everyone.

SHAEF <u>Supreme Headquarters Allied European Forces</u> Under General Eisenhower and his unusual multinational staff, SHAEF planned and executed Operation OVERLORD, the Normandy and other landings across the English Channel. In December 1944, Eisenhower permitted British and American Quakers to meet with French Quakers to plan our own multi-national relief effort under the aegis of Secours Quaker.

UJA <u>United Jewish Appeal,</u> headquartered in New York. The UJA raised large sums for relief of hard pressed Jewish communities and individuals and organizations like the JDC during World War II, and for the state of Israel once it was established. It also found jobs for new arrivals into the United States.

UNRPR <u>United Nations Relief for Palestine Refugees</u> Established in November 1948 by the United Nations General Assembly and initiated by the UN Secretary General's office, organized emergency assistance to Palestinian refugees in the Gaza strip and neighboring Arab countries during and after the first Arab-Israeli war. Originally its headquarters was in Geneva, but later Beirut proved more practical. It continued until 1950.

UNRRA <u>United Nations Relief and Rehabilitation Agency</u> mobilized and distributed aid to peoples devastated by World War II. Some 52 countries participated, contributing some 2% of their GNPs as of 1943, while the undevastated United States provided roughly half. Established in 1944, with Governor Herbert Lehman of New York as the first director, its work in Europe ended in 1947 and continued in China for two more years.

UNRWA <u>United Nations Relief and Works Agency</u> Developed by the UN Secretariat in 1950 to replace UNRPR in recognition that there was to be no short term solution to the Palestinian refugee problem.

USC Unitarian Service Committee is headquartered in Boston. In Portugal, it worked with the International Rescue Committee on behalf of political refugees.

USCOM United States Committee for European Children, founded to assist in the emigration of continental children, primarily Jewish refugees, for foster family care during World War II.

HISTORICAL CONTEXT: BRIEF CHRONOLOGY

EUROPE

1934 Nazi Nuremberg Anti-Semitic Laws provoke Jewish flight.

1938 Nazi occupation of Austria, provoking the flight of Jews from Austria.

1938, September Munich agreement hands Czech Sudetenland to Germany

1938-39 End of Spanish civil war-flight of defeated Spanish army and civilians to France and North Africa.

1939 Spring: German invasion of Czechoslovakia; flight of Jews and political refugees.

1939 September: Russia and Germany invade Poland;

 World War II begins.

1940 May/June: Collapse of France, exodus from Holland, Belgium and Paris to southern France and Portugal.

1941 December: Japanese attack Pearl Harbor bringing US into WW II.

1941 Greece: German advances and British retreat provoke thousands of Greeks to flee with departing British troops to Cairo.

1942 July: Deportation of stateless refugees from France to Germany, Poland and Auschwitz.

1942 North Africa: October: Battle of El Alemein near Cairo begins German retreat.

1942   November: Allied Landings, on Moroccan and Algerian beaches.

1943   Americans and British liberate southern Italy, Mussolini falls, Allies jointly fight their way north. Jews deported from northern Italy to Auschwitz.

1943   Yugoslavia: fighting between resistance groups and Germans leads to thousands of Dalmatian refugees fleeing to Italy, many subsequently moved to Cairo in 1943-44.

1943   United Nations Relief and Rehabilitation Administration (UNRRA) founded.

1944   June 6: Allied landings in Normandy.

1945   May 7: German armies surrender.

1945   Sept 2: Japan surrenders.

PALESTINE

During World War I, British and French, in Sykes-Picot agreement (1916), divide the remnants of the Ottoman Empire between them; France to have Syria and Lebanon and Britain Palestine and TransJordan. Under wartime pressures, Britain also promises independence to Arab leaders who revolt against the Ottomans (1915), and promises to Zionists a "homeland" in Palestine (Balfour Declaration 1917).

1922   League of Nations confirms British Mandate over Palestine, including a Jewish homeland; end of Arab independence.

        Gradual rise of Arab nationalism.

1935   Jewish immigration into Palestine increases following Nuremberg Laws and Jewish persecution.

1936-39 Arab revolt against both British rule and surge in Jewish immigration is repressed.

1939   British "White Paper" responding to Arab protests, limits Jewish immigration as Nazi pogroms intensify.

1939-44 Cairo becomes haven for Greek, Yugoslav and other refugees from European war.

1942   October battle of El Alemein near Cairo, start of German retreat.

1946   End of World War II revealed extent of Nazi extermination-of 6 million Jews; Arab-Zionist conflict intensifies in Palestine.

        British ask UN to find an answer.

1947   November: UN majority report recommends partition; Arabs oppose, Jews accept majority report gaining, 55%.

1948   May 14: State of Israel declared; recognized by President Truman, invaded by Arab armies. Arab armies divided; Israel gains additional territory

1948   November: United Nations Relief for Palestine Refugees (UNRPR) approved by General Assembly; replaced in 1950 by a longer-term organization, UNWRA.

1949   Armistices between Israel and Arab states provided the only negotiated agreed status quo until 1967, second Arab-Israeli war.

ENDNOTES

Chapter 1

1. There are also groups of Quakers who have paid ministers. As Friends moved west they often found themselves in areas with very few co-religionists. To gather a congregation they often accommodated their neighbors by agreeing to appoint a pastor.

2. For details of how the AFSC was created and its overseas activities begun, see Rufus M. Jones, A Service of Love in Wartime: American Relief Work in Europe 1917-1919 (New York: Macmillan, 1920).

3. London Yearly Meeting Epistle, 1804.

4. Sydney B. Fay, The Origins of the World War (New York: Macmillan, 1928).

5. Richard B. Gregg, The Power of Non-Violence (Philadelphia: J. P. Lippincott, 1934).

6. A Quaker from Kansas, Clarence Pickett attended Hartford Theological Seminary and taught at Earlham, a Quaker college in Richmond, Indiana. He was appointed executive secretary of the AFSC in 1929. For a biography, see Lawrence McK. Miller, Witness to Humanity (Wallingford, Pa.: Pendle Hill Publications, 1999). His autobiography well captures the quality of the man and his view of his and the AFSC's mission. See Clarence E. Pickett, For More Than Bread (Boston: Little Brown, 1953).

7. For details of the heroic activities of Varian Fry, who worked for the International Rescue Committee in the early 1940s, see his revealing memoir, Surrender on Demand (New York: Random House, 1945; reprint, Boulder, Colo.: Johnson Books, 1997).

Chapter 2

1. Philip Conard had long worked with the YMCA in Latin America, and was fluent in Spanish and Portuguese.

2. Erich Remarque, The Night in Lisbon (New York: Harcourt Brace, 1964), 79.

3. For background on modern Portugal see R. H. Robinson, Contemporary Portugal: A History (London: Allen and Unwin, 1979); also Tom Gallagher, "Controlled Repression in Salazar's Portugal," Journal of Contemporary History 14, no. 3 (July 1979).

4. Consul Aristides de Sousa Mendes "singlehandedly rescued thousands" and was soon recalled and dismissed from the service. Michael R. Marrus, The Unwanted: European Refugees in the Twentieth Century (New York: Oxford University Press, 1985), 263.

5. Antonio Tabucchi, Pereira Declares: A Testimony (New York: New Directions, 1995).

6. For background on United States immigration policy, see David S. Wyman, Paper Walls: America and the Refugee Crisis 1938-1941 (Amherst, Mass.: University of Massachusetts Press, 1968); also Richard Breitman and Alan M. Kraut, American Refugee Policy and American Jewry 1933-1945 (Bloomington: Indiana University Press, 1987).

7. Cited by Doris Kearns Goodwin, No Ordinary Times (New York: Simon and Schuster, 1994),173.

8. By going directly to President Roosevelt, Kennan succeeded in blocking an overly ambitious effort by the U.S. Navy to develop a huge base in the Azores. The move would have breached Portuguese neutrality and might have precipitated a Portuguese appeal to Britain for support. Later, of course, Kennan distinguished himself as the original formulator of the "containment" policy which played such a critical role in shaping U.S. foreign policy for the next forty years. He also helped conceptualize key policies of the Marshall Plan. George F. Kennan, Memories 1925-1950 (Boston: Little Brown, 1967), ch. 6, 11, and 14.

9. Franz Kafka, The Castle (New York: Alfred A. Knopf, 1948), 83, 224.

10. She had grown up in Spain where her father had been a diplomat, and was fluent in Spanish, Portuguese and English. She could take shorthand from Phil in Spanish or Portuguese and produce the required correspondence in any of the three languages.

11. Kennan 143.

Chapter 3

1. Howard Kershner directed AFSC's operations in France from 1939 until early 1942. For a description of how Children's Colonies were organized and goods supplied to them and to French schools, see Howard E. Kershner, One Humanity: A Plea for Our Friends and Allies (New York: G. P. Putnam, 1943)

2. Robert O. Paxton, Vichy France: Old Guard and New Order 1940-1944, rev. ed. (New York: Columbia University Press, 2001). Now a classic, his "Prologue, Summer 1940" captures the effects of the collapse of France. Also see Jean Pierre Azema, From Munich to Liberation 1938-1944 (New York: G. P. Putnam, 1943).

3. Arthur Koestler, Scum of the Earth (New York: Macmillan, 1941), 96-150.

4. Fifty years later I learned the full story in the AFSC archives. By signing that procès verbal I unwittingly created the sole documented link between AFSC and what was in fact an unauthorized and dubious freelance transaction.

5. For an account of the arguments in Washington leading to the decision about 1,000 children's visas, see Breitman and Kraut 160-64.

Chapter 4

1. Roderick Davidson had grown up in Turkey in a missionary family and later became a specialist in Ottoman history.

2. Gilbert White and Russ Ritchie declined to go with the others. Instead they managed to transport by truck Quaker supplies that had just arrived on the Marseille docks to Gaillac, an inland town near Toulouse where they expected the German presence to be much less intense, since it was the coastal region the Germans were guarding most carefully. To their surprise, they encountered German staff officers eating on the opposite side of the hotel's one dining room. The two AFSC workers quietly went about their business, distributing these civilian supplies to the Secours Quaker delegations. A message from the German officer in charge told the American Quakers they could continue their distribution for now. It seemed that as a young boy the general had been fed in the *Quakerspeisung* organized after WWI—so the refugees and children in France benefited from this unexpected case of bread on the waters. When all their supplies were distributed, they were told to hasten to Lourdes for the last train to Lisbon. The train they were ushered onto went east instead to Baden Baden, where they were interned with the others. Gilbert White, a geographer, later became president of Haverford College and a renowned specialist on water resources.

3. Personal communication from London. When she was nine years old, she was sent back to England to join her mother, with whom she was never reconciled for having torn her from her foster family in the States.

4. David Blickenstaff later became personal assistant to Andrew Cordier, a fellow member of the Church of the Brethren, who became Executive Assistant to the United Nations Secretaries General. Later, David became coordinator of all UN programs in Indonesia.

5. Seven years later, in graduate school, I discovered that E. H. Carr's book, The Twenty Years Crisis (London: Macmillan, 1946), first published about the same time as the articles, had become a book important for students to read and criticize.

Chapter 5

1. For details of what was really happening see William L. Shirer, The Rise and Fall of the Third Reich (New York: Simon and Schuster, 1960); Martin Gilbert, The Holocaust: A History of the Jews of Europe during the Second World War (New York: Holt, Rinehart and Winston, 1985) and Raul Hilberg, Destruction of the European Jews, 3 vols. (New York: Holmes and Meier, 1985).

Chapter 6

1. See Robert Murphy, Diplomat Among Warriors (Westport: Greenwood Press, 1964) for a detailed report by a participant in these and many other politico-military developments in the region.

2. Murphy 111.

3. For details see M. A. Abitbol, The Jews of North Africa during the Second World War, trans. C. T. Zentelis (Detroit: Wayne State University Press, 1989).

4. I later learned that these French-citizen "Libyans" returned to Libya to pick up the pieces of their former lives. However, riots against Jews followed Israeli military success in the 1967 war, and most fled to Israel.

5. The incredible reports about extermination camps were not yet confirmed so far as we then knew.

Chapter 7

1. Later, Michael was asked to join the UNRRA staff and still later became head of the UNRRA mission to Yugoslavia. Afterwards, in England, he became a productive scholar on the British left.

2. Voluntary societies have had a role in British national emergencies for generations. The Knights of Malta and St. John, for one notable example, had provided medical assistance since the time of the Crusades! During World War I, the American Field Service ambulance corps had served with the British Army, and was again active in World War II. So the British military were used to semi-autonomous bodies working in the areas the British controlled. I later learned that after the war the FAU were among the first to enter pestilential camps in Poland, and an FRS team helped prepare Bergen-Belsen for burning. Clifford Barnard, Two Weeks in May 1945 (London: Quaker Home Service, Friends House, 1999).

3. Tegla Davis put it well in his report of FAU activities during World War II:

Potentially there was no lack of official machinery. But official organizations, however comprehensive their plans, could never render superfluous the efforts of voluntary societies which, operating on a much smaller scale, could move more rapidly and be at work while official machinery was still being ponderously geared for action. Moreover, there were always pockets of distress that for one reason or another did not fit the official pattern. Voluntary societies had a contribution of personal service to render, even if their impact was on a small front and the material supplies that their funds could provide would not bear comparison with those provided by intergovernmental action. (Tegla Davis, Friends Ambulance Unit [London: Headly Brothers, 1947], 351-52).

Chapter 8

1. For these chapters on Italy, I referred first to a report by Louise Wood, "Italy Report" (AFSC, Philadelphia, July 1970). Otherwise, the most detailed source was Wriggins, "Italian Operation: AFSC May 1944-January 1945," dated February 15, 1945, and personal letters home. Other documents from the AFSC archives were also helpful.

2. The outstanding woman journalist of the day, she pumped him on

the state of the different refugee communities, while he pumped her vigorously in return about her impressions of the confusing Italian political scene. She feared that the Allied Control Commission would try to retain detailed control of political life for too long, and argued that the rations then being doled out to the Italian people were too stingy.

3. For a vivid account of the sea journey and their year held at the army base in Oswego, N.Y., see Ruth Gruber, Haven (New York: Three Rivers Press, 1984). For the policy debate in Washington, see Breitman and Kraut, 194-98.

4. The AFSC was among the relief agencies that had helped the Fort Oswego refugees accommodate to their last internment camp life. AFSC also organized a summer camp for the children. Gruber 232.

5. For a detailed discussion of deportations and other aspects of Nazi policy toward the Jews in Italy at this time, see Richard Lamb, War in Italy (London: John Murray, 1993), ch. 3.

Chapter 9

1. For a report on the FAU participation in the Abruzzi project, see Davis 387-90.

2. The memo called for the Allied Financial Agency, a part of the Allied Control Commission, to advance cash to individual foreigners not to exceed L 4,000 per person or L 12,000 per family per month. These amounts would be advanced to allied nationals, and to those recognized as stateless, through local banks.

3. Sam Keeny later played an important role in UNICEF's work in Southeast Asia.

4. In the late spring of 1945, Louise was transferred to the Marseille Secours Quaker office in France, where she helped administer the child-feeding program for pre-tubercular school children.

Chapter 10

1. These were called "delegations" to suggest the autonomy and distinctiveness each regional office had had from the beginning. As seen from Paris, we sometimes acted as if they were really branch offices, while they often thought of themselves as quasi-independent parts of a loose federation. I have since discovered the same differing perspectives in loosely-knit NGOs in the United States.

2. She had been a journalist before joining AFSC. Based in Paris before the war, Margaret Frawley had helped when so many French and others had fled before the German onslaught.

3. Henry Van Etten of France Yearly Meeting, a key member of the French Quaker community and leader of the Quaker prison service program in Paris. He wrote a number of Quaker pamphlets and the only extensive account of the French Quaker group that I am aware of. See his Chronique de la vie Quaker Française - 1745 to 1945 (Paris: Société Religieuse des Amis

[Quakers], 1947).

4. Based at Friends House in London, the Friends Relief Service had a distinguished history. One of its predecessors had been the Friends War Victims Relief Committee, active during and after World War I. Its members carried forward a tradition from the Franco-Prussian War of 1870-1875 and the Balkan wars of 1877-1879. From the start of World War II, the FRS provided emergency paramedical and other civilian services, including hostels for evacuees from the London blitz. In addition to their work with Secours Quaker, when the Continent opened FRS organized services in Germany, Austria, Greece, Poland, Palestine and the Netherlands. For details see Roger Wilson, Quaker Relief: An Account of the Relief Work of the Society of Friends, 1940-1948 (London: Allen and Unwin, 1952).

5. After World War I, British Friends encouraged a small group of pacifists and Protestants interested in Quaker worship to draw together and form France Yearly Meeting. Never more than 150 members throughout the country, they took up the longstanding Quaker concern for prisoners. Their headquarters at rue Guy de La Brosse near the university was known as a place where friendly people would help those in trouble. Secours Quaker became the service arm of this indigenous group, assisting stateless and other refugees as well as prisoners. By the end of the war, the Paris Secours Quaker and the southern delegations had won widespread respect for their humanitarian relief of suffering people regardless of their nationality, their ethnic or political affiliations.

6. Report from the Southern Delegations to Secours Quaker General Meeting with AFSC and FRS Present, Paris, November 1944. AFSC archives.

7. Wilson 135.

8. Robert O. Paxton's Vichy France: Old Guard and New Order is still one of the best analyses of the Vichy period. See also Jean Pierre Azema's From Munich to Liberation, 1938-1944.

Chapter 11

1. I am indebted to John Baskin's careful work on his planned biography of Buritt Hiatt, the last head of the American Quaker program in southern France just before the Occupation. His book is to be published by Houghton Mifflin.

2. Paxton estimated 76,000 Jews were deported from France, about a quarter of them were French citizens, of whom only 2,600 returned (183). For the other side of the coin, see Philip Hallie, Lest Innocent Blood be Shed: The Story of the Village of Le Chambon (New York: Harper and Row, 1979), which tells of Pastor Trocmé and his village that hid and protected Jewish children.

3. Told to me much later by Micheline Salmon, my French secretary, who had been among the workers in Toulouse before coming to Paris. She recalled how one night, helping the team on the train platform, she was horrified to see a friend and her parents standing helplessly at the door of the cattle car. Micheline gave them what limited help she could. Later she learned

that her friend had survived, but both parents had died in the camps. Her friend said that for all three the sight of Micheline helping to assuage their suffering had been a source of strength during their incarceration.

4. Note found in the AFSC archive.

5. Antony Beevor and Artemis Cooper, Paris after the Liberation 1944-1949 (New York, London: Doubleday, 1994), 151.

6. She was a tall, thin, upright woman, clearly a no-nonsense person. Trained as a nurse, she had come to Spain during the Spanish civil war and in 1937-1938 retreated to France with the refugees.

7. Although we did not get to Marseille on this trip, in the interests of completeness it should be mentioned that the Marseille Secours Quaker program also involved pre-tubercular child feeding programs, supplies sent to children's colonies, attention to prisoners and stranded POWs. In addition, the office handled movement of supplies from the Marseille docks to the other three southern delegations.

8. Drawn from a report of damage in Normandy by Helga Holbek to Secours Quaker in November 1944 and from the diary of Harvey Buchanan, who joined the Le Havre delegation in the spring of 1945.

9. Wilson 140.

10. Charlotte Brooks was an early member of the Caen team who later came to Paris to assist me. She had strong Quaker family roots and was a great help in all kinds of ways.

11. This looks remarkably little, but recall that we were offered our apartments often free of charge, the volunteers were unpaid except for a very austere allowance for pocket money, and the cost of food shipped to us from the UK or the States was not charged to our budget.

Chapter 12

1. Bernard Walker later became a solicitor in the City of London.

2. I am indebted to Eunice Clark for this recollection. She retired to New Hampshire.

Chapter 13

1. Unfortunately, Lois Jessup was with us for less than two months before she had to fly home to care for her husband, professor/diplomat Philip Jessup, Truman's Ambassador to the United Nations, who was down with pneumonia. I missed her good sense and knowledge of the AFSC's New York support.

2. For evocative detail about the ETU, see Madeline Yaude Stephenson and Edwin "Red" Stephenson, Journey of the Wild Goose: A Quaker Romance in War-torn Europe (Pasadena, CA: Intentional Productions, 1999).

3. See note 3, Chapter 10.

4. For a report on FAU assistance in Sandbostel concentration camp, not as horrible as Bergen-Belsen, see Clifford Barnard, Two Weeks In May

(London, Quaker Home Service, 1999).

5. Jo Nobel was a tall, friendly, vigorous woman, a great cook with a lively sense of humor. With considerable administrative experience behind her, she nevertheless had much patience and accepted the sometimes slower Quaker way of making decisions.

Chapter 14

1. For a sketch of the political background leading up to the General Assembly's Partition Plan see the Appendix to Chapter 14. For details of Dr. Ralph Bunche's mediation efforts and negotiations of armistices between Israel and the Arab states see Brian Urquhart, Ralph Bunche, An American Life (New York: W. W. Norton, 1993), ch. 14 and 15; also Saadia Touval, The Peace Brokers: Mediators in the Arab-Israeli Conflict 1948-1979 (Princeton: Princeton University Press, 1983). See also A Compassionate Peace, A Future for the Middle East: A Report to the American Friends Service Committee (New York: Hill and Wang, 1982).

2. For a succinct account of the first Arab-Israeli war, see Nadav Safran, From War to War: The Arab-Israeli Confrontation (New York: Pegasus, 1969). I later learned that prior to the conflict Golda Meir and King Abdullah of Trans-Jordan had agreed that Trans-Jordan would occupy the West Bank. This eased the rivalry between Israel and Trans-Jordan but did not avert a stiff conflict between them as each sought control over Jerusalem. The understanding intensified jealousies among the Arab states. Moreover, they had made no joint military plans in advance. For a more detailed account, see Benny Morris, Righteous Victims (New York: Alfred A. Knopf, 1999), 16-259.

3. Jackson later wrote a book, Meeting of Minds, about international mediation (New York: McGraw Hill, 1952); he also wrote Middle East Mission: The Story of a Major Bid for Peace in the Time of Nasser and Ben Gurion (New York: Norton, 1983). In the Kennedy Administration, he and I worked in different parts of the State Department.

4. Griffis owned Brentano's and a share of Madison Square Garden. For a lively, irreverent memoir see Stanton Griffis, Living in State (Garden City: Doubleday, 1952).

5. Griffis 251; multiply by ten to calculate today's equivalent cost.

6. For the full text of the "nineteen points," see Foreign Service Executive Committee Minutes, FX 107, Nov. 17, 1948.

7. For details of this episode, see Miller ch.15, "The Truce of God." Also see Jackson, Middle East Mission.

8. She later joined the team in Gaza and married Alan Horton, an anthropologist with a special interest in Arab society and politics. A Harvard Ph.D., he was later Dean of the University of Cairo and executive director of the University Field Staff based in Hanover, N.H.

9. At the time the refugees were full of Deir Yassin; only later was it confirmed. See, for example, Benny Morris's The Birth of the Palestinian Refugee Problem, 1947-1949 (Cambridge: Cambridge University Press, 1987) for a detailed and documented account. For a more succinct analysis, see his

Righteous Victims, especially 252-58.

      10. Don Peretz's Israel and the Palestine Arabs (Washington, D.C.: The Middle East Institute, 1958) provides a useful politico-sociological analysis of the collapse of the Arab Palestinian society, especially pages 6-8.

      11. Report of "Visit of the Quaker team to Faluja," February 6 to March 6, 1949, by Ray Hartsough and Corrine Hardesty, March 6, 1949. AFSC archives, Philadelphia.

      12. International Red Cross, undated memorandum in AFSC archive, dated in ink "December 1948."

      13. Paul Cossali and Clive Robeson, Stateless in Gaza (London: Zed Books, 1986), 14.

      14. AFSC Oral History interview #602, Josina Vreede Berger, 8.

      15. From Lee Dinsmore, in a personal communication.

      16. King Farouk was deposed in 1952 by a military coup.

Chapter 15

      1. For a detailed account of the activities of the hapless Conciliation Commission and an assessment, see David Forsythe, United Nations Peacekeeping: Conciliation Commission for Palestine (Baltimore: Johns Hopkins University Press, 1972). Also see Neil Caplan, Futile Diplomacy, vol. 3 (London: Frank Cass, 1983-), ch. 4.

      2. Alvin and Edele continued a remarkable joint career. I later learned that after a spell with the United Nations Relief and Works Administration, successor to the UNRPR, Alvin served as Comptroller of the American University in Cairo. Later they both became, as the New York Times's obituary of Edele put it, "much needed surrogate parents and defacto booking agents and accountants" for the Alvin Ailey dance troupe.

      3. Don Peretz headed the Acre AFSC team. He later became a Professor of Middle Eastern Studies at the State University of New York, Binghamton.

      4. For a vivid account of the influence exerted by the Israeli Ambassador's links to the Truman White House, see George McGhee, Envoy to the Middle World (New York: Harper and Row, 1983), 37.

BIBLIOGRAPHY

Abitbol, M.A. *The Jews of North Africa during the Second World War.* Detroit: Wayne State University Press, 1989.

Azema, Jean-Pierre. *From Munich to Liberation 1938-1944.* New York: Cambridge University Press, 1984.

Bauer, Yehuda. *American Jewry and the Holocaust.* Detroit: Wayne State University Press, 1981.

Beevor, Antony and Artemis Cooper. *Paris After the Liberation 1944-1949.* New York, London: Doubleday, 1994.

Breitman, Richard and Alan Kraut. *American Refugee Policy and European Jewry 1933-1945.* Bloomington: Indiana University Press, 1987.

Brinton, Howard. *The Religious Philosophy of Quakerism.* Wallingford, Pa.: Pendle Hill Publishers, 1973.

Caplan, Neil. *Futile Diplomacy.* London: Frank Cass, 1997.

Carr, E. H. *The Twenty Years Crisis.* London: Macmillan, 1939.

Cossali, Paul and Clive Robeson. *Stateless in Gaza.* London: Zed Books, 1986.

Davis, Tegla. *Friends Ambulance Unit.* London: Headly Brothers, 1947.

Fay, Sidney B. *The Origins of the World War.* New York: Macmillan, 1925.

Fisher, Ernest F., Jr. *Cassino to the Alps.* Washington,:Center of Military History, US Army, GPO, 1977.

Forsythe, David P. *United Nations Peacekeeping: The Conciliation Commission for Palestine.* Baltimore: Johns Hopkins University Press 1972.

Fry, Varian. *Surrender on Demand.* Preface by Warren Christopher. Boulder, Colo.: Johnson Books, 1997 (orig. 1945).

Gallagher, Tom. "Controlled Repression in Salazar's Portugal," Journal of Contemporary History, Vol. 14, #3, July, 1979.

Gilbert, Martin. *The Holocaust: A History of the Jews of Europe during the Second World War,* New York: Holt, Rinehart and Winston, 1985.

Goodwin, Doris Kearns. *No Ordinary Times.* New York: Simon and Schuster, 1994.

Griffis, Stanton. *Living in State.* Garden City: Doubleday, 1952.

Gruber, Ruth. *Haven.* New York: Three Rivers Press, 1984.

Hilberg, Raul. *Destruction of the European Jews.* (3 vols.) New York: Holmes and Meier, c.1985.

Jackson, Elmore. *Meeting of Minds.* New York: McGraw Hill, 1952.

---. *Middle East Mission: The Story of a Major Bid for Peace in the Time of Nasser and Ben Gurion.* New York: W.W. Norton, 1983.

Jones, Rufus. *A Service of Love in Wartime: American Relief Work in Europe 1917-1919.* New York: Macmillan, 1920.

Kafka, Franz. *The Castle.* New York: Alfred Knopf, 1948.

Kaspi, André. *La Mission de Jean Monnet à Alger, Mars-October, 1943.* Paris: Editions Richelieu, 1971.

Kennan, George F. *Memoirs 1925-1950.* Boston: Little Brown, 1967.

Koestler, Arthur. *Scum of the Earth.* New York: Macmillan, 1941.

Kraut, Alan M. and Richard Breitman. *American Refugee Policy and European Jewry 1933-1945*. Bloomington: Indiana University Press, 1987.

Lamb, Richard. *War in Italy*. London: John Murray, 1993.

Linkletter, Eric. *The Italian Campaign*. London: H.M. Stationery Office, 1977.

Marrus, Michael R. *The Unwanted: European Refugees in the Twentieth Century* New York: Oxford University Press, 1985.

---. *The Holocaust in History*. Hanover, N. H.: University Press of New England, 1987.

McClelland, Grigor. *Embers of War:Letters from a Quaker relief worker in war-torn Germany*. London: British Academic Press, 1997.

McGee, George. *Envoy to the Middle World: Adventures in Diplomacy*. New York: Harper and Row, 1983.

Miller, Lawrence McK. *Witness for Humanity: The Biography of Clarence E. Pickett*. Wallingford, Pa.: Pendle Hill Publications, 2000.

Morris, Benny. *Righteous Victims: A History of the Zionist-Arab Conflict 1881-1999*. New York: Knopf, 1999.

---. *The birth of the Palestinian refugee problem, 1947-1949*. New York: Cambridge University Press, 1987.

Murphy, Robert D. *Diplomat Among Warriors*. Westport: Greenwood, Press, 1964.

Paxton, Robert O. *Vichy France: Old Guard and New Order 1940-1944*. Rev. ed. New York: Columbia University Press, 2001.

Peretz, Don. *Israel and the Palestine Arabs*. Washington, D.C.: Middle East Institute, 1958.

Remarque, Erich M. *The Night in Lisbon*. New York: Harcourt Brace, 1964.

Report to the American Friends Service Committee. *A Compassionate Peace: A Future for the Middle East.* New York: Hill and Wang, 1982.

Robinson, R.A.H. *Contemporary Portugal: A History.* London: Allen and Unwin, 1979.

Rodenbeck, Max. *Cairo: The City Victorious.* New York: Knopf, 1999.

Safran, Nadav. *From War to War: The Arab-Israeli Confrontation, 1948-1967.* New York: Pegasus, 1969.

Shirer, William L. *The Rise and Fall of the Third Reich.* New York: Simon and Schuster, 1960.

Silone, Ignazio. *Fontamara.* New York: H. Smith & R. Haas, 1934.

Stephenson, Madeleine Yaude and Edwin "Red" Stephenson. *Journey of the Wild Geese - A Quaker Romance in War-torn Europe.* Pasadena, Cal.: Intentional Productions, 1999.

Tabucchi, Antonio. *Pereira Declares, A Testimony.* New York: New Directions, 1995.

Touval, Saadia. *The Peace Brokers, Mediators in Arab-Israeli Conflict 1948-1979.* Princeton: Princeton University Press, 1982.

Toynbee, Arnold J. *A Study of History.* London: Royal Institute of International Affairs, Oxford University Press, 1934-61.

Urquhart, Brian. *Ralph Bunche, An American Life.* New York: W. W. Norton, 1993.

Von Borries, Achim. *Quiet Helpers: Quaker Service in Postwar Germany.* (translated from German, introduction by Brenda Bailey and Donn Gann). Philadelphia: American Friends Service Committee and London: Quaker Home Service, 2000.

Van Etten, Henry. *Chronique de la vie Quaker Française 1745-1945.* Paris: Societe Religeuse des Amis (Quakers), 1947.

West, Jessamyn, *The Quaker Reader*. Wallingford, PA: Pendle Hill
Productions, 1992.

Wilson, Roger, *Quaker Relief – An Account of the Relief Work of the
Society of Friends, 1940-1948.* London, Allen and Unwin, 1952.

Wyman, Davis S. *Paper Walls: America and the Refugee Crisis, 1938-
1941.* Amherst, Mass., University of Massachusetts Press, 1968.

ABOUT THE AUTHOR

Howard Wriggins, the Bryce Professor of International Relations, Emeritus, of Columbia University in the City of New York, grew up in Philadelphia where he attended the Germantown Friends School. The Quaker values he learned there and at the Friends Meeting he attended played an important role in his choosing to declare himself a conscientious objector at the beginning of World War II. Once he had graduated from Dartmouth College, he began graduate work at the University of Chicago. His study of political science there was interrupted by a call from the American Friends Service Committee to join their relief operation in Europe at the height of World War II.

Young Wriggins, an idealistic 23-year-old, moved around the Mediterranean area, from Portugal to North Africa to Italy to France as a relief administrator for the next four years. The letters he wrote home at that time form the basis for the memoir he has prepared, *Picking Up The Pieces From Portugal To Palestine: Quaker Relief in World War II.*

Returning to the United States after the war, he resumed his studies, this time at Yale, only to be called by the Quakers again, this time to Gaza where the Palestinian refugees were being sheltered after the creation of Israel. He spent the next year observing, feeding, housing and educating hundreds of thousands of refugees there.

These two experiences, one during the war, the other immediately after it, informed Wriggins's lifelong concern with the interactions of governmental, military and charitable agencies. His work as a political scientist brought him to the Library of Congress and the National Security Council in Washington DC; to the US Ambassadorship to Sri Lanka under Jimmy Carter; and finally to a distinguished career as a scholar and teacher at Columbia University.

Today Professor Wriggins lives with his wife, Sally Hovey Wriggins, an expert on medieval Buddhism, in Hanover, New Hampshire. He is an accomplished photographer and sailor.

INDEX